Autobiographical Comics

FIGURE 0.1 *"Autobio Panel Autobio" from Dustin Harbin's* Diary Comics *(2015), #178. © Dustin Harbin. Used with permission.*

BLOOMSBURY COMICS STUDIES

Covering major genres, creators and themes, the Bloomsbury
Comics Studies series are accessible, authoritative and
comprehensive introductions to key topics in Comics Studies.
Providing historical overviews, guides to key texts, and important
critical approaches, books in the series include annotated guides
to further reading and online resources, discussion questions,
and glossaries of key terms to help students and fans navigate the
diverse world of comic books today.

Series Editor
Derek Parker Royal

Forthcoming Titles
Children's and Young Adult Comics, Gwen Tarbox
Webcomics, Sean Kleefeld
Superhero Comics, Christopher Gavaler

Autobiographical Comics

Andrew J. Kunka

Bloomsbury Academic
An imprint of Bloomsbury Publishing Plc

B L O O M S B U R Y
LONDON · OXFORD · NEW YORK · NEW DELHI · SYDNEY

Bloomsbury Academic
An imprint of Bloomsbury Publishing Plc

50 Bedford Square   1385 Broadway
London   New York
WC1B 3DP   NY 10018
UK   USA

www.bloomsbury.com

BLOOMSBURY and the Diana logo are trademarks of Bloomsbury Publishing Plc

First published 2018

© Andrew J. Kunka, 2018

Andrew J. Kunka has asserted his right under the Copyright, Designs and Patents Act, 1988, to be identified as Author of this work.

No responsibility for loss caused to any individual or organization acting on or refraining from action as a result of the material in this publication can be accepted by Bloomsbury or the author.

British Library Cataloguing-in-Publication Data
A catalogue record for this book is available from the British Library.

ISBN: HB: 978-1-4742-2785-8
      PB: 978-1-4742-2784-1
      ePDF: 978-1-4742-2787-2
      eBook: 978-1-4742-2786-5

Library of Congress Cataloging-in-Publication Data
Names: Kunka, Andrew, 1969- author.
Title: Autobiographical comics / Andrew J. Kunka.
Description: New York: Bloomsbury Academic, 2017. | Series: Bloomsbury comics studies | Includes bibliographical references and index.
Identifiers: LCCN 2017005671| ISBN 9781474227858 (hardback) | ISBN 9781474227841 (pb)
Subjects: LCSH: Comic books, strips, etc.–History and criticism. | Autobiographical comics–History and criticism. | Biography as a literary form. | Autobiography in literature. | Graphic novels—History and criticism. | BISAC: LITERARY CRITICISM / Comics & Graphic Novels. | SOCIAL SCIENCE / Popular Culture.
Classification: LCC PN6714 .K86 2017 | DDC 741.5/9–dc23 LC record available at https://lccn.loc.gov/2017005671

Series: Bloomsbury Comics Studies

Cover design by Eleanor Rose
Cover image © Laura Perez

Typeset by Fakenham Prepress Solutions, Fakenham, Norfolk NR21 8NN
Printed and bound in the UK

To find out more about our authors and books visit www.bloomsbury.com. Here you will find extracts, author interviews, details of forthcoming events and the option to sign up for our newsletters.

CONTENTS

SERIES EDITOR'S PREFACE

The *Bloomsbury Comics Studies Series* reflects both the increasing use of comics within the university classroom and the emergence of the medium as a respected narrative and artistic form. It is a unique line of texts, one that has yet to be addressed within the publishing community. While there is no shortage of scholarly studies devoted to comics and graphic novels, most assume a specialized audience with an often-rarefied rhetoric. While such texts may advance the scholarly discourse, they nonetheless run the risk of alienating students and representing problematic distinctions between "popular" and "literary." The current series is intended as a more democratic approach to comics studies. It reflects the need for more programmatic classroom textbooks devoted to the medium, studies that are not only accessible to general readers, but whose depth of knowledge will resonate with specialists in the field. As such, each volume within the *Bloomsbury Comics Studies Series* will serve as a comprehensive introduction to a specific theme, genre, author, or key text.

While the organizational arrangement among the various volumes may differ slightly, each of the books within the series is structured to include an historical overview of its subject matter, a survey of its key texts, a discussion of the topic's social and cultural impact, recommendations for critical and classroom uses, a list of resources for further study, and a glossary reflecting the text's specific focus. In all, the *Bloomsbury Comics Studies Series* is intended as an exploratory bridge between specialist and student. Its content is informed by the growing body of comics scholarship available, and its presentation is both pragmatic and interdisciplinary. The goal of this series, as ideal as it may be, is to satisfy the needs of novices and experts alike, in addition to the many fans and aficionados upon whom the medium popularly rests.

Derek Parker Royal

LIST OF FIGURES

ACKNOWLEDGMENTS

I first want to thank series editor and podcasting partner-in-crime Derek Parker Royal for having faith in me to do this project in the first place. The University of South Carolina Provost's Office provided a Humanities Grant that allowed me to conduct research and complete an enormous chunk of this book. My colleagues at the University of South Carolina Sumter—including Hayes Hampton, Mary Ellen Bellanca, Ray McManus, Park Bucker, and Michele Reese, as well as Academic Dean Eric Reisenauer and Dean Michael Sonntag—were indulgent and supportive during the composition of this book. I'm also incredibly appreciative of the enormous assistance I received from Aidan Sullivan, who really stepped up in the clutch on several occasions, including some ace transcribing, and without whom this project would have taken a lot longer to complete. At the very least, my stress level would have been exponentially greater without her help. And speaking of clutch performances, John DiBello came through with some research assistance that I thought might be impossible, and Mike Sterling pointed me toward some sources in underground and alternative comics that became important additions to this book. I'm also grateful to Craig Yoe and Clizia Gussoni for generously providing images from old public domain comics, including the original art for the *Mutt and Jeff* strip that came from their personal collection. In addition, I appreciate the generosity of creators who personally gave me permission to use their work in this book and even provided high-resolution images, including Justin Green, Tom Hart, Ryan Claytor, Stu Campbell, and David Chelsea. Special thanks also to Ed Kanerva at Koyama Press for his enthusiastic assistance in getting some image permissions worked out.

I feel incredibly lucky to be working in the field of Comics Studies at this moment in its development, not least because of the generous and supportive colleagues and friends who work in the field. Qiana Whitted, Brannon Costello, Charles Hatfield (who also provided a last-minute image assist), Craig Fischer, Corey Creekmur, Brian Cremins, Marc Singer, Carol Tilley, Jared Gardner, Ian Gordon, Frederik Byrn Køhlert, Michael Chaney, Aaron Kashtan, and others may not be aware of the help and support they provided, even if it was just to listen to me kvetch over beers at a conference.

Comics Studies is also lucky to have two amazing libraries with extraordinary resources for conducting research: Ohio State University's Billy Ireland Cartoon Library and Museum, and Michigan State University Library's Special Collections. My total gratitude goes out to everyone at the Billy Ireland Cartoon Library and Museum, including Jenny Robb, Caitlin McGurk, and especially Susan Liberator, who regularly checked on me during my research visits and offered very helpful suggestions. They also gave me access to the Jay Kennedy Collection of underground and independent comics, which at that point had been only partially cataloged. This help fell well outside my expectations, and everyone there turned my research trip into a genuine nerd vacation. Also, Tom Spurgeon took me out for beers when I was in Columbus, which was really nice of him. Randy Scott is a national treasure whose generosity, kindness, and knowledge made the week I spent at Michigan State University Library's Special Collections a pleasure.

Finally, and most important, my undying love and gratitude goes out to Jennifer Liethen Kunka. Your love and support during this process went beyond anything I could expect or ask for. This book is dedicated to you.

And I promise that I will never ever make an autobiographical comic about our marriage.

1

Introduction: What are Autobiographical Comics?

The centrality of autobiography

In recent years, autobiographical comics have drawn an enormous amount of critical attention. Many comics scholars identify auto-biography as a central genre in contemporary comics. In *Alternative Comics*, Charles Hatfield (2005) summarizes both the centrality of autobiographical comics and the critical issues the genre raises:

> Autobiography, especially, has been central to alternative comics—whether in picaresque shaggy-dog stories or in disarmingly, sometimes harrowingly, frank uprootings of the psyche—and this has raised knotty questions about truth and fictiveness, realism and fantasy, and the relationship between author and audience. (x)

Elisabeth El Refaie (2012a) reiterates Hatfield's point: "Autobiography has become the genre that most defines the alternative, small-press comics production in North America and Western Europe today" (36). Thierry Groensteen (2007) also comments that "the proliferation of autobiographical comics is a remarkable phenomenon of recent years, stemming from America, where the works of Robert Crumb, Art Spiegelman, and Harvey Pekar, notably, have opened the door" (19). Comics scholars have directed much of their critical attention at three key works: Art

Spiegelman's *Maus* (1986, 1991), Marjane Satrapi's *Persepolis* (2004, 2005), and Alison Bechdel's *Fun Home* (2006). The autobiographical comics that get the most critical and scholarly attention often deal with trauma (the Holocaust, the Iran–Iraq War, a father's suicide), so scholars have theorized how comics can be an effective medium for communicating traumatic experiences. As Hillary Chute (2010) states of the works discussed in *Graphic Women*, though applicable to a wide range of autobiographical comics in general,

> each ... insists on the importance of innovative textual practice offered by the rich visual-verbal form of comics to be able to represent trauma productively and ethically. For this reason, graphic narrative, invested in the ethics of testimony, assumes what I think of as the *risk of representation*. (3)

Whereas much of the critical discussion of trauma narratives has traditionally focused on the unspeakable or unrepresentable nature of the traumatic experience, the combination of visual and verbal elements of comics can make such experiences visible to the reader. Thus, for Chute, comics offers new ways of talking about trauma.

However, many autobiographical comics also address the mundane, quotidian, often humorous experiences of daily life. While it is difficult to quantify how different media measure up in a direct comparison (is comics better than other media in addressing trauma or the quotidian?), comics does seem well suited to capture the charms of everyday experiences, much in the way that comics can be an effective communicator of traumatic experiences. The interactive nature of comics, as described by Scott McCloud (1993) in *Understanding Comics*, can help develop a sympathetic connection between reader and subject, enhancing the intense experience of trauma or the humor of the mundane. As McCloud explains, the borders or "gutters" between panels require readers to perform an act of "closure" to fill in the narrative gap—an act that requires significant active participation on the reader's part (68–9). In addition, McCloud argues that the style of figural drawing, which he lays out in a "picture plane" that covers realistic, abstract, and iconic styles, can impact a reader's engagement with the narrative (51–3). The more abstract a figure, the more the reader is "pulled in" to the narrative to sympathize with characters' experiences (29–31). This sense of connection has been controversial, as one could argue a variety of exceptions (racial caricatures that fall on the abstract side of the spectrum but don't pull the reader in; realistic art styles that still allow for reader sympathy and engagement, etc.). However, autobiographical comics can exercise a power to universalize the creator's individual experience, whether it's through art style, panel layouts, or other narrative techniques. Comics can be unflinching in the fact of historical trauma, as Chute (2008a, 2016) argues, but they can also be unflinching in the face of overwhelming cuteness, like a quirky date or the common experiences shared by new parents, as we see in comics by Liz Prince, Jeffrey Brown, and others. In fact, quotidian, slice-of-life stories have served some of the most popular autobiographical comics, including the work of Harvey Pekar, Gabrielle Bell, Joe Matt, Julia Wertz, and a slew of diary and web comics.

Both Hatfield (2005) and El Refaie (2012a) stress the centrality of autobiography to "alternative" comics: that is, comics that followed out of the underground comix movement of the 1960s and 1970s through the small press and DIY (do-it-yourself) movements of the 1980s and 1990s to offer readers alternatives to the limited genres (mainly superheroes and science fiction) offered by mainstream comics publishers (mainly DC and Marvel). However, we are at a point in comics history where the term "alternative" can be erased from Hatfield's and El Refaie's quotes above: the autobiographical genre is central to comics, full stop. Superheroes still dominate the mainstream comics industry, especially the comics put out by DC and Marvel and sold through specialty comic book shops, but that genre's stranglehold on the upper echelon of comics publishing has been challenged in recent years by horror and science fiction, especially series published by Image Comics (see, most notably, Robert Kirkman, Tony Moore, and Charles Adlard's multimedia juggernaut, *The Walking Dead*).

This focus on publishers like Marvel, DC, and Image, however, is a rather myopic view of the comics industry, limited to the marketplace established by comic book stores, where loyal fans have followed the same genres, series, publishers, and creators for decades. Step outside the comic book shop and look into the worlds of book stores, libraries, and classrooms, and a different story comes to light. The aforementioned *Maus, Persepolis,* and *Fun Home* appear frequently in K-12 standards (including Common Core) and on college syllabi. Young adult sections of book stores are dominated by displays of Raina Telgemeier's enormously successful graphic autobiographies, *Smile* (2010) and *Sisters* (2014), each of which has sold hundreds of thousands of copies. Telgemeier's works have spent years occupying what looked to be permanent spots on the *New York Times*'s bestsellers list for graphic novels, until the *Times* discontinued the graphic novels list in early 2017. Major trade publishers such as Random House, Holtzbrinck, and others offer graphic novel imprints that include many of the most successful autobiographical comics. While graphic novels may have their own unique section in book stores, the major book store chains regularly include autobiographical comics in their "Biography" and other nonfiction genre sections. These academic and commercial moves in recent years demonstrate a clear, mainstream acceptance of autobiographical comics, even if that acceptance is not reflected in most comic book stores.

The centrality of autobiography becomes even more apparent when we take into consideration the world of web comics, where many creators have sought out and found wide audiences for their diary comics and other personal projects, with the benefit of being able to reach their readers directly and with an immediacy unavailable in traditional print publication. The democratic potential of web comics is most visible in the enormously popular phenomenon of the "rage comics" meme, which began in 2008. These crudely drawn comics by anonymous creators follow a similar style and formula, where the subject often experiences a common indignity that concludes with a close-up of a face in a paroxysm of rage (known as "rageguy") screaming "FFFFFFFUUUUUUUU." Amateur creators have been able to easily produce their own works through "rage comics generators" (also known as "rage makers") that virtually automate the creation process. These comics have been produced by countless anonymous creators and viewed by millions of readers through platforms such as 4chan and reddit, making them, inarguably, the most popular comics produced in decades. As the meme progressed, more common images and faces were produced that allowed creators to expand the types of stories they told in this style. With rage comics and rage makers, anyone can become an autobiographical cartoonist.

Of course, with all of this new attention and wider dissemination comes additional public scrutiny. Underground and alternative comics in previous decades could often (though not always) escape such scrutiny because their marginalized status allowed them to fly under the radar. Now, autobiographical comics in schools and libraries regularly face calls for censorship and outright banning. Public libraries have seen works by Phoebe Gloeckner, Alison Bechdel, Marjane Satrapi, and others frequently challenged. Bechdel's *Fun Home* seems to be a particularly common target of conservative crusaders who object to the book's depiction of homosexuality: colleges in South Carolina and North Carolina have received national attention for the use of *Fun Home* in First-Year Reading Experience programs. The South Carolina legislature even threatened to cut the College of Charleston's funding for using the book in such a program.[1] While autobiography does still dominate the worlds of small press and self-published comics that define the "alternative," it is now firmly established as a mainstream genre, with all of the attendant benefits and dangers that the status entails.

The study of autobiography

As is obvious from the genre's name, the study of autobiographical comics is informed by two areas: Autobiographical or Life Writing Studies and Comics Studies. Comics Studies focuses on the medium, a form of communication that encompasses multiple modes and genres. Autobiographical Studies centers on a genre without specifying a particular medium, though most scholarship has traditionally dealt with prose. A standard definition for "autobiography" comes from Philip Lejeune's *On Autobiography* (1989): "Retrospective prose narrative written by a real person concerning his own experience, where the focus is his individual life, in particular the story of his personality" (4). Through this definition comes Lejeune's concept of the "autobiographical pact": an understanding on the part of the reader that the author, narrator, and protagonist of an autobiography are all the same person (22). As a part of this pact, the reader also understands that the autobiography references an external reality that can be verified. This lends a kind of testimonial nature to autobiography, where such a text could be put "on trial" in order to verify its truthfulness, or at least, it seems, find a consensus. When this pact is violated, as was the case with James Frey's 2003 prose memoir of addiction and recovery, *A Million Little Pieces*, scandal can erupt and literary reputations can be damaged. Lejeune's definition is also problematic for comics from the outset because it's meant to apply to prose narratives, which almost always have a single author, or at least the sense of one, even if the autobiographical subject is filtered through an invisible "ghost writer." Most autobiographical comics conform to this notion of a single author or creator as well, with cartoonists who both write and draw their experiences. However, comics is also often a collaborative medium, much more so than prose, where various duties in the creation of a text can be shared by multiple people. What, then, do we do with collaborative autobiographical comics, such as the works of Harvey Pekar and Dennis Eichhorn, who rely on a slew of artists to tell their stories, or Percy Carey and Ronald Wimberley's *Sentences* and John Lewis, Andrew Aydin, and Nate Powell's *March*?

"Autobiographical comics," therefore, affects our sense of both terms and puts pressure on accepted definitions of them. These works often offer innovative ways of using the comics medium to tell stories, exploiting the potential of the medium's inherent characteristics of multimodality, sequentiality, and image–text interactions. This is evident in the way that Rocco Versaci (2007) compares prose memoirs to comics:

> Like their prose counterparts, comic memoirs take a variety of shapes and forms, but comics are capable of demonstrating a broader and more flexible range of first-person narration than is possible in prose ... [T]he best prose memoirs complicate the issue of truth-telling both implicitly and explicitly; for their part, autobiographical comics undermine simplistic notions of "truth," and they do this through their unique formal elements ... (36)

Jared Gardner (2008) further addresses the main problems in applying the kind of verifiability that Lejeune describes to comics, which contrasts the ways in which text-based autobiography operates:

The comics form necessarily and inevitably calls attention through its formal properties to its limitations as juridical evidence—to the compression and gaps of its narrative (represented graphically by the gutterspace between panels) and to iconic distillations of its art. The kinds of truth claims that are fought over in the courts of law and public opinion with text-based autobiography are never exactly at issue in graphic autobiography. The losses and glosses of memory and subjectivity are foregrounded in graphic memoir in a way they never can be in traditional autobiography. (6)

For Gardner, both the artistic rendering of the events in the artist's individual style and the fragmentation of the narrative into panels separated by gutters challenge the verifiability of events represented in the comic.

Assessment of the genre/medium relationship leads to one of the fundamental problems facing comic scholars in this area: can an autobiographical comic tell the truth? Does the very nature of comics as mediated texts that combine words and drawings effectively undermine their truth-telling ability? Hatfield (2005), Gardner (2008), and Chute (2010) have all argued that many autobiographical comics creators foreground these very questions in a variety of ways. Some creators, like Joe Matt, Seth, Julie Doucet, Gabrielle Bell, and others, willingly and playfully undermine the "truthfulness" of their work. Another comparison between prose and comics is warranted here. A prose author working in autobiography may use figurative language without it challenging the veracity of the autobiography, as in "I felt like a mouse in a trap" or "I was a mouse, caught in a trap." Readers remain aware that the subject is not literally a mouse because they are familiar with the conventions of figurative language. However, the visual aspect of comics can potentially render the figurative as the literal. The Jews are not *like* mice in Spiegelman's *Maus*; they *are* mice, which we know is not a literal truth. The mental process that the visual allegory requires for readers to decode the narrative is different from and more complex than the tools available to the prose autobiographer. The allegorical potential of comics as visual texts provides a significant artistic tool for the comic autobiographer, though it also challenges the delicate, fragile line between truth and fiction. This tool helps creators access something more like an "emotional truth," where "some graphic memoirists are much more interested in reflecting their feelings toward their own past in an authentic manner than in claiming to portray the 'absolute truth'" (El Refaie 2012a: 44). Frederik Byrn Køhlert (2015) goes even further than this:

> [I]mpervious to truth claims [through the nature of the comics form], comics autobiography allow the artist to structure the narrative to correspond to a larger, emotional truth, and to visually externalize subjectivity on the page in a way that is constitutive of selfhood while remaining true to dominant ideas of the self as fragmented and multiple. (127)

That is, the comics form allows creators to prioritize that more significant "emotional truth" while also representing the poststructuralist concept of the fragmented self (which is also a challenge to Lejeune's autobiographical pact).

As Gardner's (2008) earlier point makes clear, an artist's style can get in the way of a comic's referentiality in relation to an external reality, especially if the style is not on the realistic end of the spectrum. The New York of Julie Doucet's *New York Diary* (1999) is often a nightmarish world that bears little resemblance to the reality of New York City or to any other comic representation of the place. An artist's drawing style, especially in the representation of characters, also affects this idea of referentiality and verifiability: the more iconic, abstract, or nonrepresentational the style may be, the more distant it may seem from the truth or reality. In a sense, every artist's style, no matter how photorealistic, is divorced to some degree from reality, so we can conclude that comics, by nature of being a hand-drawn visual medium, already challenges the connection between an autobiographical text and an ideal notion of reality.

Add to this the repetitive nature of the process of creating comics: the artists must draw themselves over and over again, perhaps hundreds or even thousands of times, as they create a single work. Some creators address this by creating a consistent avatar for themselves. For example, Seth usually draws himself with the same or similar suit, hat, glasses, and accompanying ubiquitous cigarette. Ditto for Robert Crumb, minus the cigarette. On the other end of the spectrum, Aline Kominsky-Crumb rarely draws herself consistently from panel to panel, going so far as to arbitrarily change outfits from one panel to the next. El Refaie (2012a) describes this repetitive self-representation as "pictorial embodiment," and it has the advantage of offering creators "the opportunity for them to engage explicitly with their own body images and with sociocultural assumptions and values that render bodies meaningful" (91). This is yet another type of "truth" that autobiographical comics can offer. However, Gardner argues that this visual representation of the self creates a profound split between artist and subject: the drawn subject can be distinct from the artist in significant ways:

> With comics, the compressed, mediated, and iconic nature of the testimony (both text and image) denies any collapse between autobiography and autobiographical subject ... and the stylized comic art refuses any claims to the "having-been-there" truth, even (or especially) on the part of those who really were. (12)

Such a claim resists the value of embodiment that El Refaie (2012a) argues, as well as the testimonial nature of the representation of traumatic experiences that Chute (2010) finds valuable in comics.

The multimodal nature of comics as (usually) image–text combinations also has an impact on the ways in which autobiographical comics can challenge truth claims. Formally, many autobiographical comics rely heavily on caption boxes containing the first-person narration of the autobiographical self. Often, illustrations duplicate or complement descriptions in the captions, as is the case with many of the strips in Lynda Barry's *One Hundred Demons* (2002), where the caption box can take up half or more of the panel. However, the relation between verbal narration and image offers yet another place for playful experimentation. In *Fun Home*, Alison's grandmother tells a story of how three-year-old Bruce Bechdel (Alison's father) became stuck while walking through a muddy field. The grandmother explains, through caption boxes, how Mort Dehaas, the mailman, just happened to spot the toddler in the field and came to his rescue. However, Bechdel's visual depiction of the story shows a milkman pulling Bruce from the mud, not a mailman. A parenthetical aside, also in a caption box, explains, "(I know Mort was a mailman, but I always pictured him as a milkman, all in white—a reverse grim reaper.)" (41). This set of images and captions presents a complex interplay of words and pictures: the pictures don't match the "truth" of the grandmother's story, but for Alison the narrator, the milkman in his white outfit represents her own emotional truth of the story. So, an additional caption box is necessary to further explain the contradictory image–text relationship with the grandmother's narration.

Therefore, the conclusion scholars arrive at so often is reduced to this: the truth that autobiographical comics reveal is that "truth" is always mediated and unreliable and can never be absolute. As Charles Hatfield (2005) points out, autobiography in general "inevitably mingles the factual and the fictive" (112), but comics foreground this mingling, occasionally to the point that the only "truth" remaining is the impossibility of total truthfulness in comics autobiography, which Hatfield terms "ironic authentication" (125).

The slipperiness of truth and authenticity in autobiographical comics calls into question a conventional understanding of "autobiography" and leads to some fundamental questions: What is an autobiographical comic? And how do we know a comic we're reading is autobiographical?

What is an autobiographical comic?

El Refaie (2012a) offers a pretty straightforward definition of "autobiographical comics" as "a loose category of life writing through the use of sequential images and (usually) words" (48). This combines standard definitions of each term: "autobiography" as "life writing" and "comics" as both images in sequence and word–picture combinations. Therefore, we should simply know an autobiographical comic when we see one. But how does an autobiographical comic identify itself as one?

The answer to this question seems obvious, but also tautological: a work is autobiographical because it tells us, in some way, that it is autobiographical. In other words, the text offers cues, either within the text or in some paratextual form, that reveal its autobiographical nature. With paratexts—text associated with the book but not part of the actual narrative, like title and publication pages, back cover summaries, author information, acknowledgments, and review blurbs—the book may be subtitled "A Memoir" or "A True Story" on the cover or title page; the publisher may have categorized the book as an autobiography; a blurb may give it away. In the text of the narrative itself, the correspondence between the author's name and the main character's name can also function as a signal. Or the reader may combine paratextual and textual information: the author's photo on the back cover resembles the visual depiction of the main character.

We could continue a list of obvious cues, all of which relate to a commonly held understanding about the nature and definition of autobiography that most readers bring to a text. However, many autobiographical comics, including some of the most influential and frequently studied, challenge that conventional understanding and push the boundaries of the genre. For example, in the seminal autobiographical comic, Justin Green's *Binky Brown Meets the Holy Virgin Mary* (1972), the protagonist does not share a name with his creator. To complicate this further, Green does appear in a framing sequence as a cartoonist, bound and suspended upside down over his own drawing board, drawing pages with a brush in his mouth while a sickle aims precariously between his legs (see Fig. 1.1). In a direct address to the reader, the Justin avatar explains how the following story is true. Here, Green relies on and calls attention to a long tradition in comics, where artists depict themselves in front of their drawing boards and serve as narrators for their stories, autobiographical or otherwise. Those artists usually engage the reader in a friendly chat before the story begins. Green's avatar, however, while friendly, is forced to create his story, apparently against his will and at some risk. Green uses this familiar convention to symbolically represent his own personal sense that his story must be told—and must be told in comics form. Other cartoonists use the convention of depicting themselves at the drawing board as a means of creating a sense of autobiographical authenticity, as we see in Lynda Barry's *One Hundred Demons*, Art Spiegelman's *Maus*, Chester Brown's "Showing Helder," and countless other examples. In fact, this convention may be so common as to achieve the status of cliché.

The genre of autobiography has permeable, hazy boundaries, yielding such terms as "semi-autobiographical" and "*roman à clef*" to define those border cases between fiction and nonfiction. In the medium of comics, these boundaries are even more indistinct and

FIGURE 1.1 *The frontispiece to Justin Green's* Binky Brown Meets the Holy Virgin Mary. © *Justin Green. Used with permission of the artist.*

permeable. We might think of the "autobiographical" in "autobiographical comics" as always having an invisible, understood prefix "(semi-)" attached to it. After all, Art Spiegelman's parents weren't really mice; Aline Kominsky-Crumb probably didn't swim through a flood with her husband Robert on her back as depicted in *Dirty Laundry Comics* (1993: 30); young Marjane Satrapi likely didn't meet God (2003: 13); and Justin Green's fingers didn't turn into penises (1972: 26). At a most fundamental level, the artists' depictions of themselves (sometimes referred to as "avatars" or, to borrow Michael Chaney's [2011a] term, "I-cons" [23]) only partially resemble their physical appearance, and sometimes not at all. These examples and many others discussed in this book raise the important question: how far can genre conventions be bent before a work ceases to be classifiable as autobiography?

Subtitles for many works evince the anxieties about the generic classification of autobiographical comics: "an illustrated novel" (Craig Thompson's *Blankets* [2003]), "a comic-strip memoir" (Chester Brown's *The Playboy* [1992] and *Paying for It* [2013]), "a comic-strip narrative" (Chester Brown's *I Never Liked You* [1994]), "a picture-novella" (Seth's *It's a Good Life, If You Don't Weaken* [2011]), "an account in words and pictures" (Phoebe Gloeckner's *Diary of a Teenage Girl* [2002]), "a family tragicomic" (Alison Bechdel's *Fun Home* [2006]), and "An Autobiographical Novel, with Typographical Anomalies, in which the Author Does Not Appear as Himself" (Eddie Campbell's *The Fate of the Artist* [2006]). Many of these examples challenge both the generic classification of "autobiography" and the medium-specifying "comics."

These taxonomic anxieties have led both scholars and creators to try out other terms that could more accurately capture the nature of autobiographical comics. In their essay "Self-Regarding Art" (2008), Gillian Whitlock and Anna Poletti use the term "autographics," which Whitlock had previously coined in a 2006 essay for *Modern Fiction Studies*. They define "autographics" as "Life narrative fabricated in and through drawing and design using various technologies, modes, and materials. A practice of reading the signs, symbols and techniques of visual arts in life narrative" (v). "Autography," therefore, is not limited to comics, but involves any medium in which visual or multimodal elements are used in life writing, including fine arts, social networking pages, graffiti, and so on. The tension between "auto" as "the self" and the traditional understanding of "graphics" as drawing or visual design makes the term particularly appropriate for the type of work done in autobiographical comics, and several scholars have picked it up as well.

Creators also occasionally come up with their own terms for the type of autobiographical work that they do. In his introduction to Mary Fleener's *Life of the Party* (1996), Ray Zone explains that Fleener calls her work "autobiographix." Zone applies this term for the entire movement of autobiographical comics from the immediate post-underground era in which Fleener began her work. Zone connects the trend to the work of Justin Green and R. Crumb as "forebears" and claims that this work "was a necessary byroad for graphic narrative to explore in order for it to 'mature' into a legitimate means of artistic expression" (9). Like "autography" (as well as Leigh Gilmore's [1994] phonetically similar "autobiographics," which did not originally apply to comics), Fleener's term emphasizes the "graphic" or visual nature of the comics. In addition, the "x" in "autobiographix" shows the fluid connection between Fleener's work and that of her "forebears" in the underground.

Perhaps most notable, however, is Lynda Barry's designation of her memoir *One Hundred Demons* as "autobifictionalography," as indicated on the publication page of the book. On the table of contents page, a note in Barry's handwriting asks, "are these stories true or false?" Boxes next to both options are checked. Then, the first two panels of the introduction ask, "Is it autobiography if parts of it are not true? // Is it fiction if parts of it are?" (7). Though the term may be read as tongue-in-cheek, it demonstrates how unstable categories of fiction and nonfiction are when it comes to graphic autobiography.

Some creators completely dismiss the designation of "autobiography" altogether, which creates even more difficulty in setting borders around the genre. Miriam Libicki, in her comics essay "Jewish Memoir Goes Pow! Zap! Oy!" (2016), originates the term "gonzo literary comics" to encapsulate autobiographical comics and the type of comics journalism or reportage that she and creators like Joe Sacco and Sarah Glidden produce, where the creator is visually present in the work. The presence of the creator in the work, she argues, resembles the gonzo journalism of Hunter S. Thompson and others. "Gonzo literary comic," then, is a hybrid of autobiography and literature, or "autobiography disguised as literature," as Libicki describes it (47). The "literary" component allows the creator some flexibility in playing with the "truth" in ways that strict autobiography normally cannot; in addition, the reader's relationship with the narrator in a literary text is much different from the one in autobiography.

Phoebe Gloeckner (2011) famously challenges the designation of her work as autobiographical, arguing that the generic designation devalues the story in significant ways. As she describes her work, "This is not history or documentary or a confession, and memories will be altered or sacrificed, for factual truth has little significance in the pursuit of emotional truth" (179). Again, we see how "emotional truth" is privileged over, and at odds with, "factual truth." Gloeckner is especially slippery when describing the character Minnie Goetze in interviews, alternatively using the pronouns "her" and "me." Other creators may deliberately undermine autobiographical readings of their work. For example, in the semi-autobiographical *Bumperhead* (2014), Gilbert Hernandez seems to set the story during his own teenage years in the early 1970s, yet one character, Lalo, carries around an anachronistic Internet-connected tablet device throughout. So, "autobiography" as a genre can have porous boundaries through which creators can find openings to challenge and play with generic conventions.

This book and how to use it

While autobiographical comics have proliferated over the last thirty years, the boundaries of the term are not easily delineated, and many creators work to resist, undermine, or challenge the genre's conventions and to push or rupture those already perforated boundaries. Many of the more genre-defying works are the ones that have generated the most critical attention over the years, especially if they point to unique ways in which the medium of comics intersects with the genre. My job with this book is not necessarily to clarify or throw a lasso around the concept of "autobiographical comics," but instead to embrace the genre's instability because that, in my mind, is what makes the topic so interesting. Much of this book, then, will involve discussing such challenging works so that we can see why autobiographical comics has become such a worthy area of study for scholars, students, and creators.

Also, readers can use this book in multiple ways. Moving straight through the book from beginning to end will give readers a broad understanding of the genre and its many facets. To this end, the book is organized from the general to the specific, beginning with a history of the genre and critical questions about it to specific contexts and texts. However, readers may also pick out individual sections to read as appropriate to their research or areas of interest related to autobiographical comics. With this in mind, the individual sections of the book are heavily cross-referenced. For example, a reader interested in Art Spiegelman's *Maus* may start with the section devoted to the work in Chapter 5, "Key texts," but then that reader will be directed to relevant topics related to the book, like "Trauma" and "Race and ethnicity" in Chapter 4, "Social and cultural impact," or to *Maus*'s role in Chapter 2, "The history of autobiographical comics."

After the introduction, Chapter 2 of this book offers a **history of autobiographical comics.** While most such histories, like Jared Gardner's "Autography's Biography" (2008) and relevant chapters of Charles Hatfield's *Alternative Comics* (2005), start with Justin Green's *Binky Brown Meets the Holy Virgin Mary* from 1972, I want to go back further into the early decades of the twentieth century to trace autobiographical elements that have been around almost from the beginning. Though *Binky Brown* is undoubtedly the beginning point for the trend in autobiographical comics that continues to this day, many of the conventions of and approaches to autobiography have their origins even earlier in the history of the medium. This history then highlights the key developments in the genre that lead to its centrality in today's comics industry.

Chapter 3, **"Critical questions,"** will address some broad ideas about the genre in relation to various critical, methodological, and pedagogical approaches. Questions to be addressed here include the following:

- What critical questions seem to dominate the scholarship on autobiographical comics?
- Are there particular methodologies that seem well suited to the analysis of autobiographical comics?

- How does the relationship between image and text function in autobiographical comics?
- What characteristics of the comics medium lend themselves to autobiographical and confessional expression?
- What unique terminology do scholars use when discussing autobiographical comics?
- In what classes do the use of autobiographical comics seem particularly appropriate?

Chapter 4, "**Social and cultural impact**," offers individual attention to various key topics and trends that have emerged from autobiographical comics over the years. Some of these are areas that have garnered significant critical attention as well. Issues covered include trauma, graphic medicine, quotidian or mundane experiences, gender, sexuality, race and ethnicity, adolescence, and the censorship and controversies surrounding autobiographical comics. In addition, the impact of the means of production related to self-publishing and web comics will also be discussed.

Following these key topics, this book offers discussions of various **Key texts** in the genre, which will be covered in chronological order. For the sections of Chapter 5, I have picked works that have some significance in more than one of the following areas: historical and/or cultural importance, influence, experimentation in form and/or genre, scholarly attention, and educational value. The number of works that fit within these criteria far exceeds the spatial limitations of this book, so further narrowing was necessary. This is by no means an attempt to argue for a canon of autobiographical comics. However, for better or for worse, a small canon has already formed, mostly based on critical attention, scholarship, and pedagogical value. As mentioned earlier, Art Spiegelman's *Maus*, Marjane Satrapi's *Persepolis*, and Alison Bechdel's *Fun Home* have risen to this position. One could argue that Justin Green's *Binky Brown Meets the Holy Virgin Mary* deserves a spot in this pantheon primarily for its historical importance and profound influence on generations of creators. I will admit that outside of these four works, some subjectivity was involved in the decision about which works to include as "key texts" in this chapter. Many works came in and out of that section as this book progressed. I'm sure that readers will have different choices that they would include there.

Finally, the **Appendices**, **Glossary**, and **Resources** sections offer readers supplementary information for further study of autobiographical comics, including extensive primary and secondary source bibliographies and materials that expand on topics covered in earlier sections of the book. The first appendix presents an edited transcript of a panel discussion featuring pioneering autobiographical comics creators Justin Green, Aline Kominsky-Crumb, Carol Tyler, and Phoebe Gloeckner. This freewheeling conversation gives readers a sense of how creators talk about their craft and also how they see each others' work. The second appendix digs deeper into the creation of autobiographical comics through an interview with Jennifer Hayden, creator of *The Story of My Tits* (2015), a recent graphic memoir of her experience with breast cancer. Finally, the appendices conclude with two comics excerpts in dialog with one another. The first, from David Chelsea, explores the choices that a creator makes involving perspective or point-of-view. The second, by Ryan Claytor, challenges Chelsea's argument and considers these choices further. While most of the book focuses on how the genre of autobiographical comics is discussed in academic scholarship, these items in the appendices provide readers with a sense of how the creators of such comics think about and discuss their work.

In the end, my ultimate goal with this book is to provide readers with a valuable resource that introduces them to the wide-ranging, expanding, and exciting world of autobiographical comics. Readers already familiar with the genre will also find new ways of thinking about autobiographical comics and perhaps be able to make connections to other works that they were not familiar with.

Writing a book like this comes with some inherent difficulties. One is comprehensiveness. With the proliferation of autobiographical comics as a worldwide, multimedia phenomenon, it would be extraordinarily difficult, if not impossible, to be completely comprehensive in this discussion of the genre. In her study of autobiographical comics, Elisabeth El Refaie (2012a) admirably covers eighty-five different works, making it the most comprehensive study to date. That number only represents the tip of the iceberg, and even more works appear on a monthly basis. A perusal of any random issue of *Previews*, the monthly catalog of new comics distributed to comic shops by Diamond, will reveal at least a half-dozen or more new autobiographical works every month. This does not even account for the web comics, self-published mini-comics, and non-Anglophone comics not covered by Diamond's distribution. This is a long way to say that some works are going to be left out, perhaps even ones that have some significance to the genre. I have striven for coverage of the diverse array of autobiographical comics that we find today, but one significant and unfortunate gap is that I have been limited largely to works published in English. I have worked to fill this gap partially through secondary sources that deal with non-Anglophone comics that have not been translated. Also, after much internal debate, I chose not to include a discussion of comics journalism and reportage. Comics journalism certainly overlaps in significant ways with autobiography—Joe Sacco makes himself a visible, central component of his works, for example—but, in the end, I felt that this growing and vibrant area within the comics medium might be best dealt with in a separate volume. In the end, I am sure that many readers will have a favorite autobiographical comic that gets little or no attention in this book: for that, I offer those readers my heartfelt apologies.

I want to alert readers to some conventions of writing about autobiographical comics, or about comics in general. It often becomes necessary to make clear distinctions between the author/cartoonist and the autobiographical subject. When discussing the specific cartoonists, their style, choices, and so on, I will use the creator's full name (Lynda Barry, Marjane Satrapi, Alison Bechdel) or last name (Barry, Satrapi, Bechdel). When dealing with the autobiographical subject or character within the text, I will use the first name (Lynda, Marjane or Marji, Alison). Of course, those cases where a creator uses a pseudonymous autobiographical subject offer an exception to the rule (Phoebe Gloeckner's Minnie Goetz, Justin Green's Binky Brown). (For mononyms like Seth or Marinaomi, the reader is just going to have to figure it out.) This is a convention I borrow from Hillary Chute (2010), who uses it specifically in *Graphic Women*, though others have followed it as well.

Quoting text from a comic can often be a challenge. Text can appear in word balloons, thought bubbles, and caption boxes. A single sentence may run through several word balloons within a panel or even from one panel to another. These are all stylistic choices a creator can make, but they can be difficult to duplicate when describing in pure prose. For quotes that run through multiple balloons or captions, I will use a forward slash ("/") to indicate a transition from one balloon to the next within a single panel. If the text runs over two or more panels, I will use two forward slashes ("//") when the quote crosses a panel border. Lettering styles prove to be an even bigger challenge. Unless absolutely necessary to convey the meaning of a passage, I will not indicate font or other lexical changes to the text (such as bold, all caps, cursive, etc.).

In Comics Studies it has also become conventional to use "comics" as a singular noun when referring to the medium, as in "Comics is a medium." In referring to the physical publications, I will use "comic books" for the periodical pamphlets, and "graphic novels" as the square-bound book form, either collections of previously published comic books or original publications. Perhaps confusingly, "web comic" is the singular form used for electronic, online comic series.

Note

1   As a faculty member at a state institution in South Carolina, I have seen firsthand the chilling effect this controversy has had on higher education administrators afraid of cuts to already paltry state funding.

2

The History of
Autobiographical Comics

When tracing the origins of autobiographical comics, scholars and historians identify Justin Green's 1972 comic, *Binky Brown Meets the Holy Virgin Mary*, as the seminal work in the genre. Joseph Witek (2011) asserts the revolutionary nature of this one comic: "the influence of a single work on any art form can rarely be traced so directly and so explicitly" (227). In fact, the genealogy of most late twentieth-century autobiographical comics goes back to *Binky Brown*. Many autobiographical comics creators cite Green's comic as a primary influence, including Art Spiegelman, Aline Kominsky-Crumb, Robert Crumb, and Phoebe Gloeckner.[1] While this chapter will trace that influence in detail, I would also like to address the strains of autobiography that existed in the comics medium earlier than Green's groundbreaking work. Such strains were indeed rare, and some only vaguely connect to the autobiographical genre as we know it today, though they are worth noting, as they indicate, at the very least, that the potential for comics to serve as a venue for autobiographical stories was apparent early on, and some of the key conventions of the genre were established prior to Green's work.

Early examples:
Proto-autobiographical comics

To some degree, readers can find elements of autobiography in most comics, if not in most fiction altogether, whether it's early Superman stories reflecting Jerry Siegel and Joe Shuster's politics, Walt Kelly using his *Pogo* strip to express his concerns for the impact of human pollution on the environment, or Grant Morrison entering the world of his comics as a character through his concept of a "fiction suit."[2] Such instances would be too numerous to mention, but early comics history did show some sparks for the potential of the medium to tell deeply personal stories.

Perhaps unsurprisingly, some of the earliest of what we might call "proto-autobiographical comics" dealt with the lives of cartoonists. Most cases were instances of self-portraiture or even self-parody rather than strictly autobiographical stories. Comic strip creators occasionally appeared in their own comics, struggling with creativity, chastising or being chastised by their creations, or otherwise suffering for their art. In the anthology *Comics about Cartoonists* (2013), editor Craig Yoe provides several examples of such strips. For example, Winsor McCay often depicted the life of a cartoonist in his earlier strips. This makes sense for a cartoonist who foregrounded the act of creation through his vaudevillian quick-draw performances and later experiments with animation where he, as creator, interacted with his characters, like Gertie the Dinosaur. In *Dream of the Rarebit Fiend*, under the nom de plume "Silas," McCay occasionally commented on the creative, professional, and personal demands placed on successful cartoonists in strips where "Silas" would appear. Yoe also cites a February 12, 1919, *Mutt and Jeff* strip in which creator Bud Fisher depicts himself constantly harangued by different competing groups making contradictory demands on him (see Fig. 2.1). Republicans criticize him for "boosting" President Wilson, while Democrats complain that he isn't featuring Wilson enough. Readers support and reject "Bolsheviki" items in the strip. And an African-American janitor expresses enjoyment of a "colored gen'leman" in the strip, but the editor warns that such images will cause them to lose their "colored circulation." Fisher maintains the same expressionless look through the first few panels. Finally, facing such

FIGURE 2.1 *Bud Fisher's* Mutt and Jeff *strip from February 12, 1919. Printed from the original art from the collection of Craig Yoe.*

irreconcilable, contradictory demands, Fisher runs a hose from the office gas pipe to his mouth and gives up (18–19).

So early in the history of the comics medium, Fisher's strip already exhibited key tensions in the ways in which comics can do autobiography: we know that this is not a "real" event in Fisher's life, but it does speak to a truth that Fisher experienced as a cartoonist. The dark comedy of the final panel shows just how irresolvable these demands are for cartoonists. Later autobiographical creators would also explore at length these tensions over the "truths" that comics can tell.

Other creators regularly depicted themselves interacting with their creations in notable ways. Will Eisner appeared in the May 3, 1942, *Spirit* comic titled "Self Portrait," where he is beset by editors demanding late work from the cartoonist. Eisner, however, is dependent on the Spirit to provide the "true" tale of his latest adventure. The cartoonist, whose face never appears in the story, laments his own adventureless life and wishes for a reversal of roles: the Spirit would create the comic based on Eisner's adventures. The story ultimately lampoons the act of creating comics as Eisner pokes fun at himself for having an inflated view of his own talents. In a later strip ("Happy New Year," December 31, 1950), Eisner's assistant, Jules Feiffer, murders the creator of the Spirit and turns the strip into something more resembling Feiffer's own creation, Clifford.

In 1948, *Collier's* magazine ran a series of one-page cartoonist autobiographies, where each cartoonist told the story of his start in the business and the creation of his famous characters. Such luminaries as Ernie Bushmiller (*Nancy*), Ham Fisher (*Joe Palooka*), Milton Caniff (*Steve Canyon*), and Chester Gould (*Dick Tracy*) contributed to the series. These strips, with titles like "Dick Tracy and Me," often showed the cartoonists in humorous interactions with their characters. However, they also dealt with more straightforward autobiographical elements, such as documenting key events in the lives of the cartoonists, than the more humorous self-portraits that were common when creators appeared in their comics.

Two sustained examples of "proto-autobiographical comics" or at least semi-autobiography in comics are worthy of note: Sheldon Mayer's *Scribbly* series and Quality Comics' *Inkie* feature. Both demonstrate how the lives of cartoonists could be depicted in comics, even if exaggerated for humorous purposes.

Scribbly was created by nineteen-year-old Sheldon Mayer and first appeared as a one-page strip in issue 2 of Dell Comics' *The Funnies* (November 1936) and later in the series *Popular Comics*. Mayer began working as a professional cartoonist in 1932 at the age of fifteen, and four years later he would use this experience as a "boy cartoonist" to create *Scribbly*. As Mayer recalled, "Scribbly was a thing I dreamed up during my lunch hour one day in a noisy cafeteria ... I followed the old rule of writing only what you know about. What was more natural than writing about the adventures of a boy cartoonist?" (qtd in Goulart 1990: 322–3). Ron Goulart also explains the relationship between the *Scribbly* strip and Mayer's own experiences: "Mayer has maintained that the strip was a blend of autobiography and fantasy and that some of the elements that seemed most true were the most unreal" (323). Scribbly Jibbet is a young man with ambitions to become a famous cartoonist like his hero, Ving Parker. Parker discovers Scribbly's cartoon work as graffiti on neighborhood walls and fences, something that the young Mayer did as well. Soon, the young artist ends up staying in Parker's mansion, and Parker even introduces Scribbly to such real-life cartoonists as Lank Leonard (*Mickey Finn*) and Milt Gross (who also often included himself in his own strips) (see Fig. 2.2). Scribbly then starts producing his own comic, "Why Big Brothers Leave Home," which we see as a strip running at the bottom of each *Scribbly* page. That strip is based on Scribbly's own experiences with a pestering little brother and even features a boy named Scribbly as the main character. Therefore, though the strip *Scribbly* is only loosely based on Mayer's experiences as a young cartoonist, the diegetic strip that Scribbly creates is purely autobiographical and demonstrates an early awareness of the potential for comics as a vehicle for autobiographical stories. Later, the "Why Big Brothers Leave Home" strip was turned into a kind of "reader participation" feature, where young readers could earn money by sending in their horrifying or amusing experiences with younger siblings for Scribbly to draw.

Once the character Scribbly was established as a celebrity boy cartoonist, the series addressed the challenges of balancing school life with cartooning work. He also runs into problems drawing source material from real life. When he caricatures his teacher in a strip, she sends him to the principal for disciplining. The principal, however, has cartooning ambitions of his own. Rather than disciplining Scribbly, the principal taps him for drawing lessons. Ultimately, the principal creates his own autobiographical strip, "Scene in P.S. 83 as Seen by the Principal."[3] With this storyline, *Scribbly* addresses the personal dangers of mining one's life for source material—a danger that many autobiographical comics creators would address later.

FIGURE 2.2 *"Gettin' Up in th' World" from* Scribbly *by Sheldon Mayer. Originally appeared in* The Funnies *8 (May 1937).*

When Mayer began working for Max Gaines at All-American Comics (which would merge with National Periodical Publications and eventually become DC Comics), he took Scribbly with him. The *Scribbly* feature ran in *All-American Comics* 1–59 (1939–44), though the boy cartoonist ended up as second fiddle to the popular supporting character "Ma" Hunkel, a.k.a. the original Red Tornado, who would also eventually share the feature's title. Goulart (1990) explains that "There really was a Ma Hunkel, and in real life Mayer had a room in her house, which he used as a studio" (323). Ma Hunkel first appeared in the third issue of *All-American* and became the Red Tornado in issue 20 (November 1940); she ultimately began sharing the bill with Scribbly in 23 (February 1941). Mayer even appears in *All-American Comics* 45 (December 1942) in a story reminiscent of the early Bud Fisher strip discussed above, where Mayer, despondent over criticism of his comics, breaks through the panel border on the top tier of the page and attempts suicide by leaping to the bottom tier. The Red Tornado manages to rescue him by running down the stairs, changing into costume, and arriving at the final panel just in time to catch her creator (see Fig. 2.3). This is a rather ingenious and imaginative way to demonstrate the tensions between creator and creation. Scribbly later received his own comic book, which ran for fifteen issues from 1948 to 1951. Other autobiographical cartoonists would follow Mayer by creating pseudonymous stand-ins to tell their life stories, including Justin Green's Binky Brown, Aline Kominsky-Crumb's Bunch, and Phoebe Gloekner's Minnie Goetze. Such creations allowed the cartoonists to blur or challenge generic boundaries of autobiography, yet we see that such challenges occurred in the earliest examples, before a tradition of autobiography even starts in the comics medium.

The feature *Inkie* was a humor series appearing in Quality Comics' *Crack Comics* 28 (March 1943) to 60 (May 1949), originally created by cartoonist Al Stahl and heavily influenced by Max Fleischer's 1918–29 animated series, *Out of the Inkwell*, featuring Koko the Klown. Early strips in the series served as sharp and often surreal satires of the comics industry in general, and of Quality Comics in particular. In the first installments, Inkie, a tiny boy made out of ink, emerges from the comics page because he is dissatisfied with the quality of stories in which he appears. Late at night, he comes to life in order to create more satisfying stories. In some

FIGURE 2.3 *Sheldon Mayer's* Scribbly and the Red Tornado *(December 1942). From* All-American Comics 45 © *DC Comics. Used with permission.*

of the early episodes, Inkie also befriends the artist who works on his strip at the time, including series creator Al Stahl as well as later fill-in artists Jack Cole and Milt Stein. Each creator would appear overworked and beset upon by a blustery, demanding, cheap, and dictatorial boss, who may be a caricature of Jerry Iger, the owner of the studio that initially produced the strip. In one of Jack Cole's contributions, from *Crack Comics* 34 (Summer 1944), Cole is frequently interrupted by notes from the editor demanding the appearance of Inkie in the story. Cole responds by quickly drawing a picture of Inkie and holding it up to the reader before returning to the story at hand (see Fig. 2.4). Often, the cartoonist becomes enmeshed in a crime, and Inkie comes to the rescue. But like some of the other contemporaneous representations of the industry, the creation of comics appeared to be grueling, thankless work with little reward. The story from *Crack Comics* 35 (Autumn 1944), drawn by Milt Stein, depicts the Quality offices: the boss is hitting on a buxom, bespectacled young secretary, while an artist shows off his stick-figure drawings. The early strips in this series created a sense of a "bullpen" responsible for the production of comics, anticipating *Mad*'s "Usual Gang of Idiots" in the 1950s and the Marvel bullpen that Stan Lee would perpetuate in the 1960s and later. These metafictional plots and industry satires continued through issue 39 (Autumn 1945), at which point the series became a generic humor strip about "the world's smallest boy." Though Al Stahl remained the series creator until the end, he no longer appeared in the strip and no one mentions that Inkie is a boy made of ink.

Another significant precursor to later autobiographical comics appeared in EC's *Weird Science* 22 (1953). "My World," written by Al Feldstein and drawn by Wally Wood, features a series of panels with caption boxes that explain how each image represents an aspect of the narrator's "world." The six-page story begins, "This is my world. This is the world I love," and the final panel shows an artist at the drawing board, with the word balloon,

> For my world is the world of science-fiction … conceived in my mind and placed upon paper with pencil and ink and brush and sweat and a great deal of love for my world. For I am a science-fiction artist. My name is Wood.

FIGURE 2.4 Inkie *from* Crack Comics *34 (Autumn 1944). Published by* Quality Comics.

We see on the drawing board the very page we are looking at in the process of creation (a concept later discussed in Chapter 3 as *mise en abyme*). Like other early examples, this may seem like a minor occurrence of autobiography. However, the influence of EC Comics, especially the work of Wally Wood, on later underground and mainstream creators is profound.

As with *Scribbly* and *Inkie*, throughout the history of comics, creators continued to depict themselves entering the world of their characters, usually for humorous effect rather than any kind of autobiographical revelation. Stan Lee and Jack Kirby try to crash the wedding of Reed Richards and Sue Storm in *Fantastic Four Annual* 3 (1965), only to be given the bum's rush by Nick Fury and his Howling Commandos. This moment began a long tradition of Marvel creators appearing in the comics, with the idea that the Marvel Comics offices, complete with its bullpen, existed in the Marvel universe and produced comics based on the real adventures of these heroes. During this same "Silver Age" period, in the pages of DC Comics' *Green Lantern* and *The Atom*, artist Gil Kane would often directly address the reader from his drawing board. And in what amounts to a darker version of *Inkie*, an egomaniacal Kane is sucked into his own horror story after killing editor Joe Orlando in "His Name Is ... Kane" from *House of Mystery* 180 (May–June 1969), written by Mike Friedrich. Though the title is primarily a reference to Gil Kane's groundbreaking adventure comic, *His Name Is ... Savage* (1968), one can also read in the title a reference to the final line of Wally Wood's "My World": "My name is Wood." While such a story is pure fantasy, it offers what may be only a slight exaggeration of the tensions at work between members of a comic book's creative team. And as in the Wood story, the autobiographical trope of the artist addressing the reader from his drawing board would later be exploited by Justin Green, Lynda Barry, Art Spiegelman, and many others as a signal for the autobiographical mode. It also may be no accident that such an experimental story in a mainstream comic appeared at the onset of the underground comix movement.[4]

Other rare instances of autobiographical comics precede underground comix. Henry Yoshitaka Kiyama's *Four Immigrants Manga* (also known as *Manga of the Four Students*), self-published in Japan in 1931, tells of the creator's immigrant experience, along with his three friends, in San Francisco from 1904 to 1924 (English translation by Stone Bridge Press [1998]). In 1946, Miné Okubo published *Citizen 13660* (1983), her illustrated memoir of life in a Japanese-American internment camp during World War II.[5] With full-page illustrations and accompanying text, *Citizen 13660* more resembles an illustrated story than a comic, but its historical significance, resistance to contemporary racial stereotypes, and influence on later graphic narratives make it a frequent part of discussions about graphic memoirs. In 1961, manga creator Shinji Nagashima created *The Cruel Story of a Cartoonist* (*Mangaka Zankoku Monogatari*), which addresses the creator's frustrations with the Japanese comics industry. Such frustrations have been the subjects of autobiographical comics from the genre's inception. Comics scholar Mark McKinney has found an early 1960s memoir by Coral (Laroque Letour), who chronicled his life in prison and far-right nationalist beliefs using journals in comics form (cited in El Refaie 2012a: 227 n.16). None of these works had the popularity or cultural penetration to kick off a trend in autobiographical comics, however. The potential for autobiographical comics has always existed in the medium, much as the potential for any genre would in any medium. In this sense, these early forays into autobiography are unremarkable. None of the examples from the early 1900s to the 1960s rose to the level of influence that would firmly entrench the genre in the medium. Nor do they have the intimate, confessional power that marked Justin Green's work and those that followed him. Instead, the examples from popular comics sources function on a playful, metafictional level. Thus, these works often go unmentioned in historical discussions of autobiographical comics, which might gesture toward the existence of early examples but instead focus on the clearer and more significant underground influence. Nonetheless, they demonstrate the potential for the medium to allow for personal creative expressions and even establish some of the basic conventions of the genre that would become significant later.

Underground comix

So, while Justin Green's *Binky Brown* did not appear *sui generis* as the first comic to feature autobiographical elements, it is safe to say that this seminal work spawned a tradition of autobiography, especially confessional autobiography, in comics form.

That tradition had its origins in the experimental, boundary-pushing work found in the underground comix movement. Joseph Witek (1989) defines "underground comix" as "cheaply and independently published black-and-white comics which flourished in the late 1960s and early 1970s as outlets for the graphic fantasies and social protests of your counterculture" (51). These "comix" likely first appeared on American university campuses, often self-published by contributors to the local campus newspapers and college humor magazines, like Frank Stack's *The Adventures of Jesus* (1964) and Jaxon's (Jack Jackson) *God Nose* (1964), both at the University of Texas. By 1966, free underground newspapers, most notably the *East Village Other* in New York and the *LA Free*

Press in California, included strips by the first wave of underground cartoonists. In 1968, copies of Crumb's *Zap Comix* 1 were sold from a baby carriage in San Francisco's Haight-Ashbury district.[6] Soon after, underground comix—many produced by dedicated publishers like Last Gasp Eco-Funnies, Kitchen Sink Press, Print Mint, and Rip-Off Press—could be found in the head shops of the Haight-Ashbury district of San Francisco during the height of the counterculture movement, to which they were intensely connected. As Roger Sabin (1993) describes it, the counterculture was both a social and artistic movement, led by "a generation that viewed society as essentially reactionary and bellicose, and which instead interested itself in pacifism, sexual freedom, minority rights and, perhaps most notoriously, the benefits (spiritual or otherwise) of drugs" (36). As a part of the counterculture, the underground comix were defined by their resistance to censorship and the cultural norms of the time, and they flaunted taboos often for the sake of exposing otherwise forbidden topics, with the added irony of appearing in a medium that was closely associated with children. Witek (1989) explains that, because comics was already such a "specially circumscribed cultural space," the early underground creators found that "the comics medium offered a particularly fruitful ground for iconoclasm" (50–1). No subject was off limits in these books: graphic sex, violence, drug use, racism, resistance to authority, the Vietnam War.

A particular target was the Comics Code, the restrictive self-censorship regime that mainstream publishers committed to in the wake of Fredric Wertham's *Seduction of the Innocent* (1954) and the infamous Senate hearings on the relationship between comics and juvenile delinquency. Hence, the "x" in "comix" emphasized their distinction from conventional comics and signaled their adult or "X-rated" content. Underground creator Spain Rodriguez explained the overt antagonism toward mainstream comics' self-censorship: "We were able to kick the despicable Comics Code in the teeth" (qtd in Mazur and Danner 2014: 29). In one notorious example, in S. Clay Wilson's "Head First" from *Zap Comics* 2 (1968), a pirate lops off and eats a fellow pirate's penis. In the same issue, Wilson also has an untitled short story in which a naked man flings his own feces at some onlookers. Such graphic imagery was certainly boundary-pushing, and the "anything goes" mentality of these creators would open the door for more works that would challenge the status quo, even if those works were not so overtly shocking.

Charles Hatfield (2005) argues that, in addition to the taboo-breaking content, one of the lasting influences of underground comix was to make the comic book as a publication a viable commodity for adults (7). Hatfield sees a direct line from this particular revolution to the development of, among other things, autobiographical stories as content for comic books: "It was through the underground comix that comic books *per se* became an adult medium, and the self-contained nature of these 'books' ... made the medium an ideal platform for kinds of expression that were outrageously personal and self-regarding" (7). In turn, that potential personal expression also led to a kind of "auteurist" approach to comics, where individual creators achieved a status in which their work was sought out by readers. And so, many of the most popular underground cartoonists created their own individual comic books, like various works by Crumb, Kim Deitch's *Corn Fed Comix*, and Gilbert Shelton's *Fabulous Furry Freak Brothers*. Thus, a work like Justin Green's *Binky Brown*—a stand-alone, book-length autobiographical story by a single creator—fits logically into this auteurist sensibility.

Furthermore, underground publishers followed models that challenged corporate publishing strategies and creator contracts. For example, underground creators retained the rights to their creations and received royalties on sales, benefits that were virtually unheard of in the mainstream comics industry. Many of the most popular underground comix went through multiple printings, so they could conceivably always appear on store shelves, unlike the more ephemeral nature of the monthly periodical comic. Therefore, these publishing models also fomented and encouraged a culture in which creators could tell personal stories because they could also own their stories.

In this creative environment, autobiographical comics emerged as one of the ways that the medium and the prevailing culture could be challenged. In addition, the work of underground creators was already intensely personal, and figures like Robert Crumb rose to the level of celebrity quickly within the movement. Therefore, the rise of autobiographical stories seems inevitable as an obvious form of personal expression. In the earliest underground comix, the autobiographical mode manifested through vivid descriptions of intense LSD-trips, as Jared Gardner (2012) explains: "Comics, with its emphasis on the nonverbal and its openness to nonlinear storytelling, was also latched on to as the ideal medium to tell the unique and uniquely untranslatable experience of taking LSD" (120). Crumb and Art Spiegelman were among those who created "acid trip" comics to convey their experiences, though through semi-autobiographical avatars.

Crumb, as Gardner (2012) also points out, dabbled in autobiographical expression in his earliest comics, even drawing himself into stories in *Foo*, the fanzine that Crumb produced with his brother Charles in 1958 (115). Into the mid-1960s, Crumb continued to produce "semiautobiographical stand-ins" as he worked through his neuroses and anxieties on the comics page. By 1972, he was using "R. Crumb" as a character in his comics to address concerns about his own celebrity status, as in "The Confessions of R. Crumb" (*The People's Comics*, 1972a) and "The Many Faces of R. Crumb" (*XYZ Comics*, 1972b).

Justin Green explains how his first exposure to the work of R. Crumb changed his life and led him to move to San Francisco and join the underground scene. While studying classical art in Rome during his senior year at the Rhode Island School of Design, Green received a copy of an underground newspaper from another American: "Little did I know that therein was a cartoon by a fellow named Crumb that was to change my life" (qtd in Rosencranz 2008: 94). This self-described "epiphany" inspired Green to shift his focus from fine art to cartooning, and it ultimately led him to move to San Francisco in order to pursue a career in comics.

Every history of autobiographical comics (Hatfield [2005], Gardner [2008], Chute [2010], El Refaie [2012a], and others) has identified Justin Green's *Binky Brown Meets the Holy Virgin Mary*, a 1972 forty-four-page one-shot published by Last Gasp Eco-Funnies, as the seminal autobiographical underground comic. In addition, Aline Kominsky-Crumb, among others, cites Green's work as her inspiration for not only entering the world of underground comix, but also for creating her own autobiographical work. In "More of the Bunch" from *Twisted Sisters* 1 (1976a), Kominsky-Crumb's avatar, the Bunch, reads *Binky Brown* as her first experience with underground comix: she thinks, "Hey this is heavy shit. This kid's got problems ... and so do I!" She's then inspired to make her own similar comic, deciding that she will be the main character. Most notably, Art Spiegelman (1995), in his introduction to *Binky Brown*, states that "without [Green's] work there could have been no MAUS" (n.p.). Spiegelman's inspiration came even before Green's book was published: he saw the pages in progress while hanging out at Green's apartment. He then went on to produce the proto-*Maus* story that appeared in *Funny Aminals* 1 (1972) just a few months after *Binky Brown*. Regardless of any debates about its designation as "the first," *Binky Brown* inspired many creators to see comics as a viable medium for their own autobiographical stories.

Binky Brown receives more detailed attention in Chapter 5, but a brief description is warranted here. In addition to being a seminal autobiographical comic, this was also the longest sustained narrative in underground comix to this point in time. Justin Green uses the character of Binky Brown (a name derived from a childhood nickname Green had received from an uncle, combined with a color) to explore his experiences with what would later be diagnosed as obsessive-compulsive disorder related to his adolescent involvement in the Catholic Church. Specifically, Brown is obsessed with impure thoughts directed at the Virgin Mary, and he believes these thoughts radiate from his penis and, later, all of his appendages, which take the form of penises in the comic. For example, he fears that these penis rays will destroy a church if they are directed at the building, even from a distance.

From the outset, *Binky Brown* does not read like a straight autobiography. Green utilizes a symbolic or allegorical style as a means of autobiographical expression: his fears and obsessions are literalized in the book's imagery. Therefore, the experimental potential of comics to tell autobiographical stories in a unique way is evident in this early work.

Other creators quickly followed suit with their own short autobiographical works, and some would make sustained efforts at creating a body of personal stories. Robert Crumb and Aline Kominsky-Crumb continued their prolific output of autobiographical comics, both separately and together. Their collaborative *Dirty Laundry Comics* (1974 and 1977, collected in 1993) features tales of their off-beat relationship in which the artists draw themselves. Art Spiegelman continued to dabble in autobiography, most notably with the original "*Maus*" story in *Funny Aminals* (1972), and "Prisoner of the Hell Planet" from the first issue of

Short Order Comix (1973a). He also produced a variety of short dream comics, sometimes using his cartoon stand-in, Skeeter Grant. Manuel "Spain" Rodriguez was another notable contributor to the genre, whose autobiographical works were later collected in *My True Story* (1994). Spain told stories of his experiences with the Road Vultures motorcycle club during the 1950s and 1960s and also created some of the earliest examples of comics journalism, like his coverage of the 1968 Democratic Convention in Chicago for the *East Village Other*.

Many creators influenced by Green also became editors of some of the more prominent underground and post-underground periodical comics anthologies that frequently published autobiographical comics. Robert Crumb and later Aline Kominsky-Crumb edited *Weirdo* (1981–93), and Art Spiegelman co-founded and co-edited *Arcade* (1975–6) and *Raw* (1980–91). Spiegelman and co-founder Bill Griffith published seven issues of *Arcade: The Comics Revue*, through San Francisco underground publisher Print Mint. Despite its short run, the magazine contained important autobiographical work by significant underground creators, including Spiegelman, Crumb, Aline Kominsky-Crumb, Bob Armstrong, and Diane Noomin. In addition, *Weirdo*, especially under the editorship of Kominsky-Crumb (issues 18–28, 1986–93), became a significant venue for the publication of autobiographical comics from both underground creators and the next generation.

Autobiographical stories also flourished in the pages of comix devoted to groups underrepresented in the mainstream comics industry, both behind the scenes and on the page. While series like *Wimmen's Comix*, *Tits & Clits*, *Twisted Sisters*, and *Gay Comix* did not exclusively deal with autobiography, these series had a high concentration of personal stories that addressed topics not otherwise covered in mainstream popular culture or the more male-dominated underground comix industry, like promiscuous sexual activity, menstruation, masturbation, sexual abuse, domestic violence, and coming out. Even when not dealing with dramatic events, they exposed readers to sympathetic portrayals of otherwise marginalized groups, usually in a frank and honest way. These four series, along with Mary Wings's one-shots—*Come Out Comix* (1973) and *Dyke Shorts* (1978)—require more considered attention because of the significant roles they played and long-term impact they had in this history. The sheer concentration of autobiographical stories that these series offered was a part of their contribution, but they also served as vehicles (or even launching pads) for many of the key creators in the genre. These works will also be discussed in the "Gender and sexuality" section of the "Social and cultural impact" chapter.

Wimmen's Comix and *Tits & Clits* survived the underground comix crash, though they experienced sporadic publication. The seventeen issues of *Wimmen's Comix* published from 1972 to 1992 bridge the time from the publication of *Binky Brown* to the completion of Art Spiegelman's *Maus*, and, as such, the series both influenced and was influenced by trends in autobiographical comics during this period. *Tits & Clits* continued irregular publication until its seventh issue in 1987. *Gay Comix* (1980–98, created by Howard Cruse and initially published by Kitchen Sink) arrived much later than the other two series, but it followed the same format, anthologizing a mixture of autobiography, real life, humor, and fantasy stories focused on themes dealing with sexuality and gender.

Many female creators felt excluded from the underground comix movement as both creators and readers. The taboo-breaking ethos of the undergrounds led male creators to graphic stories of misogyny, rape, and violence toward women, often played for laughs. Male-dominated anthologies rarely had room for female cartoonists, and so women often had to create their own routes to publication. However, the underground also offered the potential for new creative outlets that didn't exist in the mainstream comics industry. Hillary Chute (2010) explains the importance of comix for women:

> The growth of the underground comix movement was connected to second-wave feminism, which enabled a body of work that was explicitly political to sprout: if female activists complained of the misogyny of the New Left, this was mirrored in underground comics, prompting women cartoonists to establish a space specifically for women's work. It is only in the comics underground that the U.S. first saw any substantial work by women allowed to explore their own artistic impulses, and further, women organizing collectives that undertook to articulate the challenges and goals of specifically female cartoonists. (20)

Trina Robbins was one of the earliest female cartoonists to establish such a space, first in the all-female anthology *It Aint Me Babe*

(1970), published by Last Gasp and in association with the feminist newspaper of the same name. Robbins then went on to help form the Wimmen's Comix Collective, a group of ten female cartoonists who would each serve as contributors and rotating editors for a new anthology series, *Wimmen's Comix*.[7] From the first issues, beginning in 1972, the series featured autobiographical stories, including works by Robbins, Kominsky-Crumb, Diane Noomin, Sharon Rudahl, and others. As the series progressed, it published a vast number of autobiographical short stories, occasionally even devoting entire issues to the genre. Later autobiographical contributors included Caryn Leschen, Phoebe Gloeckner, Lynda Barry, Alison Bechdel, Carol Tyler, Joey Epstein, Mary Fleener, Leslie Sternbergh, Dori Seda, Sophie Crumb, Penny Moran, and Julie Doucet.

Three months prior to the publication of *Wimmen's Comix*, Joyce Sutton (later Joyce Farmer) and Lyn Chevli (also known as Lyn Chevely and Chin Lyvely) formed Nanny Goat Productions and released *Tits & Clits Comix*. The first two issues were created completely by Chevely and Farmer, and then the comic became a multi-artist anthology with its third issue. The series, later published by Last Gasp through its seventh and final issue in 1987, increased its autobiographical offerings through its run, featuring creators like Trina Robbins, Roberta Gregory, Chris Powers, Sharon Rudahl, Mary Fleener, Dori Seda, Joey Epstein, Joyce Brabner, and Leslie Sternbergh and topics ranging from single motherhood and adolescent sexuality to abortion rights and sexual predators.

Aline Kominsky-Crumb and Diane Noomin separated from the Wimmen's Comix Collective in 1976 to produce their own comic, *Twisted Sisters*. As Chute (2010) explains, Kominsky-Crumb was "frustrated by what she perceived as an almost superhero-inflected glamorization of women under the auspices of feminism" amongst the collective (24). The first issue cover of *Twisted Sisters* forms a kind of mission statement for the series (though the two creators provide an actual mission statement on the inside, using their characters Bunch and Didi Glitz as spokeswomen), with Kominsky-Crumb's Bunch persona sitting on a toilet and criticizing her appearance in a hand mirror. Noomin went on to use the *Twisted Sisters* title for a pair of anthologies and a miniseries in the 1990s.

Mary Wings also experienced dissatisfaction with the Wimmen's Comix Collective over the lack of lesbian representation in their comics, so she self-published *Come Out Comix* in 1973, and later *Dyke Shorts* in 1978. *Come Out Comix* tells a long, single narrative, labeled "Coming Out: One Person's Experience" and "The Story of a 'New Lesbian'," that follows Wings's avatar, Maggi (sometimes spelled "Maggie"), from her initial discovery of her lesbian identity to her first relationship with her partner, Dorothy. The issue's conclusion is unresolved, leaving the future of Maggi and Dorothy's relationship hanging, but no second issue continued the story. *Dyke Shorts* then mixes Wings's own personal stories with those of others that have been told to her.

Gay Comix, created by Howard Cruse, ran for twenty-five issues from 1980 to 1998, originally published by Kitchen Sink and later by Bob Ross. Andy Mangels, the final editor of the series, changed the name to *Gay Comics* with issue 15 (1993) in order to break away from the association with the long-passed underground movement. Though the anthology series mixed genres (including an issue featuring only gay superheroes), it offered an opportunity for a range of sensitive, personal, autobiographical stories on such subjects as dating, prejudice, AIDS, coming-of-age, and transgender identity. In addition to Cruse's autobiographical and semi-autobiographical works, other autobiographical creators included Bruce Billings, Angela Bocage, Lee Marrs, Billy Fugate, David Kottler, Julie Franki, and Alison Bechdel. Bechdel credited *Gay Comix*—the first issue of which she found in a New York gay book store in 1981—with inspiring her to become a cartoonist. Issue 19 (1993) was devoted entirely to Bechdel and included several autobiographical stories (the cover explicitly states that the issue contains no strips from her *Dykes to Watch Out For* series).

Parallel to the American underground movement, we can find significant autobiographical works in other countries. In 1972, manga artist Keiji Nakazawa published *I Saw It!* (*Ore wa Mita*), a forty-five-page memoir of his experience surviving the atomic bombing of Hiroshima when he was seven years old. The following year, he began releasing his epic, ten-volume semi-autobiographical manga series, *Barefoot Gen* (*Hadashi no Gen*), which documents the atomic bombing and post-war period in Japan. Art Spiegelman read *Gen* while working on the early chapters of *Maus*, and he cites the work as a key influence, as he explains in the introduction to the first volume of *Gen*'s English translation (2004). Other creators have also connected their experiences to historical events. In 1973, Shigeru Mizuki's *Onward Towards Our Noble Deaths* (2011) came out in Japan. The one-shot manga tells the semi-autobiographical story of Mizuki's experience in the Japanese Army, stationed on New Britain Island during World War II, where he was the only survivor of a suicide mission that resulted in the loss of his left arm. In the manga, Mizuki's alter ego, Maruyama, does not survive the mission, but the commentary on the futility and absurdity of the mission comes from Mizuki's own experience. Like Nakazawa's work, Mizuki's is sharply critical of Japan's involvement in the war and its continued sacrifice of its citizens in the face of inevitable failure. In another example, Spanish cartoonist Carlos Giménez created *Paracuellos* (2016) to document his life in orphanages during Franco's reign. The work, begun in 1975, was critical of the recently deceased dictator's regime, and, as a result, the artist's life was threatened.

Comics historians tend to end the underground era in the early 1970s, around the time when the June 1973 *Miller vs. California* Supreme Court decision handed over definitions of obscenity to local jurisdictions, and the shuttering of head shops over legal decisions on selling drug paraphernalia closed off avenues for comics distribution and caused publishers to reduce their output significantly. In *Bijou Funnies* 8 (1973), the inside front cover contains an editorial asking readers to protest the Supreme Court decision on obscenity. The text claims that this ruling will make it impossible to continue publishing the comic, and, in fact, this was the final issue of the series. Witek (1989) also adds that "much of the counterculture's political and artistic energy had dissipated" by this time as well (51). Hatfield (2005) concurs: "[T]he movement, once stretched, proved flaccid. As comix became entrenched, they lost their impetus and collective focus both politically and, eventually, aesthetically" (19). The shock value that many underground creators aimed for had also run its course, for the most part. Whatever the causes, sales of underground comix dropped. Harvey Pekar points out that his creation of *American Splendor* coincided with this conservative drawback from underground publishers, who, according to Pekar, were only going to back known quantities, like Crumb and Gilbert Shelton ("The Young Crumb Story," *American Splendor* 4, 1979). However, underground publishing and the underground spirit did not suddenly end at this time, and the surge of autobiographical comics in the late 1980s was largely a result of the work and inspiration of the underground creators. And several long-running, though infrequently published anthology series bridged the underground movement and the next wave of independent and small press comics, including *Weirdo*, *Wimmen's Comix*, *Tits & Clits*, and *Gay Comix*, which all continued into the late 1980s and early 1990s. Not only did they continue to publish work by early underground creators, but they also promoted the next generation of autobiographers like Phoebe Gloeckner, Alison Bechdel, and others. One of the most important and sustained outcomes of the underground movement, therefore, was to further democratize comics and inspire alternative venues for creators whose works did not fit the mainstream.

Post-underground and the rise of Pekar and Spiegelman

Despite the sharp decline in underground comix during the mid-1970s, the history of autobiographical comics moves fluidly from the 1970s to 1980s, possibly because autobiography remains a sustained force for most of the remaining, productive underground cartoonists. Also, some of the more significant autobiographical comics of the period come at the tail end of the undergrounds, like Harvey Pekar's *American Splendor*, which began its regular, annual publication in 1976. With a few notable exceptions, like *Binky Brown* and *Come Out Comix*, the vast majority of autobiographical comics produced out of the underground movement were in the form of short stories. This is largely due to the dominant publishing format of the anthology comic book, whether multi-artist anthology series or single artist one-shots. Most of the autobiographical stories in underground comix were rarely over ten pages long, and many were only a single page. Therefore, most of the autobiographical works that followed in the wake of the undergrounds continued the short story tradition, as can be seen in *American Splendor*, Dennis Eichhorn's *Real Stuff*, Colin Upton's *Big Thing*, Dori Seda's *Lonely Night Comics*, and various anthologized works by Mary Fleener, Phoebe Gloeckner, Carol Tyler, and others. The post-underground era also brought new experiments in publishing format that moved comics beyond the periodical comic book format to bound books or "graphic novels" as they came to be called. The graphic novel movement had considerable impact on the world of autobiographical comics, allowing creators to tell more expansive stories and reach different audiences. This impact can best be seen in the enormous critical and commercial success of Art Spiegelman's *Maus*. In addition, shorter works could be collected into book-length anthologies, thus keeping in print stories that may have faded into obscurity with long out-of-print comic books. Hatfield (2005) summarizes the influence of the undergrounds on the next generation of creators:

> [C]omix ... offered not only new economic terms and a new, more individualistic model of production but also the necessary inspiration for these in a new level of adult and achingly personal content, both fantastic and, as time went on, naturalistic. (111)

This set of influences can especially be seen in *American Splendor*, as well as the wave of confessional comics that followed in Pekar's wake.

Harvey Pekar began to self-publish *American Splendor* in 1976, just a few years after the underground comix movement had peaked. Hatfield (2005), noting Pekar's importance in the history of autobiographical comics, says that he "brought a radical appreciation for the mundane" through "a defiantly working-class strain of autobiography" (111). *American Splendor* built on the promise of the undergrounds by featuring more sophisticated, intensely personal stories and moving beyond the shock value that motivated a lot of the comix that preceded it. Following Pekar, many autobiographical comics creators would in turn build upon the personal, confessional nature of *American Splendor* to the point that no subject seemed out of bounds. Hatfield (2005) explains that "this new school of autobiographical comics has tended to stress the abject, the seedy, the anti-heroic, and the just plain nasty" (111). Pekar's significance stems not only from his subject matter, but also from his collaborative approach to autobiography and his efforts at self-publishing and distribution, which was relatively untested when he began *American Splendor* in 1976. While Pekar did often lose money on individual issues of the series, he maintained a relatively regular annual production of the comic until 1991, and each new issue was usually met with some demand for the earlier issues.

Pekar also achieved a kind of celebrity status surprising for a fringe cultural figure producing personal comics for a few thousand readers. In 1988 and 1989, he made several appearances on *Late Night with David Letterman*, ostensibly to promote his comic, though more likely for the show to exploit Pekar's eccentric personality. Pekar claimed that the appearances had little effect on the sales of his comic, but they certainly moved him from the cultural margins into a more recognizable position, plus they provided considerable material for *American Splendor*. (The series and Pekar's influence receive more extensive coverage in Chapter 5.)

One of the most important developments for autobiographical comics out of the underground comix movement is the early career of Art Spiegelman. Spiegelman's underground output ranged from darkly comic stories like his *Viper* series, retold dreams, and a handful of autobiographical stories. These autobiographical stories from the period fed directly into the creation of *Maus*. In the 1972 one-shot *Funny Aminals*, Spiegelman published a proto-*Maus* story that established the basic allegory of Jews as mice and Nazis as cats. In this story, a father mouse is telling a bedtime story to his son, Mickey, but instead of telling a nice story to ease the young mouse into sleep, the father tells of a series of harrowing escapes and final capture that led him and his wife to Mauschwitz. The story relates events that would later be retold in *Maus*, but its frame as a bedtime story creates a larger sense of irony. Perhaps Spiegelman's most famous story of the period—"Prisoner of the Hell Planet" from *Short Order Comix* 1 (1973a)—gains significance because it's reprinted in *Maus* and serves as an important plot point. In this story, Spiegelman uses a highly expressionistic style to relate his experience with his mother's suicide.

Prior to the publication of the first volume of *Maus* in 1986, Spiegelman had serialized the comic in the pages of *Raw*, the art comics periodical that he edited with his wife, Françoise Mouly, beginning in 1980. Speigelman published the serialized *Maus* as a small insert into the much larger-format *Raw*. During that serialization, *Maus* had already received significant critical attention within the world of comics (including reviews in *Comics*

Journal) as well as a mainstream review in the *New York Times*, so the publication of the first book by Pantheon was immediately met with some anticipation. This serialization is also worth noting because it shows *Maus* fitting into a larger trend of post-underground autobiographical comics that emerged in the 1980s. Therefore, *Maus*'s unprecedented mainstream critical attention may make it seem like the book came out of nowhere, but it would be more accurate to see it as a work that rose to the top of a trend that was already in play by the early 1980s.

To say that *Maus*'s impact on comics in general and autobiographical comics in particular was significant is a gross understatement. Spiegelman's work is an important historical touchstone that continues to influence comics today, especially in the public reception and acceptance of comics as a literary form and in the topics and themes that creators choose to pursue in comics form. Its publication by Pantheon, an imprint of Random House, placed *Maus* in mainstream book stores, giving it more potential popular attention than it would have received if exclusively available in comic book stores, as was the case with almost all comic books at the time. However, it proved difficult for book stores to classify, since the few "graphic novels" at the time were mostly collections of comic books and comic strips, usually shelved in the Science Fiction or Humor sections. Spiegelman had to famously petition the *New York Times* to move *Maus* from the fiction bestseller list to nonfiction. Therefore, one of its most significant influences has been to legitimize autobiographical comics by moving them into more recognizable and appropriate categories. Today, *Maus*, along with Marjane Satrapi's *Persepolis*, Alison Bechdel's *Fun Home*, and many others, can be found in book stores shelved in the Biography or History sections alongside prose works.

Maus Volume 1: My Father Bleeds History (1986) collected the first six installments of the serialized *Maus* that had been produced from 1980 to 1986. Pantheon collected the final chapters in volume 2, *And Here My Troubles Began*, in 1992. The second volume became the first graphic novel to receive the Pulitzer Prize, though it was a special award due to the continued difficulty in classifying the work. This achievement is frequently cited as a watershed moment in graphic novel history.

Maus has since been published in a variety of forms, including the multimedia *MetaMaus* project that includes production materials and a DVD. It has also garnered significant scholarly attention, much more than any other graphic novel. The work appears regularly on K-12 and college syllabi, giving it even deeper cultural penetration. At this point, *Maus* is one of the key entry points for many readers into the comics medium. Therefore, *Maus* has influenced creators to use comics as the medium to tell their personal stories, but it also has inspired readers to seek out more works like it, thus creating a cumulative effect for the popularity of graphic memoirs. The significance of *Maus* will be discussed even further in Chapter 5.

Along with Spiegelman and Mouly's *Raw*, *Weirdo*, the anthology series begun by R. Crumb and Bill Griffith in 1981, continued the spirit of underground comix while also promoting the next generation of independent cartoonists. *Weirdo* ran for twenty-seven issues until its cancellation in 1990. From the outset, the series regularly published autobiographical stories by Robert Crumb and Aline Kominsky-Crumb (including several of their collaborative "Dirty Laundry" comics), alongside a few others, including later editor Peter Bagge. For its final nine issues, under the editorship of Aline Kominsky-Crumb, *Weirdo* became a source for the cutting edge in autobiography, and large portions of each issue were devoted to such works. Beginning in issue 18, Kominsky-Crumb published autobiographical stories by Crumb, Dori Seda, Frank Stack (as Foolbert Sturgeon), Penny Moran, Justin Green, Phoebe Gloeckner, Carol Lay, and Julie Doucet, among others. *Weirdo* serves as a bridge between the underground movement, which had mostly petered out by 1980, and the independent comics movement of the late 1980s that followed the success of *Maus* and largely focused on autobiography.

Alternative comics and second wave autobiography

In an essay on Joe Matt, Chester Brown, and Seth, Bart Beaty (2011) describes two waves of North American autobiographical comics. The first consists of the underground creators described above, and the second wave emerges in the mid-1980s with such creators as those three discussed in his essay. Hatfield (2005) identifies this wave as following in the wake of Harvey Pekar, the creators' primary influence: "[T]his new school of autobiographical comics has tended to stress the abject, the seedy, the anti-heroic, and the just plain nasty" (111). In addition, "the dominant narrative modes have been tragedy, farce, and picaresque. In the wake of Pekar, these scarifying confessional comics have in fact reinvented the comic book hero" (111). This uncompromising confessional mode, therefore, offers a sharp alternative to the dominant heroic narratives of mainstream comic books. For Hatfield, Pekar's unfiltered focus on the mundane, everyday experiences of his working-class existence spawned a new wave of autobiographical artists who took their cue from this confessional mode and ran with it. Hatfield's assessment can be seen in the way Joe Matt reveals his unconventional bathroom habits (like urinating in sinks and jars), his frequent masturbation, and his general stinginess. Additionally, Julie Doucet, in her series *Dirty Plotte* (named after a Québécois slang term for a vagina) and later graphic novels, frequently deals with intimate, personal topics as well: menstruation, miscarriage, violent sexual fantasies, alcohol, and drug use. Doucet's confessional mode is certainly in keeping with her contemporaries like Matt and Brown, but it also exhibits a strong influence from the early female underground creators. Doucet also specializes in dream comics, often following a structure where the dream nature of the narrative does not become apparent until the story takes a bizarre turn following a realistic opening. For all of these creators that followed Pekar, the authenticity of their confessional work supersedes any concern for the perception of their public personae, to the point that they often depict how their dedication to authenticity has negatively affected their personal relationships.

As with any attempt to describe historical waves, this distinction between a first and second wave features porous boundaries. Underground creators continue to produce significant work throughout this period. Harvey Pekar's notoriety with *American Splendor* comes largely in this second wave, continuing into his most popular and critically significant work, *Our Cancer Year* (1994), in collaboration with his wife, Joyce Brabner. In fact, many cartoonists who began their careers in the underground continued to produce major autobiographical works well into this second wave, including many of the short comics collected in Spain Rodriguez's *My True Story* (1994) and Joyce Farmer's

Special Exits (2014). However, Beaty's (2011) division between first and second wave autobiography helps trace social networks and strains of influence both within a given period and between waves. In addition, Dominick Grace and Eric Hoffman (2013), in the introduction to their collection of interviews with Chester Brown, place Brown in a post-underground historical context that includes the early 1980s minicomics movement. They credit the availability of cheap photocopying technology for this DIY (do-it-yourself) movement that included many young autobiographical comics creators, like Brown (whose *Yummy Fur* began as a self-published minicomic, though it did not contain autobiographical stories at the time) and Doucet (who self-published *Dirty Plotte* before the series was picked up by Drawn & Quarterly as its first periodical comic). Such cartoonists distributed their self-published minicomics through local comic shops, via mail order, or at comics conventions. Therefore, the beginning of this wave can be defined by the continued influence of the undergrounds and the availability of affordable means of self-publication and distribution.

By the mid-1980s, the American comics market was also shifting away from newsstand distribution toward direct distribution to independent comic shops. This system allowed mainstream publishers to circumvent the restrictive Comics Code, which had been dictating and censoring comics content since the late 1950s. That meant publishers could aim their work at a more adult or mature audience. Smaller independent publishers also emerged during this period. While most of the fare from the mainstream and independent publishers focused on standard comics genres—superheroes, science fiction, fantasy, erotica, and horror—opportunities for more personal and experimental work also emerged. As Elisabeth El Refaie (2012a) notes, "These were typically of a satirical nature, but they also included more serious, personal, or political works, often by the same creators who had begun in the underground movement" (33). For example, Denis Kitchen's Kitchen Sink Press continued publishing the works of underground and underground-inspired cartoonists as well as Will Eisner's more personal comics. Fantagraphics, founded by Gary Groth and Mike Catron in 1976 first as the publisher of *The Comics Journal* and later, starting in 1982, as a comics publisher, has been another leader in the post-underground, alternative comics world and has also served as a key source for autobiographical comics. Fantagraphics has published and continues to publish comics by Robert Crumb, Aline Kominsky-Crumb, Carol Tyler, Debbie Drechsler, Ellen Forney, Harvey Pekar, Joe Sacco, Joyce Farmer, Mary Fleener, Ulli Lust, and many others involved in autobiographical comics. From 2004 to 2011, Fantagraphics published the quarterly anthology series of literary comics, *Mome*, which regularly featured autobiographical or semi-autobiographical comics from Jeffrey Brown, Gabrielle Bell, Jonathan Bennett, Sophie Crumb, and others. They have also been a force behind keeping classic underground comix in print, including *Wimmen's Comix*, *Zap*, and *Inner City Romance*.

Another important publisher that emerged in the second wave of autobiographical comics is Drawn & Quarterly, which handled many of the significant autobiographical cartoonists of the time. Drawn & Quarterly is a small press publisher located in Toronto, Canada, and has served since 1990 as one of the premier publishers of alternative comics. The company, founded by Chris Oliveros, began life by publishing its eponymous anthology series. The issues of the *Drawn & Quarterly* periodical anthology featured early autobiographical work by Joe Matt, Seth, Julie Doucet, Carol Tyler, Mary Fleener, Colin Upton, Michael Dougan, Ida Marx, David Collier, and other key creators of this period. Soon after these initial anthology publications, Drawn & Quarterly also published solo periodical comics, including Julie Doucet's *Dirty Plotte* (1991–8), Joe Matt's *Peepshow* (1992–2006), and Seth's *Palookaville* (1991–present). The publisher also picked up Chester Brown's *Yummy Fur* from Vortex Comics. While Brown was not known at that point for his autobiographical work, he was influenced by Joe Matt and others to begin telling his own personal stories in that series.

Though Drawn & Quarterly does not publish exclusively autobiographical comics, they have been responsible for a large percentage of the work that has appeared in the last twenty-five years. Other creators published by them include Lynda Barry, Miriam Katin, Joe Sacco, John Porcellino, David Collier, Guy Delisle, Sarah Glidden, Pascal Girard, and Joe Ollmann, among others. In addition to publishing North American autobiographical cartoonists, Drawn & Quarterly also offered several important works in translation, including the manga memoirs *A Drifting Life* by Yoshihiro Tatsumi (2009) and *Onward Towards our Noble Deaths* by Shigeru Mizuki (2011). Into the twenty-first century, other small press publishers followed Fantagraphics and Drawn & Quarterly in offering alternative autobiographical comics: Top Shelf, Picturebox, Koyama, Uncivilized Books, Retrofit-Big Planet Comics, Alternative Comics, and so on. The Joe Matt–Chester Brown–Seth nexus also demonstrates the importance of networks of friendship and influence within this second wave. Such networks were also important during the underground comix movement: many underground creators moved to San Francisco with the expressed purpose of seeking out key influences like Robert Crumb and Justin Green. In addition, the marriages of Robert Crumb to Aline Kominsky and, later, of Justin Green to Carol Tyler attest to the closeness of these networks. In the second wave, networks often emerged geographically, as with the Toronto-based trio of Matt, Brown, and Seth or the 2010–12 Brooklyn studio, Pizza Island, which included Sarah Glidden, Domitille Collardey, and Julia Wertz.

Trends in autobiographical comics also became evident in other countries as well. For example, according to Theirry Groensteen, autobiography didn't really take off in French comics until the 1990s (cited in El Refaie 2012a: 228 n.18). The French publishing collective L'Association (often shortened to "L'Asso") formed almost simultaneously with the creation of Drawn & Quarterly in 1990. This group—initially made up of Jean-Christophe Menu, Stanislas Barthélemy, Mokeït (Frédéric van Linden), Mattt Konture, Patrice Killoffer, Lewis Trondheim, and David B. (Pierre-François Beauchard)—resisted the limited genres and the dominance of the forty-eight-page hardcover graphic album in the *bande dessinèe* industry. Instead, they opted for different graphic novel formats in black and white, alternative genres (especially autobiography), and other formal experiments. The group grew out of the contributors to *Labo*, an anthology organized by Menu. Much of L'Association's output focused on autobiography and memoir, including works by Menu, Trondheim, and David B. The history of L'Association is filled with conflict and political infighting among its founders, especially directed at founding member and publisher Menu (for more on this history, see Wivel [2011]). But the publisher's early successes proved the viability of autobiography as a marketable and potentially profitable genre, and mainstream publishers soon followed suit. The group's influence was not limited to France, however: major works from L'Association were translated and distributed worldwide with considerable cultural and critical impact.

L'Association achieved perhaps its greatest success with the publication of Marjane Satrapi's *Persepolis*, released periodically in four volumes from 2000 to 2003. *Persepolis*'s US publication appeared in two volumes, subtitled *The Story of a Childhood* (2004) and *The Story of a Return* (2005), later collected in *The Complete Persepolis* (2007). The work was an almost immediate international success, gaining significant scholarly and critical attention and spawning an award-winning animated film, co-directed by Satrapi (2007). It has also become a staple in a variety of college and high school courses as one of the three key autobiographical works (along with *Maus* and *Fun Home*) that have risen to the level of "canon" in Comics Studies. Within the same realm of international significance is David B.'s *L'Ascension du Haut Mal* (1996–2003), published in English translation as *Epileptic* (2006), a work that combines Beauchard's own *Künstlerroman* with the family's struggles over his sibling Jean-Christophe's treatments for epilepsy. In addition, Lewis Trondheim's autobiographical work has been translated into English and published as part of the serial *Nimrod* from Fantagraphics (1998–2001). In this series, Trondheim depicts himself as an zoomorphic rooster, and other figures have animal or non-human appearances as well. In these stories, Trondheim often foregrounds the struggle to create autobiographical comics: "My main problems is my memory. I have some vague ideas floating around in my head. I don't remember names, and barely the settings. Just one or two memories remain clear in my head" (issue 6, 2001). Such concerns about truth and authenticity run throughout many contemporary autobiographical comics.

Other Francophone comics collectives and small presses formed in the early 1990s with the goal of pushing the medium and the industry in new, more artistically challenging directions, including Amok and the Belgian group Fréon. One such group, Ego Comme X (founded in 1994 with an accompanying anthology series of the same name), offered more experimental, intensely confessional, and expressive autobiographical comics by members Loïc Néhou and Fabrice Neaud (*Journal*, 1996–2002), among others. Néhou, for example, often experimented with minimalist style and first-person focalization, which has rarely been used in such a sustained way throughout a narrative. Unlike key works by L'Association, such as *Persepolis* and *Epileptic*, few if any of these more experimental autobiographies have been translated into English or reached a wider audience outside of Francophone readers.

Twenty-first-century autobiography

Following the genre's time in the purview of the underground and alternative comics worlds, autobiographical comics have become central to the mainstream, perhaps second only to the dominant superhero genre but often replacing it in some publishing circles. The proliferation of autobiographical comics in the twenty-first century has resulted in such an enormously varied genre for which broad trends are often difficult to distinguish, and too many significant, notable works exist to cover in a history like this. Some of the trends, though, involve the division of autobiographical comics into vibrant subgenres and niches, like coming-of-age stories, cancer narratives, diary comics, and so on. The emergence of Comics Studies as a scholarly field in the last part of the twentieth century has also helped to legitimize the comics medium in general while also raising certain works into canonical roles. Now, classes are regularly taught on autobiographical comics, special issues of scholarly journals and panels at academic conferences (if not entire conferences) have been dedicated to the genre, and scholarly anthologies and monographs have appeared to offer ways of reading and analyzing autobiographical comics. Meanwhile, opportunities for self-publishing through the DIY minicomics movement have grown exponentially with the advent of web comics. This new means of distribution has also created new opportunities for and ways of telling autobiographical stories.

In their history of comics, Dan Mazur and Alexander Danner (2014) cite the 2003 publication of Craig Thompson's *Blankets* as a significant turning point in graphic novel publishing (295). Thompson's 600-page memoir of his struggles with religion and sex as an adolescent in a fundamentalist Christian family appeared in a single volume rather than receiving serial publication first. This was a bold move: creators often used serial publication as an important income source during the long production process, which, in the case of *Blankets*, was four years. In addition, serialization allowed a creator to build an audience for the work and to generate feedback as it developed. Prior to *Blankets*, most of the major works in the autobiographical genre had been collections of previously released material, as was the case with *Maus*. The risk paid off for Thompson, who had already built a readership through his popular, semi-autobiographical work, *Goodbye, Chunky Rise* (1999). *Blankets*, originally published by Top Shelf and later by Drawn & Quarterly, has remained continuously in print and is widely taught in college classes.

Marjane Satrapi's *Persepolis* and Alison Bechdel's *Fun Home* will be covered in greater detail in separate sections in Chapter 5. However, their profound influence on autobiographical comics resonates throughout the decade that followed their publication. These two works also gained significant scholarly attention as well as more frequent appearances on high school and college syllabi, adding to the graphic novel "canon" already occupied by Art Spiegelman's *Maus*. This increased attention, however, came with increased cultural scrutiny, as both works became targets of attack by conservative groups for their alleged graphic content. Both works also followed *Maus* in that all three came out from mainstream trade publishers: *Maus* and *Persepolis* from Pantheon, and *Fun Home* from Mariner Books, an imprint of Houghton Mifflin Harcourt. These works continued to prove that graphic memoirs have popular appeal, and they have remained perennial sellers in the years since their initial publication. Both have had multimedia success as well, with *Persepolis* as an award-winning animated film co-directed by Satrapi, and *Fun Home* as a Tony-winning Broadway musical. Though many comics scholars and teachers resist the idea of a "comics canon," the volume of scholarship on these three works has put them at the center of Comics Studies.

Autobiographical comics have been central to the development of Comic Studies as a legitimate area of academic interest. The critical success and cultural visibility of Art Spiegelman's *Maus*, in particular, brought comics to the attention of scholars and, in a sense, gave permission for the academic study of comics. In fact, some of the pioneering works of Comics Studies focused on *Maus* and other autobiographical comics, most notably Joseph Witek's *Comic Books as History* (1989), which includes chapters on *Maus* and on *American Splendor*. Since then, several scholarly monographs and essay collections have been devoted, in whole or in part, to autobiographical comics, including Charles Hatfield's *Alternative Comics* (2005), Hillary Chute's *Graphic Women* (2010) and *Disaster Drawn: Visual Witness, Comics, and Documentary Form* (2016), Elisabeth El Refaie's *Autobiographical Comics* (2012a), Michael Chaney's anthology *Graphic Subjects* (2011), and Jane Tolmie's collection *Drawing from Life* (2013), among others.

As autobiographical comics have proliferated in the early twenty-first century, several key subgenres have emerged, each with a strong body of work developing. One particular area where autobiography prevails is in "graphic medicine," which uses comics to educate and inform readers about health issues through instructional comics, memoir, and reportage. As Jared Gardner (2015) explains, "graphic medicine" appeared "at the crossroads of narrative medicine and comics studies," narrative medicine being a response "of practitioners and patients to push back against the seemingly inexorable drive of late 20th-century medicine to replace patient narratives with data derived from ever more sophisticated diagnostic technologies." A wide variety of both mental and physical health matters have been addressed in comics form: cancer, Parkinson's disease, depression and bipolar disorder, PTSD, anorexia, spina bifida, and many others. (Individual works will receive greater attention in the "Graphic medicine" section of Chapter 4.) The significance of this subgenre can most recently be seen in Penn State University Press's "Graphic Medicine" series. The series launched in 2015 with the *Graphic Medicine Manifesto* co-written by the editorial collective, made up of scholars, creators, and medical professionals, including Ian Williams (who coined the term "graphic medicine"), MK Czerwiec, Susan Merrill Squier, Michael J. Green, Kimberly R. Myers, and Scott T. Smith. As the series' mission statement explains, these books

> are inspired by a growing awareness of the value of comics as an important resource for communicating about a range of issues broadly termed "medical." For healthcare practitioners, patients, families, and caregivers dealing with illness and disability, graphic narrative enlightens complicated or difficult experience. (qtd in Dunlap-Shohl 2015: n.p.)

The series includes original comics as well as scholarly work. Though not all of the comics are autobiographical in nature, several of the earliest works published in the series are first-person "graphic pathographies" such as Peter Dunlap-Shohl's *My Degeneration: A Journey through Parkinson's* (2015) and Aneurin Wright's *Things to Do in a Retirement Home Trailer Park … When You're 29 and Unemployed* (2015). This idea of "graphic pathographies" builds on the *raison d'etre* originating with Justin Green's *Binky Brown* decades earlier, where Green represents his own battles with the debilitating effects of OCD.

Part of this autobiographical boom can also be credited to the advent of web comics, which offered a cheap and easy way for creators to distribute their work online and build an audience without having to go through the trials of submission and rejection that dominate the traditional print publishing industry. Some of the most significant or notable autobiographical comics in recent years began their lives as web comics, such as Lynda Barry's *One Hundred Demons* (2002), Brian Fies's *Mom's Cancer* (2006), Jennifer Hayden's *Underwire* (2011), and Julia Wertz's *The Fart Party* (2007). In many cases, the web comic leads to print publication, but not always. For some creators, web publication is sufficient, and its benefits outweigh those of print. The sheer volume of autobiographical comics on the web makes them extraordinarily difficult to catalog.

Many autobiographical web comics take the form of diaries that are published on a regular schedule. Diary comics have an earlier history—Joe Matt's *Peepshow* (2003) began as one-page diary entries, and much of Julie Doucet's work takes the form of diary entries—but the web comics medium allowed creators an unprecedented sense of immediacy and timeliness, where their work could reach its online audience quickly and often on a daily basis. In one of the most significant examples, James Kochalka published a daily diary comic, *American Elf*, on his website from 1998 to 2012. Others have followed his model, though for shorter periods of time or on a regular schedule that is not as prolific as Kochalka's, including Julia Wertz's *The Fart Party* (2005–11), Erika Moen's *DAR!* (2003–9), and Dustin Harbin's *Dharbin* (2010–present). In addition, Gabrielle Bell's diary comics often focus on contained events, like travels or convention appearances.

One of the most significant autobiographical comics in recent years, Raina Telgemeier's *Smile* (2010), first appeared as a weekly web comic on the site Girlamatic.com, in 2004. Telgemeier built an audience through her successful comics adaptation of the young adult book series, *The Baby-Sitters Club*, for Scholastic's Graphix imprint. The first 120 pages of *Smile* came out on the web, but then Telgemeier completed the book for print publication in 2010. *Smile* covers 4½ years in Telgemeier's adolescence, from the time she accidentally knocked out her two front teeth in sixth grade through various trials with orthodontics to fix the resulting dental problems. *Smile* has become one of the most successful graphic novels ever published, spending more than 175 weeks on the *New York Times* "Paperback Graphic Books" bestseller list as of this writing, with over 1.5 million copies in print, and around 240,000 copies sold in 2015 alone, after selling 240,000 copies in 2014 (Hibbs 2015, 2016). Telgemeier followed *Smile* with *Sisters* in 2014, a memoir of an eventful family trip that occurs within the time covered by *Smile*. *Sisters* shares similar success with the previous memoir, having sales of around 220,000 copies in 2015 and 1.4 million copies in print as of 2015 (Hibbs 2016), while spending over sixty weeks on the same bestseller list.[8] This is an astounding publishing success that will have a long-ranging effects on publishing decisions, comics scholarship, the cultural impact of comics in general, and autobiographical comics in particular.

These enormously popular coming-of-age memoirs deal with fairly normal but no less dramatic events of adolescence. The ability of young adult readers to associate with Raina's trials has inspired an enormous fan base and has spawned a cottage industry of young adult graphic novels focused on young women going through adolescence. For example, Colleen Frakes's *Prison Island* (2015) details her childhood growing up in the unique circumstances of the McNeil Island prison facility in Washington state while her father worked there as a guard. Liz Prince's *Tomboy* (2014b) addresses the topic of gender identity as young Liz tries to resist the socially constructed norms for how a young girl should behave and dress. Both *Tomboy* and *Prison Island* were published by Zest Books, a small publisher that specializes in young adult nonfiction. In addition, Maggie Thrash's *Honor Girl* (2015) combines *Fun Home*'s subject matter with Telgemeier's light-hearted sensibility to describe Thrash's discovery of her sexual identity while at a summer camp for girls.

The influence of Telgemeier's success has only begun to be felt in the publishing industry: we could be on the verge of a whole generation of young cartoonists with their own personal stories to tell. In addition, the recent success of *Fun Home* as a Broadway musical, winning five Tony Awards, including Best Musical, and drawing sold-out performances, indicates that autobiographical comics have become a part of mainstream American culture. In 2015, the film adaptation of Phoebe Gloeckner's *Diary of a Teenage Girl* met with considerable critical acclaim. The "mainstreaming" of autobiographical comics indicates that such works have limitless opportunities to reach new and wider audiences as past associations or stigmas for comics fade away.

Notes

1   See the panel discussion with Green, Carol Tyler, Aline Kominsky-Crumb, and Phoebe Gloeckner in Appendix 1 for a conversation on the influence of *Binky Brown*.

2   Grant Morrison (2011) describes his concept of the "fiction suit" in *Supergods*, where he explains how he became a character in his series *Animal Man*, drawn by Chaz Truog: "This was a way of 'descending,' as I saw it, into the 2-D world, where I could interact directly with the inhabitants of the DC universe on their own terms, in the form of a drawing" (254).

3   This storyline originally appeared in *All-American Comics* 8 and 9 (November–December 1939), and was reprinted in Spiegelman and Mouly, eds, *The Toon Treasury of Classic Children's Comics* (2009), 61–7.

4   DC Comics had a history of creators inserting themselves into their superhero universe. In several DC *Justice League of America* and *Flash* stories from the early 1970s, DC editor Julius Schwartz and writers Cary Bates and Elliot S! Maggin traveled from our universe (known as Earth-Prime in DC's cosmology) to interact with heroes on the parallel earths, Earth-1 and Earth-2. This is the model for what Grant Morrison (2011) would later term the "fiction suit."

5   For more on *Citizen 13660* as a graphic narrative, see Chiu (2008) and Zhou (2007).

6   The passive voice here is intentional because different versions of this legendary story exist. The most common version has Crumb

and his first wife, Dana, selling the comics from a baby carriage on February 25, 1968. This version is cited, for example, in Mazur and Danner (2014), 23. Underground comix historian M. Steven Fox (2013), however, offers the correction that Don Donahue (the publisher of *Zap* 1 through his newly formed company, Apex Novelties), Dana, and her friend Mimi were the ones that sold the comic on that day (82 copies, total). Fox references a cash envelope that contained sales totals for Don, Dana, and Mimi. Donahue concedes that Crumb "may have joined Dana and Mimi [at] some point during their sales efforts." In Rosencranz (2008), Donahue tells a slightly different story, affirming that he, Crumb, and Dana, pregnant at the time, did sell some comics via a baby carriage on that day. Donahue did explain, though, that thousands of copies of the first printing were sold to a national distributor (74–5).

7   Robbins also put out her own solo comic, *Girl Fight Comics*, through Print Mint in 1972.

8   In total, as of this writing, Telegemeier occupies five of the ten spots on the *New York Times* "Paperback Graphic Books" bestseller list, with her fictional work *Drama* and two *Baby-Sitters Club* adaptations accompanying the two memoirs. According to comics retailer Brian Hibbs (2016), in his annual report of BookScan sales numbers for book stores (from which all of my data on Telegemeier's sales figures come from), Raina Telegemeier's books accounted for $11 million in total sales for 2015.

3

Critical Questions

This chapter offers various ways in which we can analyze autobiographical comics, using the tools, terminology, and approaches established by scholars of the genre.

Autobiographical comics and autobiographical theory

The genre of autobiographical comics raises issues and challenges to the broader study of autobiography and life writing. That is, much of the theorization of autobiography has been understandably limited to prose autobiography. When those theories or concepts are applied to the multimodal form of comics, they require some refining, as ideas that apply to prose become more complicated when the visual elements of comics are added. Considerable academic work on autobiography has been done in the last few decades, but only in recent years has comics entered the discussion. However, journals associated with the study of autobiography and biography have devoted special issues to comics, including the 2008 issue of *Biography* on "Autography" edited by Gillian Whitlock and Anna Poletti (31 [1]), which demonstrates the contributions that comics can make to this larger area of study.

Certain questions and challenges arise when comics enter into the discussion of autobiography. When readers encounter the generic classification "autobiography" or "memoir," they come to it with a set of expectations. As David Herman (2011) notes, "Readers orient differently to stories that make a claim to fact, or evoke what is taken to be a (falsifiable) version of our more or less shared, public world, than they do to fictional narratives" (232). One of the expectations is that the work will tell some kind of verifiable "truth," whatever that slippery term might mean. Yet comics, by its very nature as a medium that includes both text and drawn images, does not present documentary evidence in the same way that other media can, like prose, photography, and film. This is not to say that these other media have special access to the "truth" that comics does not have, but audience members are less likely to question those sources unless confronted with glaring evidence to the contrary. Therefore, the discrepancy between comics and other media when it comes to truth-telling lies primarily in the fact that comics are drawn, and so the autobiographical experience is more transparently filtered or mediated through the artist's consciousness and style. In other words, the stylistic and story-telling choices that go into representing events in comics form seem more overtly subjective because stylistic representations are so clearly idiosyncratic to the artist involved. Photography and film seem more objective, or create the illusion of objectivity, because they appear to be the result of dispassionate machines passively recording events unfolding before them. Comics, alternately, is a highly and nakedly personalized medium. Yet, as Hillary Chute (2016) notes, citing Spiegelman's *Maus* and the comics journalism of Joe Sacco,

> The essential form of comics—its collection of frames—is relevant to its inclination to document. *Documentary* (as an adjective and a noun) is about the presentation of evidence. In its succession of replete frames, comics calls attention to itself, specifically, as evidence. Comics makes a reader access the unfolding of evidence in the movement of its basic grammar, by aggregating and accumulating frames of information. (2)

Chute touches here on the primary purpose and appeal of comics as a form of documentary in a variety of nonfiction genres, including journalism, history, and autobiography. She identifies the unique nature of comics form and the reading experience of that form as what makes it suitable and even desirable as documentary.

When we start asking a question like, "Do autobiographical comics tell the truth?" then a whole series of questions cascade from that initial query. These questions get at the heart of autobiographical comics' significance as a medium and its desirability as a means of telling personal stories.

The autobiographical pact and the problem of first-person narration

One initial question to start with: who is the "I" or first-person narrator of the autobiographical comic? When we think of a first-person narrator in prose, we think of the consciousness through which the narrative is filtered: what is called in narrative theory "focalization."[1] Rocco Versaci (2007) identifies five ways in which first-person narration can occur in comics: direct address, thought bubbles, text boxes (or caption boxes), an "alter ego" for the creator, and the artist's style (39–44). Identifying the "alter ego," or autobiographical avatar or protagonist of the story, in this category presents a challenge to any kind of conventional understanding of first-person narration: "The use of an alter ego suggests distance between writer and character, but the visual dimension of comics allows these memoirists to communicate to the reader that the narrative is memoir as opposed to fiction" (41). Versaci uses *Binky Brown* as an example, but this may be problematic, as the Justin Green avatar on the splash page of that story has to identify Binky as the author's alter ego. In Versaci's estimation, then, *Binky Brown* has two first-person narrators: the character in the story and the speaking artist who frames the narrative (see Fig. 1.1). As others have noted, it may be more useful to separate the first-person narrator from the story's protagonist, even while keeping in mind that both are extensions of the creator.

Philip Lejeune's concept of the "autobiographical pact," which runs through many discussions of autobiographical comics, states that, for a work to be considered an autobiography, the reader must be able to accept that the author, narrator, and protagonist are the same person. Citing David Herman (2011), El Refaie (2012a) breaks these three figures down to their roles in relation to the autobiographical narrative: "the self in all life writing can be said to be tacitly plural, including a divergence between, at the very least, the *real-life I* (the author), the *narrating I* (the self who tells), and the *experiencing I* (the self told about)" (53).[2] Christian W. Schneider (2013) summarizes opposition to the autobiographical pact: "Lejeune's dictum has been rightly criticized by post-structuralist approaches for being too essentialist and too focussed on referentiality" (321). However, Lejeune's concept often serves as a starting point for discussing autobiographical comics because the medium raises special problems. In a prose autobiography, readers may have pictured in their imaginations a sort of idealized version of the author at different ages, perhaps supplemented by photographs included in the work. With comics, the protagonist doesn't even need to look like the author, and so the connection implied in the pact can be disrupted. Many of the examples discussed in this book play with the issue of authorial representation: *Maus*, *Binky Brown*, Aline Kominsky-Crumb's "Bunch" stories, and so on. In the latter two examples, the creators are often inconsistent with the depiction of their avatars throughout their work[3]; in *Maus*, Art Spiegelman draws himself as a human with a mouse head and as a human wearing a mouse mask. Later, Speigelman's *In the Shadow of No Towers* (2004) features the *Maus* avatar as a retrospective narrator; however, a human self-portrait appears in past recollections.

The use of caption boxes in autobiographical comics usually indicates the presence of the narrating I, the present version of the author who retrospectively tells the story. Many creators rely extensively on caption boxes for their narration. For example, in *One Hundred Demons* (2002), Lynda Barry includes caption boxes in almost every panel, and in many cases, these boxes dominate the space of the panel, squeezing out the image, which is usually the domain of the experiencing I. Herman (2011) also points out that the presence of narrative caption boxes often dictate the reader's understanding of the events and their importance, while the absence of such narration can create a more ambiguous effect (as happens in Jeffrey Brown's works, such as *Clumsy* [2002] and *Unlikely* [2003], which contain no captions). The narrating I can have a visual component as well, as when the narrating artist appears at the drawing board and directly addresses the reader. But, as El Refaie (2012a) explains, direct address requires a sense of eye contact between the speaker and the reader (194). Because comics can allow for a shift into direct address without breaking the flow of the story, the protagonist could fluidly shift between experiencing I and narrating I within a single scene. This happens quite a bit in Joe Matt's comics, where Joe speaks his thoughts aloud while alone in his room.

Direct address and caption boxes are just some of the ways in which autobiographical comics can foreground first-person narration. Both function on the verbal or textual register of comics form. Several comics scholars (including Fischer and Hatfield [2011] and Pedri [2015]) have applied to comics narrative theory's concept of "focalization" and the concept of "ocularization" normally used with film.[4] In this application, "focalization" refers to the consciousness through which the narrative is filtered; this can have either a verbal or visual function. Therefore, caption boxes would be a function of focalization. "Ocularization," then, focuses on the visual perspective through which we see the story unfold. Nancy Pedri (2015) makes the case that focalization encompasses ocularization (13). The separation of these terms, however, is useful for comics, especially autobiographical comics, because of the varying techniques available for first-person narration or focalization. With ocularization, then, the image in the panel would have to contain the view as seen through the eyes of the narrator, and so, the narrator could not be seen in the panel, except perhaps through a mirror. It might be more useful to consider a more specific term, "internal ocularization," to distinguish the images that appear to be the representation of the autobiographical subject's visual field from those images that contain the autobiographical subject, which would then be considered "external ocularization" (sometimes referred to as "zero ocularization"). El Refaie (2012a) discusses the difficulty of a true first-person point of view, or internal ocularization, in comics (194). In his story "Everybody Gets It Wrong!" (2008, part of which is reprinted in Appendix 3), cartoonist David Chelsea demonstrates this difficulty, even though such perspective would be "true to experience."[5] In fact, only a handful of autobiographical comics sustain a first-person perspective or internal ocularization throughout the narrative: Dan Clowes's "The Stroll" (*Eightball* 3, 1990) and Danny Gregory's *Everyday Matters* (2003) being two examples.

With comics, then, the autobiographical pact is more challenging and problematic. The reader's acceptance of certain conventions

related to comics may stand in contradiction to the autobiographical pact. Perhaps the most significant of these challenges is
an artist's visual style, which Versaci (2007) identifies as one of the
markers of first-person narration, in that the highly personalized
style can serve as a unique "voice" for the creator. In fact, Thierry
Groensteen (2011) identifies a narrator responsible for the image
as the *monstrator* (see 84–6). However, the visual representation
of real people cannot exactly match their real appearance, no
matter how photorealistic an artist's style, so style can be seen as
a barrier to the truth if we are privileging photographic evidence.
And with regards to Scott McCloud's (1993) "picture plane"
(51), or spectrum of art styles that run from iconic or abstract
to realistic, a significant number of autobiographical cartoonists
employ a style on the iconic or abstract end of the spectrum, such
as the simple linework of John Porcellino and Guy Delisle, the
humorously cartoonish caricatures of Joe Matt, the expressionistic abstraction of Julie Doucet, and the Picasso-like "cubismo"
style of Mary Fleener. With these creators, individual characters
may be more identifiable based on the consistency of the artist's
depiction than by a firm relationship between that depiction and
the person's physical appearance. For example, in *Persepolis*,
Satrapi uses an iconic art style, but she is able to distinguish the
teenage and older Marjane by the inclusion of a beauty mark to
the side of her nose. This way, through changes in hairstyles or in
scenes where she wears a hijab that may make her indistinguishable
from other similarly clad women, the reader can still identify the
story's protagonist (more on Satrapi's iconic style in the section on
Persepolis, Chapter 5). Even more challenging is when a creator
will use zoomorphic or nonhuman figures to represent real people,
as Art Spiegelman in *Maus*, James Kochalka in *American Elf*, and
Lewis Trondheim in *Nimrod* do. In these cases, does the value
of the allegorical representation overcome any questions that the
representations might raise with regards to documentary truth?
   The issue of style as a sign of first-person narration becomes
problematic, however, when we take into consideration those
autobiographical works that are collaborations between writers
and artists. The most well-known example of such collaborations
is Harvey Pekar's *American Splendor* (discussed at greater length
in Chapter 5). Pekar employed a variety of artists who represented
Harvey in different styles. Witek (1989: 139) and Hatfield (2005:

126) highlight how these different representations of Harvey exemplify the multiplicity or instability of identity. Perhaps the closest comparison to Pekar, Dennis Eichhorn's series *Real Stuff*, also employed a wide variety of independent and underground artists for its stories. Other important autobiographical collaborations include US Representative John Lewis's *March* series, co-written by Andrew Aydin and drawn by Nate Powell; Percy Carey's *Sentences: The Life of MF Grimm* (2007), drawn by Ronald Wimberly; and John Leguizamo's *Ghetto Klown* (2015), drawn by Christa Cassano and Shamus Beyale. Note that each of these examples involves a collaboration between a celebrity or public figure and comic artists.

The unspoken agreement, the autobiographical pact, between reader and author also promises a level of verifiability with the events depicted in the work: that the "I" narrator or autobiographical subject of the text is the author, and that the story the author tells can be verified in some way, as if it might "hold up in court," so to speak. This sort of verifiability can even be established outside of the autobiographical narrative itself, in what is known as the "paratext": the information that is not a part of the narrative but appears in a book, on the cover, or even external to the physical book still affects our reading of it. Paratexts can include back cover or dust jacket copy, the "about the author" text, blurbs, and so on. For example, many books will cue the reader to their genre (also letting book stores know where the book should be shelved) as "memoir," "autobiography," or more generally "nonfiction," often on the back cover. Such a designation lends a sense of credibility to the work even before the reader opens the book, like a guarantee from the publisher that the work is indeed truthful. In another example, the dust jacket copy for David Small's *Stitches* (2009) declares that it is "a life story that might have been imagined by Kafka": so, despite the extraordinary and bizarre nature of the events recounted in *Stitches*, the reader should know from the outset that this is, indeed, "a life story." Chester Brown's *Paying for It* (2013), about his experiences with prostitutes, contains blurbs not only from well-known comic professionals (R. Crumb, Alan Moore, Neil Gaiman) and reviewers in mainstream media outlets (*New York Times*, National Public Radio), as one would expect, but also from sex worker rights activists, former prostitutes, and academics who study the sex worker trade. These latter "blurbers" contribute their expertise and experience to establish the work's veracity.[6] This paratextual information, therefore, provides a kind of testimony to the autobiography's veracity.

Violating the autobiographical pact

We have well-known examples of what can happen if an author violates the autobiographical pact. Perhaps the most notable example in recent years is the public shaming experienced by James Frey when his successful 2003 prose memoir of addiction and recovery, *A Million Little Pieces*, came under close scrutiny by journalists and critics, who discovered that many key events in the book had been vastly exaggerated or even completely fabricated. The book landed on the top of the bestsellers list after Oprah Winfrey named it Oprah's Book Club Selection in 2005. The revelation of Frey's fabrications and inconsistencies led to a condemnation of the author, a public apology on Oprah Winfrey's talk show, and other negative consequences. Frey has become a textbook example of the consequences incurred when a memoir is fabricated. Though nothing like this has yet happened with an autobiographical comic, it illustrates how seriously readers and publishers take the inherent trust they have in the genre.

Some comic creators, in fact, intentionally violate or play with the autobiographical pact so often that it becomes an expected part of their style. Gabrielle Bell does so frequently with her diary comics. In an interview with Jack Baur at the 2012 American Library Association convention, Bell explained that she "uses memoir as a springboard to tell fantastical stories." For example, in her entries from Friday, July 26 and Saturday, July 27, 2013 (reprinted in *Truth Is Fragmentary* [2014], 138–41), Gabrielle realizes that she has not completed any comics work for the day, so she goes to a health food store to get some energy pills. The clerk sells her on some "brain booster" capsules, which have the added benefit of improving memory. Once she takes the pills, she remembers where she left her car, but she also ends up remembering multiple families that she had and has abandoned, including a marriage to a polar bear. Bell lures the reader into these diary entries with an experience that seems plausible in the life of a cartoonist: a day spent without getting any work done. Even the trip to the health food store seems legitimate. The veracity of the story falls apart, however, when the reader is introduced to the first of three abandoned families. As the pill wears off, she immediately forgets that the baby she's holding is her own child. Another pill unveils the existence of a second family, and so on. The tone of the narration remains steady throughout: she is even unfazed by the memory of the polar bear family. Bell often makes this transition from autobiography into fantasy in her diaries, so readers cued to her works will come to expect it. New readers, though, require some immersion in her work before this technique becomes "normal." Yet the mixture of autobiography and fantasy is part of the charm and appeal of Bell's comics and not really a detriment to the reader's relationship with the author.

Even more playful with this mix is Eddie Campbell's *The Fate of the Artist* (2006), with the subtitle, *An Autobiographical Novel, with Typographical Anomalies, in which the Author Does Not Appear as Himself.* The narrative involves an investigation into the disappearance of the artist Eddie Campbell and includes such elements as testimony from Campbell's real-life daughter, Hayley, in the form of photographs combined with word balloons.

As with Frey's memoir, comics can also violate the autobiographical pact without cuing the reader to the fact that a violation has taken place, creating even more problems for authenticity and verifiability. One other way to think about this issue is to ask the question "What happens when autobiographical comics lie?" Now, some fabrication is expected and usually goes without controversy. For example, authors create composite characters and compress timelines in order to streamline narratives. These are common conventions of autobiography in general. However, there seems to be a line that autobiographers cannot cross, or they will face a trial in the court of public opinion, as was the case with James Frey. Two examples of more extensive fabrication in autobiographical comics can highlight the complex relationship between reader, text, and creator when such a violation occurs: Will Eisner's *The Dreamer* (reprinted in *Life, in Pictures* [2007], originally published in 1986) and Seth's *It's a Good Life, if You Don't Weaken* (1996).

The Dreamer is a loosely-veiled memoir of Eisner's earliest experience in the comic book business, from the founding of the Eisner and Iger Studio to the creation of *The Spirit.* Eisner changed the names of the people involved in the story (Jack Kirby is "Jack

King," George Tuska is "Gar Tooth," and so on) and glossed over some of the shadier aspects of the comics business in the early days. Though the work is loosely fictionalized, Eisner relates one story that became a standard part of his biography. In *The Dreamer*, Eisner's stand-in, Billy Eyron, produces a new superhero comic called "Heroman" at the behest of a client, Vincent Reynard. Reynard makes it clear to Billy that he wants Heroman to be a direct copy of Bighero, the very successful superhero character published by Reynard's former employer, Bang Comics, run by Don Harrifield. After *Heroman* is published, Harrifield sues Reynard for copyright infringement. Reynard convinces Billy to take the stand and lie on the publisher's behalf, claiming that Billy came up with the idea for Heroman. On the stand, however, Billy cannot lie, and he testifies that Reynard conceived of Heroman. Reynard loses the suit and stiffs Eyron's studio the $3,000 he owes for the *Heroman* comics.

This story has been understood to be Eisner's version of the lawsuit between Superman publisher Harry Donenfeld and Wonder Man publisher Victor Fox. Following his own honesty and conscience, Eisner went against his self-interest and told the truth about Wonder Man's creation in court, knowing full well that he and Jerry Iger would lose the money owed to them by Fox. Denis Kitchen relates these details in his annotations to *The Dreamer*, an addition to Eisner's text that lends further sense of verifiability to the comic. Eisner's biographers Bob Andelman and Michael Schumacher both relate this story with *The Dreamer* as their source. However, years following Eisner's death, the court transcripts for the *Superman vs. Wonder Man* suit surfaced. As Paul Levitz points out in his biography of Eisner, "The transcripts told a different tale: Eisner had denied the Superman connection and tried to protect Fox" (28). This revelation alters not only the reader's relationship with the text, but it also makes a fundamental change to Eisner's biography in general.

Seth's *It's a Good Life, if You Don't Weaken* is another text that creates an illusion of verifiability, though with a different effect. In what he refers to as a "picture-novella," Seth becomes obsessed with the work of an obscure gag cartoonist named "Kalo" after coming across a single *New Yorker* cartoon from the 1950s. His continued investigation yields only a few more cartoons in both popular and obscure magazines from the late 1940s to early 1960s.

All of these cartoons appear in an appendix to the book. Through further detective work, Seth discovers that Kalo was the pen name for a Canadian cartoonist named Jack Kalloway, and Seth manages to track down his surviving family and put together the pieces of his brief cartooning career.

Kalo, however, doesn't exist, and little in the book indicates this. One of the book's final pages features a photograph of Kalo, "circa late '40's/early '50's." On close inspection, the figure in the photo looks remarkably like Seth. Very early in the book, Seth shows a Kalo cartoon to fellow cartoonist Chester Brown, who remarks, "he kinda draws like you" (19). Nonetheless, it is the presence of Chester Brown in this work that lends an air of verifiability to the story. Seth and Chester Brown, along with Joe Matt, regularly feature each other in their comics. Their network serves as a kind of mutual verification society, with all of their stories falling into the same autobiographical comics "universe."[7] Seth has frequent conversations with Chester about Kalo, and Chester even finds an obscure magazine of gag cartoons that contains some previously unknown Kalo work. Most of all, Seth's obsession with Kalo makes sense: Seth's artistic style, his fashion choices, and his collecting obsessions all indicate his strong nostalgia for that 1930s–1950s period in American popular culture. The book gives little reason to doubt the story's veracity. Only through researching outside of the text will a reader even know that Kalo didn't exist. In an interview with Kim O'Connor (2012), Seth justified the creation of Kalo:

> If anything, it was simply a device to make the tale more engaging ... It was never my intention to put anything over on the reader. I was seriously failing in my earlier autobio attempts to get at the heart of my own life or personality. By adding a fictional plot, I ended up getting much closer to a true portrait. It was still a rough inaccurate portrait, but nearer than before.

Thus, Seth approached a "true portrait" of himself through this fabrication, and we end up with a kind of hierarchy of truth, where some lies are justified if they help the creators achieve a more personal sense of truth about themselves.[8]

What does it mean to the reader when the autobiographical pact is violated? Clearly, there is not a universal response. None of

the cases discussed above ever rose to the level of, say, the James
Frey scandal, but none of them had the cultural penetration that
Oprah's Book Club offered. For the most part, critics and scholars
tend to look for other ways that the autobiographical comic reveals
some kind of "truth" through the fabrication.

The problem of authenticity

While there are some instances of creators playing with the expectation of truthfulness in autobiography, most want to encourage
readers to believe in their veracity. How, then, do comics creators
overcome the challenges that the medium presents to truthfulness,
verifiability, and authenticity? Comics has an added burden when
it comes to establishing a sense of "authenticity," and how comics
does this is a key question raised by several scholars, including
Charles Hatfield (2005), Jared Gardner (2008), and Elisabeth
El Refaie (2012a). In most general autobiographies, the authors
establish authenticity by virtue of proving, in some way through
evidence, that they were present at the events being described.
(Of course, this is not true for *all* events recounted in an autobiography.) For example, we may accept a celebrity actor's account
of the making of a particular film as authentic because we know
the actor appeared in the film—we can verify this fact through
evidence, though that evidence is external to the autobiographical
text. This can happen in comics as well. We know from historical
records that Representative John Lewis was present at the March
on Washington and other civil rights events depicted in the *March*
series of graphic memoirs. There is very little justification for
thinking that these graphic memoirs are not "true." But aside from
the external verification of the facts in an autobiography, how can
comic creators establish their authenticity within the comic itself?

    John Porcellino makes an interesting gesture toward authenticity
in *The Hospital Suite* (2014). In detailing the effects of his bout
with debilitating illness, Porcellino describes how he had become
so thin that his wedding ring slipped off his finger. However, John
reads Harvey Pekar and Joyce Brabner's *Our Cancer Year* (1994),
and he notices that the book contains a similar scene. Despite this
similarity, John decides to leave his scene in his story because it

did happen to him. By acknowledging that the astute reader might recognize the similar scene from Pekar and Brabner, Porcellino gives himself a measure of credibility—his dedication to the truth of his own story is more important to him than the potential accusation of plagiarism.

We have already seen how an artist's style can be a marker of his or her unique voice or identity, but we can also see style as an indicator of authenticity. El Refaie (2012a) borrows the term "visual modality" from social semioticians, which refers to "the extent to which an image resembles its objects of representation," with visual or non-linguistic modes serving "the same communicative function as language, but in their own distinctive forms" (152). These "modality markers" can include precise detail, background, color, lighting, and so on. The "truth value" of these modes vary, but Western cultures in particular value a kind of photographic realism or naturalism (153). Yet, in analyzing artist's styles along McCloud's (1993) "picture plane" (51), from realistic to iconic (El Refaie uses Max Cabanes's *Heart Throbs* [1991] and Miriam Engelberg's *Cancer Made Me a Shallower Person* [2006], respectively), El Refaie discovers,

> Although the visual style of a comics artist *is* an important authentication strategy, it often draws its power less from its iconic resemblance to reality than from the indexical clues it seems to offer about the artist's genuine characteristics and intentions. (155)

That is, Engelberg's sketchy, amateurish art seems more "authentic" than refined and realistic art because it seems more spontaneous and artless. Therefore, El Refaie argues, "stylistic realism is not the most common cue to authentic intention" in autobiographical comics (155). We could extend this consideration to other artists, like John Porcellino, Jeffrey Brown, Liz Prince, James Kochalka, and others. Their work also looks hand-made and spontaneous. Brown, for example, leaves in mistakes, like speech balloons where the text runs outside the border because the balloon was not initially drawn large enough.

Alternately, manga artists like Keiji Nakazawa (*Barefoot Gen* [2004–9] and *I Saw It!* [1972]) and Shigeru Mizuki (*Onward Toward Our Noble Deaths* [2011]) combine iconic or cartoonish figures with realistic backgrounds and objects. Though this is a common technique in Japanese comics, the net result of this combination of styles fixes their World War II-era stories in a specific time and place. Such details do seem to add credibility to their historical narratives, though the disjunction between styles may seem jarring to Western readers not used to the manga conventions.

Photography in autobiographical comics

Though an artist's style may be seen as more authentic the less realistic it is, many autobiographical comics creators use photography in their stories as a gesture toward authenticity. As El Refaie (2012a) writes, "Unlike most of the more common comics genres, graphic memoirs frequently include photographic images and other forms of 'documentary evidence' in their work, either in their 'pure' form or in a graphic rendering" (158), and "it is undoubtedly the photograph that plays the most significant role in performing authenticity in the graphic memoir genre" (159). In *Can't We Talk about Something More Pleasant?*, Roz Chast (2014) uses photographs for a particular effect when she is describing the task of cleaning out and organizing her elderly parents' apartment after they have moved to an assisted living facility. At first, she is excited about the potential "treasures" she might uncover, but the reality sets in quickly:

> There was no buried treasure. No Hermès scarves, no Chanel purses. No first editions, no Braque etchings. No heirloom china. (My mother believed in plastic plates—they were lightweight and didn't break.) It was pretty much dusty old junk (108).

To give a sense of the obsolete stuff she found, as well as the general state of clutter in the apartment, Chast shifts to a series of photographs. These include old electric razors, "random art supplies," an old milk carton stuffed with pencils, a 1950s blender, a kitchen drawer full of jar lids, a collection of empty Styrofoam egg cartons in the refrigerator, and defunct brands of health supplies in the medicine cabinet. Other photographs show how every surface of the house is covered with clutter: books, magazines, mail, notebooks, office supplies, all stacked precariously (109–18). Chast's captions reinforce the uncanny nature of the mess: "Why was there a drawer of jar lids?" (115). Following the photographs, Chast catalogs "What I Rescued and Decided to Keep" (119). However, on this page, Chast has drawn all of the objects rather than photograph them. The shift to photography in this book, then, more effectively reveals the sheer level of clutter that existed in the apartment. Chast could have rendered these details in her own drawing style, but the photographs say, essentially, "You have to see this to believe it."

Some autobiographical comics creators incorporate photography into a larger project of collage, tying photographs in with other objects to create the feeling of a scrapbook page. We can see this technique in Aline Kominsky-Crumb's *Need More Love* (2007) and many of Lynda Barry's works, including *One Hundred Demons* (2002). Chute (2010) connects this technique in Barry to the fragmentary nature of traumatic memory (116–17), but it also evokes a hand-made quality that lends itself to a sense of authenticity.

El Refaie (2012a) also mentions that photography can function in autobiographical comics through the "graphic rendering" or drawing of photographs within the story world (158). In Nina Bunjevac's (2014) *Fatherland: A Family History*, her narrative has to skip over an entire year (1976–7) where nothing relevant to her story happens, yet she still feels the need to document that time: "The next year or so went by without much to tell, providing no anecdotes worthy of repeating. Were it not for my grandfather and his handy camera, this period would have remained undocumented and thus forgotten." Bunjevac's caption makes an essential connection between photography and memory, the latter entirely dependent on the former. What follows, however, is not a series of reproduced photographs, but a series of redrawn photographs, each with a caption stating the general season and year the picture was taken. Each photo is given its own separate page, and its "photographness" indicated by a scalloped border meant to duplicate the look of a family picture pasted in an album. Bunjevac's style throughout her work is already photorealistic, with her combination of pointillism and cross-hatching, so the images look consistent with the rest of the book.

Often, however, artists will draw the photographs in a different, more realistic style than they would normally use. In *Soldier's*

Heart, Carol Tyler (2015), documenting her father's experience in World War II, duplicates photos of her parents in a more heavily shaded, realistic style than her normal iconic, cartoony style. She also includes maps of his father's travels for basic training and his tour in Europe during the war, which is another common authentication strategy, as El Refaie (2012a) explains: "Maps perform a particularly important function in signaling the authenticity of autobiographical comics that describe someone's travels ... probably because they seem to provide clear, unambiguous links between locations in a narrative and actual places in the real world" (158).

The idea that photographs reflect authentic reality is, however, an illusion, though a trenchant one: "Despite decades of discussions surrounding the problematic relationship between photographs and the 'truth,' an inherent belief in the photograph's direct connection to reality seems to persist" (El Refaie 2012a: 159). One of the more famous examples of a challenge to the authenticity of photography in autobiographical comics appears at the end of *Maus II*. Throughout most of *Maus*, Spiegelman includes redrawn photographs, but almost all of them perpetuate the zoomorphic animal metaphor at the heart of the memoir. So, a prewar picture of Anja Spiegelman will show her in mouse form. On a few occasions, though, Spiegelman includes actual photographs. Most notable is the photograph of Vladek Spiegelman in one of the final pages (134). Vladek appears stern-faced in his striped concentration camp uniform. However, the photograph is a staged fabrication. Vladek had the souvenir photo taken after his liberation from Auschwitz, at a studio that had a clean, well-fitting camp uniform that survivors could wear. Vladek used the photo to prove to Anja, from whom he was separated at the time, that he was still alive. Hatfield (2005) thoroughly addresses the significance of this photograph. He explains how the inclusion of this image undermines *Maus*'s dominant metaphor: "The momentary defeat of metaphor in the last chapter boldly asserts the falseness of Spiegelman's drawn 'photos' throughout the text" (150). That is, if the drawn photos work to reinforce the "reality" of the animal metaphor, and if so much of *Maus* involves getting the reader to buy into the metaphor, then Vladek's photo brings that metaphor to a sudden, screeching halt. In addition, the photo is a fabrication, but a fabrication of Vladek's own self-image that he wishes to project. For Hatfield (2005), this fact reinforces the notion that what we get in *Maus* is Vladek's version of events, regardless of the metaphor that Spiegelman has laid over that story (150). For autobiographical comics in general, though, Vladek's photo serves as a reminder to readers that our trust in the veracity of photographs can be manipulated. (For more on photography in comics, see the section on *Fun Home* in Chapter 5.)

The *mise en abyme*

Another very common convention for establishing authenticity is the use of a *mise en abyme*. Michael Chaney (2011a) discusses the use of the *mise en abyme* in graphic autobiographies as it relates to Lacan's concept of the mirror stage and the formation of identity. The *mise en abyme* involves a version of the comic we are reading appearing in the diegetic world of the comic, as when an artist is seen working on the comic that we are reading or a character responds to an earlier issue of a series. Chaney (2011a) also uses the concept to discuss instances of mirrors and mirroring in a text. For example, Chaney unpacks the opening images of Satrapi's *Persepolis*, in which the initial image of Marji is then followed by near duplications of her in her classmates who appear in the class photo with her. However, the appearance of the act of creation of the work in the work is also a key manifestation of this concept. Chaney addresses as an example the opening images of Barry's *One Hundred Demons*, in which Barry pictures herself at the drawing board working on the page that we are reading. Barry's text, meanwhile, questions the nature of autobiography itself: "Is it autobiography if parts of it are not true? // Is it fiction if parts of it are?" (7). Such images can, Chaney (2011a) argues, create a sense of authenticity and truthfulness in the comic:

> Presumably, visual reference to the author's labor of creating the very text we read lends credibility to her subjective truths by hypostatizing them in the material commodity object (the finished memoir). We can be certain, moreover, that she will honestly illustrate her life, since as we hereby witness, she cannot stop herself from doing so, going so far as to draw

the metadiscursive pledge regarding the irresolvable nature of autobiographical authority, which perforates the opposition of fact and fiction. (22)

The artist sitting at the drawing board, in fact, often occurs as a common trope which signals that the work we are reading is autobiographical.

The *mise en abyme* appears in some of the earliest proto-autobiographical comics. Sheldon Mayer's character Scribbly creates his own comic strip, "Why Big Brothers Leave Home," and each *Scribbly* page features that strip running across the bottom. In other early examples, the artist would appear sitting at the drawing board and directly addressing the readers. Set on the drawing board would be a page in progress, which the readers could recognize as the page that they are reading based on panel arrangements and outlines and shapes within the panels. Despite its early entry in the genre, Justin Green's *Binky Brown* seems to parody this trope in its first page, as the bound and partially blindfolded Green is suspended over the drawing board with a brush in his mouth and a scythe poised between his legs (see Fig. 1.1). Green addresses the audience directly here to explain the autobiographical nature of the work and his own compunction to create it. In more recent cases, a creator's autobiographical persona will show other people his or her work-in-progress, or the creation of the work will be a significant part of the story itself. For example, in *Epileptic* (2006), David B.'s mother interrupts the story of David's maternal grandmother, which causes a sudden shift to the narrative present. The mother is reading the original art pages of David's comic, and she doesn't want him to tell the story of how her mother found her great-grandmother drunk and passed out. The mother fears that the readers will think the epilepsy is hereditary, stemming from the ancestor's alcoholism. She also criticizes David's drawing style as ugly, and she doesn't understand why he must dredge up these past stories. David insists on a dedication to the truth in his work, and such stories connect his ancestors' struggles in the past to his own immediate family's struggles with Jean-Christophe's epilepsy. As David's mother holds up the individual page, we see that the vague shapes and panel arrangements on that page resemble those of the previous page that we just read (95–6). Also, we know her objections go unheeded because the published book we are reading contains the page that she holds.[9]

While David B. uses the *mise en abyme* to insist on the truthfulness of his narrative, Miriam Katin, in *Letting It Go* (2013), features her work-in-progress in a way that destabilizes assumptions about the truth in autobiographical narratives. While going through security at a Jewish museum in Berlin, Miriam's husband loses his wedding ring. Later, as they are at the airport leaving Berlin, he finds the ring in his coat pocket. Further along in the narrative, Katin depicts herself at work on the pages dealing with the trip to Berlin. However, Miriam has a Skype conversation with her son in which she reveals to him that she wants the ring to stay lost in the story because, as a Holocaust survivor, she does not want to make Germany look good: "It will be meaner that way. I want it to be as nasty as possible," she explains. Yet, from reading the story, we already know that she does not choose this path for her narrative. Therefore, at some point in the creation of the work not shown in the story, she changed her mind and made a different choice. The choice enhances the reconciliatory nature of the work inherent in the title, but it also foregrounds that fact that this, and by extension all autobiographical narratives, is created by an individual moved by her whims, biases, and general subjectivity. This raises bigger questions about "truth" in autobiography and reinforces Hatfield's (2005) concept of "ironic authentication": that the only "truth" is that truth is constructed.

Chester Brown achieves a similar effect in the paired stories "Helder" and "Showing Helder" from *Yummy Fur* 19–20 (January–April 1990) and reprinted in *The Little Man: Short Strips, 1980–1995* (2006). "Helder" takes place in a boarding house where Chester lives, along with nine or ten other tenants. Helder is a strange, aggressive, confrontational, and violent boyfriend of a tenant. Chester has a series of odd encounters with Helder, and these constitute the main events of the twenty-one-page story.

"Helder" would be a curious but otherwise unremarkable story on its own, but in the following issue, Brown documents the creation of the story in "Showing Helder." In the latter story, Chester shows various friends the original pages of "Helder" from the previous issue. Each of his friends (including Kris, who features in "Helder," and fellow cartoonist Seth) offers suggestions and advice for improving the story. Some of the suggestions are minor changes: Kris, for example, asks Chester to change the clothes and jewelry she is wearing because she doesn't like what he drew. She also disagrees over dialog and makes suggestions for changes there as well. One of the most significant debates in the story involves Chester's use of a narrative device in which his character directly addresses the audience with information about the story. For example, one panel has Chester walking up the steps and saying, "I'm just getting back from work" (90). One friend objects because he would never say this in this situation, plus the information it gives is unnecessary. The friend points out to Chester that this is a frequent problem in the story: "Each time you do this it's to convey information that's either not important or repeats something that's said elsewhere" (90). Others whom Chester consults, like Seth, think that the direct address is fine and that Chester has the freedom to use narrative devices like this without having to worry that they don't reflect reality. Chester then decides to follow Seth's opinion and leave the direct address in the story. In most cases, Brown doesn't reveal in "Showing Helder" how he resolved each of these critiques. However, because readers have likely already read "Helder" if they picked up the previous issue (or if they are reading the stories consecutively in the collection), then they know the final version of the story and can see how it changed from earlier drafts. We can make one-to-one comparisons between the pages in "Helder" and the corresponding draft pages we see in "Showing Helder." In the case of the direct address, it doesn't appear in "Helder" at all, meaning a decision was made following the events depicted in "Showing Helder" to change the story in this significant way.[10] The latter story, therefore, foregrounds the creative decisions that are made in the process of creating an autobiographical story: that such decisions are often made not for the sake of accuracy or strict faithfulness to the original events, but because it works for the creator's narrative goals, because of influence from friends and fellow artists, or, in some cases, because of the caprices of those depicted in the story and concerns about avoiding conflict with them.

Perhaps one of the more playful examples shows up in Joe Matt's *Peepshow*, which may have been influenced in some ways by Brown's earlier story, since the two creators are friends (see Chapter 5 on Brown, Matt, and Seth). Within the world of *Peepshow*, Joe has created a diegetic *Peepshow* comic that resembles, but is not, in fact, the comic of the same title that we are reading. In the collection *The Poor Bastard* (1996), Joe is confronted by two friends, Andy and Kim, over their depiction as "Randy" and "Kitty" in the comic. Joe denies the connection between his friends and the characters in his comic: Andy is a musician with a shaved head and a small beard; Randy has dreadlocks. If we imagine that Andy and Kim are themselves renamed versions of Joe Matt's real-life friends who may have confronted him about their depictions in *Peepshow* as Andy and Kim, then this scene becomes the narrative equivalent of an "infinity cover," with an endless level upon level of *Peepshow* comics with different versions of these characters.[11]

Teaching autobiographical comics

All of the questions covered in this chapter, as well as the topics covered in the later chapters of this book, stem from those that scholars and critics engage with when they discuss autobiographical comics. Such questions and topics can also benefit classroom discussions on the genre as well. More and more syllabi, from middle school and high school classes to college courses, as well as across a variety of disciplines, include autobiographical comics. *Maus*, *Persepolis*, and *Fun Home* are among the most commonly taught of these texts, and many of their qualities, for example, line up with the Common Core educational standards in the US, such as analyzing different cultural experiences and diverse perspectives, as well as dealing with multimedia and multimodal texts.

Cultural experiences, diverse perspectives, and multimodal reading are just some of the classroom uses for autobiographical comics in a variety of subjects and disciplines. Hillary Chute (2008a, 2010, 2016) emphasizes the value of witnessing traumatic historical events through the comics form, making such nonfiction comics valuable tools in History classes. And as we've seen throughout this book, autobiographical comics raise questions about and challenge conventional notions of autobiography, and even "truth," so that they can serve a special place in Autobiography or Life Writing classes alongside their prose counterparts. Lan Dong's edited collection, *Teaching Comics and Graphic Narratives: Essays on Theory, Strategy and Practice* (2012), covers several different subject areas, like

American Studies, Ethnic Studies, Women's and Gender Studies, and Genre Studies, with many individual essays that cover several autobiographical works. Dong's contributors offer case studies on teaching individual comics (including the usual suspects *Fun Home* and *Persepolis*), as well as overviews of entire classes. Stephen E. Tabachnick's essay collection, *Teaching the Graphic Novel* (2009), from the Modern Language Association's Options for Teaching series, does not focus on using graphic novels in specific subject areas to the extent that Dong's collection does, but it does cover a wide variety of texts, strategies, and issues for using comics in the college classroom. Essays by Dana A. Heller and Bryan E. Vizzini deal with teaching *Maus* in American Studies and undergraduate History classes, respectively, and Nathalie op de Beeck uses Lynda Barry's concept of "autobifictionalography" from *One Hundred Demons* to address specific issues in dealing with autobiographical comics. Several works for teaching comics in high school classes also devote sections to autobiographical comics. Maureen Bakis's *The Graphic Novel Classroom* (2011) includes a section on "Looking at Memoir" that contains chapters on *Persepolis* and *Maus*. Ryan J. Novak's *Teaching Graphic Novels in the Classroom: Building Literacy and Comprehension* (2013) offers pedagogical strategies and lesson plans that meet Common Core standards for grades 7–12. Novak organizes his book by genre and includes a chapter on "Biography and Memoir."

Though many of the pedagogical guides for teaching autobiographical comics, whether in middle school, high school, or college, tend to use *Maus*, *Persepolis*, and *Fun Home* as their primary examples, the approaches used for teaching these comics can be applied to a variety of other works covered in this book as well. One of my goals with this book is to provide readers with a wide variety of examples—from the usual suspects to lesser-known but accessible web and self-published comics, as well as a range of subjects and critical approaches—so that readers, students, teachers, and scholars can see for themselves the richness and variety that the genre of autobiographical comics offers.

Notes

1   This is a vast oversimplification of what is a much more complicated and debated process and which has been addressed by such fields as narratology and cognitive linguistics. For more on focalization as it relates to comics, see Schneider (2013), Horstkotte and Pedri (2011), Mikkonen (2012), and Herman (2010).

2   To share a personal anecdote here, while interviewing Miss Lasko-Gross for the *Comics Alternative Podcast*, I asked her how co-host Derek Parker Royal and I should refer to her autobiographical protagonist when we discussed *Escape from "Special"* and *A Mess of Everything*: should we refer to her as "you" or as "Miss"? Though the author insisted we use "you," I found it difficult to do so. I wanted to allow for the possible distinction between the event as experienced and the event as depicted—in other words, to allow for a separation between the author and protagonist. Perhaps hypocritically, I have had no problem using "you" with a prose autobiographer, probably because the author I'm speaking to matches my imagination of the protagonist. What is it, then, about the visual nature of comics that tripped me up here? Does the mediation of the protagonist through drawing create a disconnect between that figure and the author?

3   For a discussion of this inconsistency in *Binky Brown*, see Hatfield (2005), 132; for Kominsky-Crumb, see Chute (2010), 31–2.

4   The concept of "focalization," originated by Gerard Genette, is enormously complicated and subject to considerable debate within the field of narrative theory. Pedri (2015) encapsulates some of the debates. See also Groensteen (2011) for a more thorough discussion of these concepts related to narration in comics, esp. 83–4.

5   Appendix 4 also contains an excerpt from Ryan Claytor and Harry Polkinhorn's *Autobiographical Conversations* (2013), in which Claytor directly engages with Chelsea's (2008) idea (as well as Hatfield [2005] on the same subject) while visually demonstrating various tools for autobiographical storytelling in comics. Chelsea and Claytor show how comic artists wrestle with these issues of perspective and narration, though free of the taxonomic debates about terminology that occur in narrative theory.

6   In an odd example of a back cover blurb, Maggie Thrash's *Honor Girl* (2015), about the author discovering her homosexuality at summer camp, contains the following from NPR's Ira Glass: "Though I am neither a teenage girl nor a lesbian, I found this story

super-real and relatable." This serves as a kind of ironic testimonial: Glass testifies to the book's veracity *because* of, rather than in spite of, the fact that he has had no personal experiences that are reflected in the book.

7   This relationship is discussed in much greater detail in Chapter 5 on Joe Matt, Chester Brown, and Seth.

8   El Refaie (2012a) covers one of the more scandalous instances of fabrication in autobiographical comics: the French graphic memoirs *1h25* (2009) and *Momon* (2010) by "Judith Forest." The first book was celebrated in the French literary scene, and the author gave many interviews and made public appearances. However, stories circulated that Forest did not, in fact, exist. The second book reveals the author's truly existential crisis, as she fears that she is not real. At the 2011 Angoulême festival, the editors confessed to fabricating Forest and hiring an actress for her interviews and public appearances (El Refaie 2012a: 176–7).

9   At the end of *Are You My Mother?*, Alison Bechdel (2012) also shares draft chapters of the book with her mother, which becomes the book's climactic moment.

10   Curiously, Brown did use direct address in his following autobiographical story from *Yummy Fur* 21–3, collected as *The Playboy* (1992). In this story, Brown's narrator is a flying, present-day version of himself with demonic wings (what Versaci [2007] calls "a visual representation of Brown's conscience" [43]), taking the reader on a trip through time and revealing the thoughts of young Chester back in 1975. Brown eschews thought balloons in favor of having the demonic narrator reveal his younger self's thoughts directly to the reader.

11   The Chester Brown and Joe Matt examples are also discussed in their section of Chapter 5 in order to show how Matt, Brown, and Seth challenge the conventions of autobiography.

4

Social and Cultural Impact

Trauma

Many of the key works in the genre of autobiographical comics demonstrate the power of comics to represent traumatic personal and historical experiences: the intensely personal narratives of childhood sexual abuse by Phoebe Gloeckner, Debbie Drechsler, Craig Thompson, and Lynda Barry; the experience of parental suicide in Alison Bechdel's *Fun Home* (2006); the witnessing of traumatic historical events in works by Art Spiegelman, Shigeru Mizuki, Keiji Nakazawa, Marjane Satrapi, Miriam Katin, and John Lewis; the sudden death of a child in Tom Hart's *Rosalie Lightning* (2015) and Leela Corman's *We All Wish for Deadly Force* (2016); a son's suicide in Willy Linthout's *Years of the Elephant* (2009). Autobiographical comics function at the intersection of witnessing, testimony, narrative, and visual representation. Several critics have addressed the important and unique relationship of comics to representations of trauma. Hillary Chute (2010) claims that the comics medium is uniquely suited to represent traumatic experiences, in that it has the power to make the private public through visual representation (3–4). Following Cathy Caruth, Chute addresses the ethical dilemma of representing trauma: "how not to betray the past" (220 n.8). That is, such a betrayal could take the form of apparent dishonesty, inaccuracy (both emotional and factual), or a lack of authenticity in the representation of events. In his essay on Phoebe Gloeckner, Frederik Byrn Køhlert (2015) argues,

[T]he formal properties of comics autobiography offer unique opportunities for the representation of the largely visual memories associated with trauma, and that the narrativizing potential of the form can be productively mobilized both for therapeutic purposes and as a means to assert agency for the victim of trauma. (124)

Køhlert cites the frequent discussion in trauma studies on the value of narrativizing the normally fragmented memory of traumatic experience, but most of trauma studies focuses on prose narration and autobiography. Because that memory is both fragmented and usually visual in nature, the fragmented, visual nature of the comics medium as a series of individual panels linked by gutters suits the representation of traumatic experience well. Gloeckner's work is likely the example par excellence for the uncompromising visual depiction of traumatic experience, but Køhlert's argument here also explains the pervasiveness of traumatic narratives in autobiographical comics.

Historical and personal trauma

For the purposes of this discussion, we can consider two different types of traumatic narratives: historical and personal. The historical narrative deals with events on a larger national or global scale. Such events can include the Holocaust in Art Spiegelman's *Maus* (1986 and 1991), Miriam Katin's *We Are on Our Own* (2006) and *Letting It Go* (2013), World War II in Shigeru Mizuki's *Onward Towards our Noble Deaths* (2011), Keiji Nakazawa's *Barefoot Gen* (2004–9), the Islamic Revolution and the Iran–Iraq War in Marjane Satrapi's *Persepolis* (2004, 2005), and the 9/11 attacks on New York City in Art Spiegelman's *In the Shadow of No Towers* (2004). In all of these works, we do get the individualized, personal perspective of those who witnessed and experienced the events, but the overall scale of the events themselves dwarf the individual experience. Personal narratives focus on the private, singular experiences of the creators, like childhood sexual abuse in Debbie Drechsler's *Daddy's Girl* (1996) and Craig Thompson's *Blankets* (2003), the loss of a loved one in Alison Bechdel's *Fun Home* (2006) and Tom Hart's *Rosalie Lightning* (2015), and marital abuse in Rosalind Penhold's *Dragonslippers* (2009). Some personal experiences may be universalizable, where readers can connect with and understand the experience through its depiction in the comic, but the experiences are not tied to larger historical events. The two categories may overlap significantly, and a creator's approach to each may be similar, but such a distinction can help us see how these different narratives function in the comics medium.

Chute (2008a) explains the important role that comics can play in representing history, and in challenging common conventions for such representations: "graphic narrative offers compelling, diverse examples that engage with different styles, methods, and modes to consider the problem of historical representation" (457). Chute argues that this is particularly true for representations of traumatic historical events, as comics on such topics, such as *Maus*, "refuse to show [the traumatic side of history] through the lens of unspeakability or invisibility, instead registering its difficulty through inventive (and various) textual practice" (459). Therefore, graphic narratives, including autobiographical comics dealing with traumatic historical events, not only say something about a specific event, but also about how such events can be represented, especially through an artist's style, as well as other formal elements of comics.

Trauma and comics' formal elements

Citing Lenore Terr, author of *Unchained Memories*, Chute (2010) describes how comics' formal elements lend themselves to representing traumatic memory: "Traumatic memory tends to be more fragmentary and condensed than regular memory—a good description of the basic form of comics" (114). Terr points to how traumatic memories are spatial, while a sense of sequence can often be lacking. Chute continues,

> Comics is deeply relevant for this mapping: authors are able to put their child bodies in space on the page. The basic structural form of comics—which replicates the structure of traumatic memory with its fragmentation, condensation, and placement of elements in space—is able to express the movement of memory. It both evokes and provokes memory: placing themselves in space, authors may forcefully convey the shifting layers of

memory and create a peculiar entry point for representing experience. (114)

Though Chute refers primarily to representations of childhood traumatic experiences here, this quote can be relevant to any representation of traumatic memory. Comics creators have an unlimited number of choices in representing their experiences. They can choose to represent the trauma graphically (in every sense of the word) in order to confront the reader directly with the shocking images, as is the case with Phoebe Gloeckner's and Debbie Drechsler's depictions of sexual abuse. These creators also deploy dramatically different stylistic choices: Gloeckner uses an exaggerated realism combined with careful text placement to force the reader's attention toward the graphic images; meanwhile, Drechsler uses a far less realistic, abstract, surreal, flat style, with heavy inks and distorted perspective while showing her father's sexual abuse. However, both Lynda Barry and Craig Thompson choose to stage the abusive experiences off-panel, leaving the reader to imagine what has happened. The latter examples support the common notion in trauma studies that the traumatic experience is unrepresentable, while creators like Drechsler and Gloeckner directly challenge that notion.

Tom Hart's *Rosalie Lightning*

One way that the formal elements of comics can lend themselves to representations of traumatic experience can be seen in a more intensely personal graphic memoir, Tom Hart's *Rosalie Lightning* (2015). The book begins with the declaration of the death of Tom Hart and comic artist Leela Corman's daughter, Rosalie, who is not quite two years old. We don't actually see the death scene here, but captions inform us that it has happened, and we see Tom and Leela in the initial stages of grief. The book moves through the aftermath, including time at a "mourning retreat" in New Mexico. However, between these two events, Hart's narrative becomes fragmented, cutting between the main plot and flashbacks to the time with Rosalie. The memories seem to overwhelm Tom at sudden moments, and some memories recur multiple times in the narrative.

Early in the book, Hart offers a series of twelve panels labeled, "Images You'll Get Used to While Grieving Your Lost Child" (See Figs. 4.1 and 4.2). These images provide a useful example of how the fragmented, panel-to-panel nature of the comics form can be used to represent the tragic, traumatic experience. The panels include, "Crackers, fruits, and meats in little gift boxes"; "Oranges peeled, never eaten"; "Your spouse on the ground"; "You on the ground" (20). The two-page spread concludes with three panels: "Past // Present // or Future" (21), accompanied by images of Rosalie picking acorns, Tom laying on the ground, and dark blackness, respectively. The final triptych is the closest we get to anything like a chronological narrative in these two pages. Otherwise, the images are connected by the category that contains them and represent fragments of the larger narrative of loss and recovery. The middle four panels show different first-person perspectives from Tom's view while lying on the ground. The first of these point-of-view images depicts the grass, trees, and buildings in the distance with all planes in focus. The next three images revise the first, with the background, middleground, and foreground planes (respectively) in focus because, as Tom's narration explains, "our eyes can only focus on one distance at a time" (21).

Thus, Hart's revisions of the initial image force the reader to grapple with the artificial, constructed nature of comics narratives: even a point-of-view shot is not realistic because it doesn't take into account the way that the eye shifts focus. Yet to present the image realistically would require three different variations, which would not be feasible. That shifting perspective is then connected to the shifting chronological perspective that the narrative is going to take, moving back and forth through past, present, and future. These early pages train the reader to follow the shifting, repetitive, fragmentary, nonlinear narrative that is to follow. The training is reinforced by the use of the second person pronoun "you": "You on the ground. // Your view of the earth and grass" (20), which also builds a sense of empathy with Tom and Leela's experience. The close reading of these two pages can also lead us to wonder how other graphic autobiographies of traumatic experiences can build a connection with readers and teach them how to experience the text in a deep and meaningful way.[1]

FIGURE 4.1 *From Tom Hart's* Rosalie Lightning *(2015), page 20.* ©
Tom Hart. Used with permission of the artist.

FIGURE 4.2 *From Tom Hart's* Rosalie Lightning *(2015), page 21.* ©
Tom Hart. Used with permission of the artist.

Miriam Katin's *We Are on Our Own* and *Letting It Go*

In the essay "Haunting Spectres of World War II: Memories from a Transgenerational Ethical Perspective in Miriam Katin's *We Are on Our Own* and *Letting It Go*," Dana Mihăilescu (2015) reads Katin's two graphic autobiographies as parts of a continuous narrative: the first (2006) relating the escape that Katin, then a toddler, made with her mother from Nazi-occupied Hungary in 1944; the second (2013) dealing with the process of reconciliation that Katin underwent when her son announced he was moving to Berlin. Thus, when taken together, Mihăilescu argues, they reveal the impact of the Holocaust on three generations: adult survivors (Katin's mother), child survivors (Katin), and the children of survivors (Katin's son, Ilan). This "transgenerational perspective" gives Katin's works a unique distinction from the most celebrated graphic memoir of the Holocaust, *Maus*, which focuses on the relation of the Holocaust between the adult survivor and his child.

Katin uses a pencil-only style in each of these works, which creates interesting and evocative effects. It has a totalizing effect of making each work seem more personal and spontaneous: the pencils give the art a rough, handmade quality, and the reader gets a sense of the pressure of the artist's hand on a page, as if transmitting the artist's emotions directly into the images. Most of *We Are on Our Own* is in black and white (or more like the gray tone of a graphite pencil); only flash-forwards to post-war scenes between an adult Miriam and her family in the United States appear in color. But even in the black-and-white portions of the book, there are gradations in the weight of her line. Mihăilescu observes that,

> throughout the narrative Katin employs stylistic variety in point of the pencil-drawn panels: the scenes presenting the initial image of cosmopolitan Budapest, before the gradual implementation of restrictive anti-Jewish laws, are delicately rendered, whereas the scenes dedicated to turbulent life on the run are drawn in heavy pencil lines. (167)

Soft pencil lines, therefore, represent security and normalcy, while heavy lines represent chaos, fear, and constant danger. Once

Miriam and her mother reach safety at the end of the narrative, and they are reunited with her father, the softness returns. However, in the final pages, young Miriam re-enacts her traumatic experience through her toys, even stabbing a male doll with a fork. In this moment, the heavy lines re-emerge, and the reader is left with the sense that young Miriam will always feel the lurking immediacy of the danger that she only so recently survived.

We Are on Our Own also follows a more rigid, traditional panel grid in its page layouts. For Mihăilescu, this traditional layout "make[s] up a well-organised, long-ruminated and thoroughly processed work, in keeping with the fact that the author's dealing with her family's Holocaust experiences and memories occurred some fifty years after the event" (167). In addition, these events are largely reconstructed from her mother's memory, as Katin was too young to remember more than some images and emotional experiences. The construction of the story in this way, then, allows Katin to work through her own emotional, fragmentary childhood memories with the more controlled narrative of her mother's experiences.

In contrast to *We Are on Our Own*, *Letting It Go* is almost entirely in color, with black and white only appearing during flasbacks to the past. In addition, *Letting It Go* uses a free-flowing, panel-less page layout for most of the book (again, with the exceptions of flashbacks). Mihăilescu points out that the less-structured page layouts allow for a greater sense of spontaneity and immediacy: Katin's pages respond to the events as they are happening, and, therefore, are unmediated by the planning and thought that go into panel design and organization (168).

Miriam resists her son's move to Berlin because she still harbors obvious resentment of the German people for the Holocaust, plus she still feels a sense of constant, lurking danger that something like the Holocaust could come back at any time. *We Are on Our Own* leaves us with this sense in young Miriam's war play, so the later book demonstrates how that feeling was perpetuated for more than sixty years. Only when Katin goes to Berlin and sees how the Holocaust is memorialized and made visible by the city does the process of reconciliation take hold. The narrative concludes with the inclusion of Miriam's work in a comic art exhibit at the Jewish Museum in Berlin, the opening of which she attends at her own expense.

Katin's works present a compelling narrative of survival and reconciliation. But the stylistic choices she makes regarding coloring, penciling, and page layouts make these works a more evocative, visceral experience. As with Tom Hart's work, Katin teaches the reader to experience her narrative in an active and meaningful way.

Trauma and authenticity

Many discussions on autobiographical comics circle around questions of authenticity, and for representations of trauma, these questions are essential, especially for creators. Many creators find that the success or failure of their work hinges on the reader's acceptance of the work's authenticity. As Jeff Adams (2008) notes, Art Spiegelman privileges the review of *Maus* he received from his cousin Lolek, a Holocaust survivor. Adams writes, "Authenticity is best measured, as far as Spiegelman is concerned, by those who actually experienced that which he had only imagined; this is seen by his audience as verifying the truth of the account" (64). Authenticity and witnessing go hand in hand here: for Spiegelman, authenticity can best be determined by witnesses, who can provide a kind of seal of approval for the work. We can also see Spiegelman's concern with authenticity in the various versions and supplements to *Maus* that he has created, especially the *Maus* CD-Rom and later *MetaMaus* multimedia project. Spiegelman has detailed the extensive research and the entire process of creation, and all this reinforces the sense that *Maus* is an authentic Holocaust account. We can even listen to his recorded interviews with his father, Vladek, which formed the basis for the dialog between the two in the book.

Spiegelman's notion of authenticity and witnessing is perhaps best applied to works about historical trauma, where an event is witnessed and experienced by multiple individuals, often on a national scale. By its very title, Keiji Nakazawa's *I Saw It!* aggressively declares its authenticity through witnessing, as he was present when the United States dropped the atomic bomb on Hiroshima at the end of World War II. Yet how do authenticity and witnessing function in the more intensely personal narratives of trauma? (Questions of authenticity and autobiographical comics receive further attention in Chapter 3.)

The topic of trauma overlaps with several other topics common to autobiographical comics and dealt with separately in this book: graphic medicine, adolescence, gender and sexuality, race and ethnicity. Considering a work like David Small's *Stitches* (2009), we can see it falling into several categories: teenage David loses his voice when he gets cancer caused by his physician father's excessive x-ray treatment; his emotionally abusive mother is a closeted lesbian. Adolescence, disease, sexuality, and traumatic experiences combine in this one work and make the divisions in this book somewhat arbitrary. And so, we will see several works that cross over different sections of this chapter.

Adolescence

Thierry Groensteen singles out childhood as one of the most common topics in European autobiographical comics from the mid-1990s, when the trend in autobiography began there (cited in Beaty 2009: 232), and the same can be said about the genre in Anglophone comics as well, though the trend started much earlier in the United States and Canada. Justin Green's *Binky Brown* (1972) is essentially a story of adolescent sexuality and religious guilt, and many of the other early autobiographical comics of the underground movement followed suit, as with Aline Kominsky-Crumb and, later, Phoebe Gloeckner, along with many of the contributors to *Wimmen's Comix* and *Gay Comix*. In the Canadian autobiographical comics movement that occurred in the mid-1980s, the early autobiographical work by Chester Brown, Seth, and Joe Matt dealt with adolescence as well. Graphic memoirs about childhood and adolescence abound and overlap with other common themes like trauma, race and ethnicity, gender, and sexuality (many of the works relevant to the topic of childhood and adolescence will also be dealt with in other sections of this chapter). Ultimately, a significant number of key texts in autobiographical comics deal with adolescence and coming-of-age narratives, including Marjane Satrapi's *Persepolis* (2004, 2005), Craig Thompson's *Blankets* (2003), Alison Bechdel's *Fun Home* (2006), David Small's *Stitches* (2009), Derf Backderf's *My Friend Dahmer* (2012), Ulli Lust's *Today Is the Last Day of the Rest of Your Life* (2013), and Raina Telgemeier's *Smile* (2010) and *Sisters* (2014).

Nostalgia

Because many autobiographical comics about childhood and adolescence are written retrospectively by adult cartoonists, they often deal in nostalgia, mainly by providing cultural touchstones to situate the work in the past. These touchstones can generate reader connection to the experience, especially those readers who are roughly the same age as the creator. John Porcellino's *Perfect Example* (2005), about his teenage years living in a Chicago suburb in the mid- to late 1980s, makes frequent references to the post-punk and alternative music scene of the time, including Camper Van Beethoven, R.E.M., Soul Asylum, the Ramones, and so on (in addition, the book's title comes from a song by Hüsker Dü). This was the soundtrack for many disaffected, white, suburban, teenage boys in the 1980s,[2] so those references can offer certain readers a frisson of pleasure in recognition while also giving the work a greater air of authenticity by capturing the milieu accurately.

In Maggie Thrash's *Honor Girl* (2015), the Backstreet Boys, and boy bands in general, serve as a motif throughout the narrative. As a teenage girl in the 1990s, Maggie has strong opinions about her favorite boy band (as well as her favorite member of her favorite boy band: Kevin Richardson of the Backstreet Boys) and argues her case seriously. Thrash establishes this debate about boy bands as a kind of heterosexual ritual for adolescent girls. Thus, when she discovers her homosexual attraction to camp counselor Erin, the shock of the transition she undergoes becomes more dramatic. Maggie has been following her friends and peers along a heteronormative path, but once she leaves that path, she also loses the touchstones that would guide her down it.

Ariel Schrag's high school memoirs—*Awkward* (2008a), *Definition* (2008a), *Potential* (2008b), and *Likewise* (2009)—are unique outliers to the nostalgic reminiscences of many autobiographical comics of adolescent development. Schrag produced a comic following each year of high school. She would then self-publish and distribute the comics to her friends and family. Following her graduation from high school, the comics were published first by Slave Labor Graphics and then by Simon and Schuster's Touchstone imprint. These books have a sense of immediacy and authenticity to them: we are getting stories of adolescence unfiltered by adulthood. Her stories are also often unflinchingly confessional: Ariel recounts her first sexual experiences, drug use, and coming out as a lesbian. In addition, the creation of her comics plays a role in her narratives, but readers also get to see the development and maturity of her style as she progresses with each book.

Bildungsroman and Künstlerroman

Most of the graphic memoirs that deal with childhood or adolescence would be classifed under the genre Bildungsroman, or coming-of-age novel.[3] These works deal with the trials and tribulations of adolescence, education, spiritual growth, sexual development, and so on. Many of the works discussed in Chapter 5 and elsewhere qualify for this category: Justin Green's Binky Brown, Keiji Nakazawa's Barefoot Gen, Joe Matt's Fair Weather, Chester Brown's The Playboy and I Never Liked You, Lynda Barry's One Hundred Demons, Marjane Satrapi's Persepolis, and Alison Bechdel's Fun Home. Within that larger genre, many autobiographical comics specifically address those experiences that led to the subject becoming a comic book artist. Such moments can include early exposure to comic books, special attention from a beloved art teacher, or the creation of comics as an outlet for adolescent anxieties. These works that deal with the development of the comics artist qualify for the category of Künstlerroman, or novel of artistic development.

Many of the cultural touchstones that create a sense of nostalgia in autobiographical comics also contribute to stories that deal with the personal and artistic development of the autobiographical subjects. This is especially true of stories that show the subject's first exposure to comics. In Phoebe Gloeckner's Diary of a Teenage Girl (2002), Minnie reads the underground comix of Robert Crumb, Aline Kominsky-Crumb, Justin Green, and others, and these become a direct inspiration for her desire to become a comic book artist—and, more specifically, to create autobiographical comics. Miss Lasko-Gross includes stories of self-publishing her own comics in A Mess of Everything (2010), and Ariel Schrag reads and creates comics throughout her high school memoirs, for example.[4] Other creators depict their growing adolescent interest in art more generally, like Craig Thompson in *Blankets* and Marjane Satrapi in *Persepolis*.

Perhaps one of the most extensive example of a *Künstlerroman* is Yohihiro Tatsumi's manga memoir, *A Drifting Life* (2013). Through his autobiographical persona Hiroshi, Tatsumi tells the story of not only his development as a creator in the post-war manga market—from four-panel gag strips to more complex, mature work—but also the history of the manga industry in this immediate post-war period. Hiroshi experiences various shifts in the manga market—for example, from "rental manga" to periodicals, from a focus on humor to drama and mystery, and from an adolescent to an adult readership. Tatsumi also recounts various stylistic shifts, like the introduction of cinematic techniques into manga storytelling. Along the way, he reveals the origins of the "gekiga" movement, which he originated to shift the manga industry away from childish humor to more mature works. Much of the book documents the conversations that various artists had about their craft and content, the conflicts with publishers who often focused on the bottom line rather than the future of the medium, the struggles to make a living and remain popular through a considerable monthly output, and the successes and failures of new, experimental work.

Raina Telgemeier's *Smile* and *Sisters*

Though autobiographical comics of adolescence have appeared frequently throughout the history of the genre, such stories have proliferated in recent years. This proliferation may be traced to Raina Telgemeier's enormously popular coming-of-age memoirs, *Smile* (2010) and *Sisters* (2014). Telgemeier's works deal with fairly normal but no less dramatic events of adolescence. These comics are always lighthearted and engaging, with an iconic, manga-influenced style.

Smile covers four and a half years in Telgemeier's adolescence, from the time she accidentally knocks out her two front teeth in sixth grade through various trials with orthodontics into high school. The braces and other orthodontic issues exacerbate typical adolescent experience involving peer pressure, teenage romance, and family. Also, the narrative has elements of a *Künstlerroman*: Raina's interest in cartooning develops as the story progresses, and it helps her through some of her teenage awkwardness, especially when she gets into high school and is able to follow a more artistically minded crowd.

Sisters covers a shorter period within the timeframe of *Smile*: a long car trip to a family reunion in Colorado. During this trip, some issues with sibling rivalry involving Raina's younger sister, Amara, come to a head. Telgemeier uses a series of flashbacks, which are cued to the reader by yellow-tinted pages, to show how the sisters' relationship has developed over the years. As with *Smile*, we see some of Raina's development as an artist, but here it's often in competition with her younger sister, who seems to exhibit greater talent early on.[5] *Sisters* also gets deeper into family issues as Raina and Amara learn of marital problems that their parents are having.

As detailed in Chapter 2, Telgemeier has had enormous success with her graphic memoirs and other work, including her comics adaptations of *The Baby-Sitters Club* series and her fictional graphic novel, *Drama* (2012). In a blog post titled "11 Million Reasons to Smile," Bart Beaty (2016) recounts that success, which totaled $11 million in sales for 2015, with *Smile* and *Sisters* selling around 400,000 copies each between 2014 and 2015. Beaty questions why, despite this financial success and cultural saturation, Telgemeier's work has not received more scholarly attention within Comics Studies beyond a few mentions in larger discussions of young adult literature.

The issue may be that Telgemeier's work, especially her autobiographical comics, doesn't fit within a lot of the key subject areas or theoretical frameworks that Comics Studies tends to focus on. With topics like orthodontics, a family trip, and sibling rivalry, she doesn't engage with the kinds of childhood traumatic experiences that creators like Phoebe Gloeckner, Debbie Drechsler, David Small, Craig Thompson, and others have dealt with. Her books don't explore sexuality or identity issues, and her style is rarely experimental. Instead, her art is engaging and humorous, and she addresses lighthearted topics that connect with a large number of readers. It seems that what makes her work so attractive and popular with her target audience may be exactly what accounts for the lack of attention from comics scholars.

This explanation is in no way meant to denigrate Telgemeier's work. She clearly connects with her readers in significant and profound ways. It is comics scholars who need to find the ways to engage with this cultural phenomenon. This will be true not only for Telgemeier's work, but also for the scores of young adult graphic memoirs that are following in her wake. As Beaty (2016) predicts, when the generation of readers in Telgemeier's target audience starts producing comics scholars, then we may see the work get the attention it deserves.

In fact, Telgemeier does subtly handle some challenging topics in *Smile*: Raina starts to feel greater empathy for people with disabilities; her female friends experience puberty at different rates, which contributes to some of the peer pressure issues; and she develops a romantic interest for an African-American boy named Sean. However, these issues all go by without significant comment, as if they were normal parts of an American childhood. By making these issues normal and unworthy of overt commentary, Telgemeier actually makes a significant comment. In the recent past, such topics might have received heavy-handed, didactic treatment in the manner of an "Afterschool Special" or "a very special episode" of a television series; in Telgemeier's hands, these previously controversial topics are mundane parts of everyday life.

Smile does ultimately conclude with a lesson for young readers: as Raina narrates,

I realized that I had been letting the way I looked on the outside affect how I felt on the inside. // But the more I focused on my interests, the more it brought out things I liked about myself. And that affected the way other people saw me! (206–7)

In high school, Raina has fallen in with an artistic peer group, and so she transitions from her middle-school friends, who seem to have become distant to her, anyway. While *Smile* does not deal with Raina's artistic development at any great length, we do see the seeds of her budding interest in art and the ways in which it can benefit her.

As discussed in Chapter 2, the comics industry is just starting to see the effect of Telgemeier's success. Young adult graphic memoirs like Colleen Frakes's *Prison Island* (2015), Maggie Thrash's *Honor Girl* (2015), and Liz Prince's *Tomboy* (2014) show the ongoing potential for such coming-of-age comics. Graphic memoirs of adolescence, however, can also graphically and unflinchingly deal with topics like teenage sexual experiences, drug use, parental and sexual abuse, and depression in significant and profound ways. For example, one of the more critically acclaimed graphic memoirs in recent years, Ulli Lust's *Today Is the Last Day of the Rest of Your Life* (2013), reveals in graphic detail Lust's experiences as a teenage runaway hitchhiking through Italy in 1984. The spectrum of adolescent experiences that run from Telgemeier to Lust reveals the diverse ways in which autobiographical comics can deal with this formative period.

The quotidian and the confessional

The quotidian

In a 2005 panel discussion at Small Press Expo (transcribed in Michael Rhode, ed., *Harvey Pekar: Conversations*, 2008), Harvey Pekar describes his motivation for creating *American Splendor*:

> I started thinking about doing stories that were realistic, and the best realistic stories I could do were autobiographical. It seemed that the more accurately I wrote about my life, the better the story came out. I also wanted to write about everyday life, quotidian life, because I felt that writers in just about every area had ignored a lot of what goes on in everyday life. (147)

As discussed in Chapter 5, Pekar's work in *American Splendor* took the underground ethos and applied it to the mundane experiences of everyday life. Pekar was able to transform such events into profound, poetic comics. Part of that success came from Pekar's unwillingness to romanticize himself or his life, and he often comes across as a cantankerous and intolerant character. However, Pekar's stories allow the next generation of autobiographical comics creators to follow a similar path of documenting the mundane experiences of everyday life, leading to a subgenre of autobiographical comics that is often referred to as "slice of life."

In this focus on the quotidian,[6] Pekar's influence can be seen in the works of Colin Upton, a Canadian cartoonist who has published several works of short, autobiographical stories. His one-shot comic book *Colin Upton's Big Thing* (1990) shows the influence of Pekar directly—it contains black-and-white short stories, appears in the same magazine-sized format as *American Splendor*, uses a similar kind of newsprint paper, and has an introduction by Pekar. Placing Upton in line with his own work, Pekar praises Upton's honesty and ability to be self-critical and self-deprecating. In "Raspberry Girls," several underage girls manipulate Colin and his friend, Steve, to buy them raspberry cider. Colin also has a tense relationship with his brother, mainly, it seems, about hockey, as seen in both "Hockey Night at Home" and "A Family Christmas in Peachland." Upton's work is definitely in the Pekar vein, focusing on very mundane daily experiences and ruminating on various political and social topics, like the Canadian election and welfare.

The influence of the quotidian can also be seen in the prolif-eration of diary comics, especially those that are created for the web. This would seem obvious: if a diary is meant to capture the everyday experiences of the creator, than it would, by definition, focus on the quotidian. Diaries such as James Kochalka's *American Elf* (1998–2012), Ryan Claytor's *And Then One Day* (2004–7), Jennifer Hayden's *Underwire* (2011), and Dustin Harbin's *Diary Comics* (2015) (all discussed further in the "Self-publishing and web comics" section of this chapter) focus on topics like family, romance, and the artistic life.

True romance

Many independent comics creators have addressed the trials, tribu-lations, and adorable cuteness of romantic relationships. Among such creators, both Liz Prince and Jeffrey Brown use episodic structures in their comics to reveal their various short-term and long-term relationships. Both also use a sketchy, intentionally amateurish style to give a sense of immediacy to the comics. For example, Prince often does not erase the structure lines that artists use to lay out the figures in a panel, and Brown leaves in mistakes such as dialog that overflows beyond the border of the word balloons or words that have been crossed out and replaced. In fact, Brown's style in his autobiographical comics differs dramatically from that which he uses in his fictional works, like *The Incredible Change-Bots* and his *Star Wars* books, revealing that the autobiographical style is a conscious choice.

Liz Prince's various autobiographical comics dealing with romance began as web comics, which were later collected in *Will You Still Love Me if I Wet the Bed?* (2005), *Delayed Replays* (2008), and *Alone Forever: The Singles Collection* (2014a). *Will You Still Love Me* and *Delayed Replays* consist of short gag strips without any sustained narratives. In each, Prince documents daily occurrences in her relationship with Kevin. These often involve snuggling in bed and/or talking about intimate bodily functions in ways that only couples in a long-term relationship can do. In one example from *Will You Still Love Me*, Liz is sitting on the toilet when Kevin comes in to hug her. Liz screams, "Don't hug me when I'm peeing!" to which Kevin responds, "But you're so cute I want to squeeze the pee out of you" (12). Prince's humor and style offer a sense of familiarity with this relationship, and she rarely deals with negative events.

Jeffrey Brown's autobiographical comics have a stronger confessional element to them, covering the ups and downs of various relationships. In fact, Brown parodies himself in his introduction to Prince's *Will You Still Love Me*: "These comics are great! It's kind of what I try to do ... // except cuter, and funnier, and without wallowing in self pity, and ..." The final two panels trail off into silence.

Brown's *Unlikely* (2003) tells of Jeffrey's first relationship and loss of virginity with his girlfriend, Allisyn. The relationship doesn't so much end as it instead trails off—Allisyn asks for some space, they continue to talk on the phone, and eventually the distance between the two increases to the point they fade from each other's lives. Later, in *Every Girl Is the End of the World for Me* (2005), Jeffrey reconnects with Allisyn after the publication of *Unlikely*, three and a half years after the relationship ended.

Though *Unlikely* documents Brown's first relationship, it is actually the second volume in Brown's "Girlfriend Trilogy" which also includes *Clumsy* (2002) and *Any Easy Intimacy* (2005, also known as *AEIOU*), with *Every Girl* serving as a kind of epilog to the series. The narratives in both *Clumsy* and *Any Easy Intimacy* follow similar patterns to that in *Unlikely*, with the relationships trailing off into a series of phone calls. *Clumsy* deals with a long-distance relationship that follows on the heels of Jeffrey's break-up with Allisyn, though in this book, she's referred to as "Kristyn." In fact, an early scene in *Clumsy* between Jeffrey and Kristyn, as their relationship is coming to an end, also appears in *Unlikely*, though in a slightly different form.

In these works, Brown does not depict his persona in a positive light—he is needy, jealous, and riddled with self-pity. The girlfriends don't come out well, either, but the books are not angry diatribes aimed at getting even with his exes. Brown's negative self-depiction, then, gives his work some sense of authenticity—a strategy used by other creators as well, like Joe Matt and Chester Brown, for dealing with their narratives of failed relationships. Other autobiographical creators who deal with the quotidian also spend time with romantic relationships, as is the case with Gabrielle Bell and Julia Wertz. Figure 4.3, from Julia Wertz's *Drinking at the Movies* (2015), illustrates a problem creators may have in using their comics to detail their romantic lives—readers may feel an unwelcome sense of connection and intimacy with the creator.

The confessional mode

Charles Hatfield (2005) argues that the popularity of the confessional mode in autobiographical comics also comes from the influence of Pekar on a later generation of cartoonists:

> Pekar has inspired a school of serialized comics autobiography, including a slew of alternative comic book titles released between the latter 1980s and the mid-1990s ... [T]his new school of autobiographical comics has tended to stress the abject, the seedy, the anti-heroic, and the just plain nasty. If the method of this school has been documentary, the dominant narrative modes have been tragedy, farce, and picaresque. In the wake of Pekar, these scarifying confessional comics have in fact reinvented the comic book hero. (110–11)

Hatfield places these creators in the context of an industry dominated by mainstream publishers focused on heroic adventures of superheroes, demonstrating how this alternative movement has directly taken on that mainstream. The new "school" of the 1980s and 1990s that Hatfield describes includes such creators as Dennis Eichhorn, Chester Brown, Joe Matt, Seth, Mary Fleener, and Julie Doucet. These creators continued the focus on mundane and quotidian subject matter from Pekar, for the most part, but added a further "scarifying confessional" element where no subject seemed to be off-limits in order to achieve an extreme sense of authenticity.

In this sense, we can also see strains of influence from Robert Crumb, Aline-Kominsky-Crumb, Justin Green, and other underground creators. Crumb's persona, as discussed in Chapter 5, reveals his sexual fetishes and challenging social attitudes about race and gender in the face of critical backlash. Kominsky-Crumb deals with a variety of confessional topics that might be considered embarrassing or taboo, even beyond those that she shares with her husband. The cover of *Twisted Sisters* 1 (1976), with Kominsky-Crumb's alter ego, The Bunch, sitting on a toilet and lamenting her appearance, reveals the body issues and unflattering self-depiction that will later influence the next generation of autobiographical comics creators.

The confessional mode differs from those works that seek to expose traumatic experiences, even though both achieve a certain level of authenticity in the way that they address otherwise taboo topics. For the confessional cartoonists, authenticity seems to be the end in itself, as well as challenging the conventional mores that render certain topics forbidden, much in the way that the undergrounds did. Traumatic autobiography also challenges social taboos, but does so in order to bring these traumatic experiences into the light or to make them "speakable." The confessional mode also allows for previously unspeakable experiences to be rendered speakable, but the topics here include masturbation, excessive drinking and drug use, sexual experiences, and revealing personal habits. With these creators, no topic seems to be off-limits.

Anti-confessional backlash

This confessional approach to autobiography so dominated the alternative comics scene in the 1990s that it generated strong satirical backlash. Much of the criticism seemed directed at the dominant clichés of the comics, where once shocking confessional topics like masturbation had become commonplace, and topics were broached more for the sake of shock than for any other value they might have. Most notably, in "Daniel G. Clowes ®™ in Just Another Day ...," a four-page story from *Eightball* 5 (1991), Clowes takes a swing at the creators of autobiographical comics, especially those who revealed sordid details of the creators' lives, as well as at the readers who experienced validation from such revelations. The story begins with eight panels of Clowes flossing, brushing, taking pills, and shaving. On the second page, an offstage director yells "Cut!" and tells the actor, Steve, to hold on while he talks to the reader. "The Real Clowes" is at his drawing board, saying to the audience,

> Look, I **know** this seems kind of boring and self-obsessed so far but the point with this kind of story is that if I show the minutiae of my daily life truthfully, no matter how embarrassing or painful maybe you'll respond to that truth and realize that we perhaps share the same unspoken human traits and you and I will have a beautiful artist/reader experience. **Dig?** (emphasis in the original)

The story resumes with the actor sitting on the toilet, taking off his dirty sock and smelling it. The director then goes back to the idea that this depiction of a mundane experience is meant to connect to the reader, who has probably done the same thing. However, this attempt at connection has all been a ruse to get the reader to admit to disgusting behavior like "sock-huffing." We learn that the scene, as depicted, never happened to Clowes. The director points to the reader and everyone on the set laughs at us for our "confession".

The next scene shows us "The Real **Real** Clowes" anxiously doubting himself at the drawing board: "What am I doing? Why am I drawing myself like this? Why am I so filled with self-hatred?? I'm no big-shot wheeler-dealer ... I'm a **sensitive artiste!**" (emphasis in the original). This Clowes explains that his self-hatred comes from all the media attention he's been getting. He says,

> It's weird trying to do comics about yourself ... it's almost impossible to be objective ... the way you depict yourself really depends on how you feel about yourself and that can change every two minutes ... // But it's even more complicated than that ... like, you have to decide how much you're willing to embarrass yourself, you have to make sure it's not just to show

what a *cool*, honest guy you are ... stuff like that ... it's an agonizing struggle!

However, each of the final five panels reveals yet another Dan Clowes, until the final caption box reads "Etc., etc.," indicating that the versions can go on into infinity.

As Hatfield (2005) argues, this short comic deconstructs the notions of authenticity with creators of autobiographical comics—even the most sordid, embarrassing confessions are merely part of a pose to generate sympathy and respect from the reader (117–19). However, Clowes also targets the reader here by breaking the fourth wall and laughing directly at the audience when we were meant to feel that the comic was laughing *with* us in a sense of solidarity over shared private behaviors.

In 1993, Scott Russo and Jeff Wong produced an even more brutal satire of autobiographical/confessional comics in "Rancid Plotte" from *Jizz* 10 (reprinted that same year in *The Comics Journal* 162 [October 1993], a special issue on "Autobiographical Cartoonists"). This four-page parody features Julie Doucet (Droolie Douché), Joe Matt, Chester Brown (Chestnut Brown), Seth (Sethpool), and Mary Fleener (Mary Fleabag), the altered names in the tradition of *Mad* magazine parodies. Wong provides dead-on mimicry of each artist's visual style, so the story has the look of a jam comic. "Rancid Plotte" takes the personal quirks of each character to their repulsive extremes.

Thus, the confessional mode, which grew out of the underground movement and its resistance to taboos, became so common within autobiographical comics of the late 1980s and early 1990s that these parodies emerged, criticizing the creators' excesses and challenging those elements that had become clichéd within a short period of time. However, confessional creators also established an approach to authenticity in autobiographical comics, where self-deprecation and self-criticism provided license to reveal intimate details about themselves and others.[7]

Gender and sexuality

As discussed in Chapter 2, the underground comix movement created opportunities for creators who came from groups that were underrepresented by the mainstream comics industry, especially women and LGBTQ creators. Their fit within the underground movement was not neat, however. Because of the taboo-challenging nature of underground comix, misogynistic and homophobic content was fair game, and many straight male creators indulged in such content to excess. On the one hand, the underground comix movement may have looked just as uninviting as the mainstream comics publishers to marginalized creators. Yet, on the other hand, the opportunities for self-expression and freedom from censorship that the underground offered became an inspiration for creators to pursue more personal stories and create their own publishing venues. Thus, creators like Trina Robbins, Lyn Chevli (sometimes spelled "Chevely" or "Chin Lively"), Joyce Farmer, Aline Kominsky-Crumb, Diane Noomin, and Howard Cruse began producing series that served these underrepresented groups, such as *Wimmen's Comix*, *Tits & Clits*, *Twisted Sisters*, and *Gay Comix*. With the exception of *Twisted Sisters*,[8] all of these series survived the underground crash of the mid-1970s and continued on into the alternative comics era of the 1980s. Long after the shock value and taboo-breaking ethos of the underground had run its course, these series were still finding an audience and producing vital stories. They also continued to feature work by the post-underground generation of independent cartoonists, like Alison Bechdel, Mary Fleener, Lynda Barry, Julie Doucet, and Phoebe Gloeckner, to name a few. Some other creators produced limited amounts of work almost exclusively in the form of short stories for these anthology series and others like them, and so their work never gained proper recognition outside of the series' readership because they never produced a full-length graphic novel or even a bound collection of their work. This section is going to focus mainly on the important impact of these early anthology series, demonstrating how they influenced the genre of autobiographical comics to the point where works like Alison Bechdel's *Fun Home* (2006) and Marjane Satrapi's *Persepolis* (2004 and 2005) are now considered mainstream.

Women's underground comix

While male creators like Robert Crumb and Justin Green were responsible for the earliest autobiographical comics in the underground era, female cartoonists recognized the potential of the genre early on, formed many of the genre's conventions, and furthered a sustainable tradition. The creation of *Wimmen's Comix* and *Tits & Clits* came within months of *Binky Brown's* release, the creators' embrace of the autobiographical and semi-autobiographical revealing this almost immediate recognition of the genre's possibilities. Ana Merino (2008) explains the differences between the male and female traditions in underground comix:

> The autobiographical comic, which developed with strength and sarcastic humor in the context of the male underground comics of the 1960s in North America, had ... its female version from which important female cartoonists learned to represent themselves and narrate their own realities. (76)

This tradition would go on to influence later female cartoonists, whom Merino calls "daughters of the underground" (77). These creators "developed the intimate autobiographical line to its limits, touching on themes such as child abuse and incest, adding an aesthetic quality and professional graphic artistry to the sordidness and suffering of their personal stories" (77). Certainly not all female autobiographical cartoonists have followed in this tradition, but the potential for intimate, personal stories developed by the early female underground creators like Trina Robbins, Aline Kominsky, Diane Noomin, Lyn Chevli, Joyce Farmer, and many others had a direct influence on later creators who would push the personal subject matter even further, as we see with Phoebe Gloeckner, Debbie Drechsler, and Julie Doucet.[9]

In 1970, Trina Robbins put together the first all-female underground anthology, *It Aint Me Babe*, through the publisher Last Gasp Eco-Funnies. The comic is largely a mixture of fantasy stories and some satire, though one two-page story, "Tirade Funnies" (1970) by Michele Brand, offers a hint at the kind of autobiographical self-expression that would come later. Brand addresses the common problem of women being catcalled, heckled, and harassed by men, and she fantasizes about ways to respond. Later autobiographical stories in the women's anthologies would also pick up on this kind of social and political commentary told through personal experience.

When Robbins and the Wimmen's Comix Collective put out the first issue of *Wimmen's Comix* in 1972, more creators took opportunities to tell their own personal stories. Aline Kominsky-Crumb's first "Goldie" story appears here, as the opening strip in the issue. Lee Marrs also provides "All in a Day's Work," a four-page strip that deals with sexual harassment in the workplace, and, like Michele Brand's story in *It Aint Me Babe*, it fantasizes about alternative choices that women can have to deal with it. Strips like this serve more as personal essays than narratives *per se*, but they share with autobiographical narrative comics the representation of personal experience and the use of identifiable cartoon avatars to serve as the author's personae.

Most significant in this first issue, however, is Trina Robbins's "Sandy Comes Out," about the "true life" experience of Robert Crumb's sister, Sandy, as she discovers her lesbian identity. In his introduction to the comics anthology *No Straight Lines: Four Decades of Queer Comics* (2012), editor Justin Hall identifies this as "the first comic about a lesbian that was neither derogatory nor erotic." This story served as an important seed in the history of queer comics. Mary Wings was inspired by it to create and self-publish *Come Out Comix* (1973), "the world's first lesbian comic book" (Hall 2012).

Later issues of *Wimmen's Comix* would also feature more and more autobiographical and personal stories[10] that dealt with issues like sexuality, abortion, spousal abuse, birth control, sexual assault, coming out, and menstruation. For example, in the third issue, Debbie Holland offers the emotionally charged story "Fucked Up," about her experiences with abortion before and after *Roe v. Wade*. Holland concludes with a clear political statement about her motivation to do the story: "I wanted to tell you my story—because abortion is still a question (instead of a right) in some people's minds & we've got to fight for our rights!" (123).

Each issue of *Wimmen's Comix* was edited by a different member of the collective and, later, by two members per issue. As the series progressed, individual issues focused on a theme, like fashion (#11), the occult (#13), "disastrous relationships" (#14), and "little girls" (#15). Autobiography became the dominant genre as the series moved through the 1980s. In her introduction to *The Complete Wimmen's Comix* collection (2016), Trina Robbins states that the series came to an end in 1992 because of distribution problems. While it did well in head shops and women's and independent book stores, it faired poorly in the comic book stores that dominated the comics industry in the 1980s and 1990s, since they tended to focus on superhero comics and male readers.

Of the early issues of *Wimmen's Comix*, Robbins (2016) explains,

> The first few issues were uneven. Many of the women who submitted work to us had never drawn a comic before, and it showed. But we were more interested in giving women a voice that in how professionally they could pencil and ink. (ix)

Ana Merino (2008) explains the value of these early feminist comics further: "The evolution of underground feminine comics was more symbolic and intimist; it never aspired to aesthetic perfection nor did it construct itself around the same type of countercultural provocation as that of its male colleagues" (74). These comics established a tradition of women's autobiographical comics that would develop through the series and beyond, but they also served as a training ground for young female creators who had few, if any, other outlets for their work in the comics industry.

The earliest issues of *Tits & Clits Comix*, begun in 1972 by Joyce Farmer (nee Sutton) and Lyn Chevli, did not contain strictly autobiographical comics, though it is clear that some stories were drawn from the creators' experiences. For example, the first appearance of the recurring character Mary Multipary, "The Menses Is the Message," by Joyce Sutton, deals with the struggles of menstruation. In the course of the story, Mary goes through several options for "feminine hygiene products," including using three tampons at a time, trying expensive pads, going back to "cotton horsies," letting a dog drink her menstrual blood, and cutting out a rubber sponge to form a homemade tampon. In such cases, the characters like Mary Multipary serve as semi-autobiographical avatars for the creators to address taboo subjects of common female experiences.

The third issue of *Tits & Clits* (1977) contains the series' first overtly autobiographical story, "Out of the Closet and into the Frying Pan" by Trina Robbins. Framed by a scene set in a futuristic 1990, the story takes an unconventional approach to autobiography. A mother in the future explains to her daughter, "it's perfectly natural to love another woman!" The daughter, however, brushes her mother off as old fashioned, exclaiming "gay is passé!" The daughter then asks the mother if she ever had sex with another woman, which begins a flashback depicting a youthful version of the mother, a young cartoonist who looks a lot like Trina Robbins. At a "woman's dance," the mother meets and is immediately attracted to Letitia, the lead singer of a band named Labia. The band's guitarist asks the cartoonist-narrator to create the group's logo. However, the potential relationship never reaches fruition. The story then returns to 1990, where the mother explains that she never did have sex with another woman, even though the desire had been there. As the story concludes, the daughter leaves on her date with Vrrst, a tentacled, blob-like alien wearing a beanie. This story projects into the future the vision that sexuality will no longer be an issue by 1990: not only is "gay so passé," but the daughter's relationship with a non-humanoid alien is not even questioned. So, the story combines autobiography with utopian science fiction about sexuality in the future, that the hang-ups Trina experienced in the present will no longer be issues.

Tits & Clits continued irregular publication until its seventh issue in 1987. The series increased its autobiographical offerings through its run, featuring creators like Chris Powers, Sharon Rudahl, Joey Epstein, Mary Fleener, Dori Seda, Joyce Brabner, and Leslie Sternbergh and topics ranging from single motherhood and adolescent sexuality to abortion rights and sexual predators.

In 1986, with much less fanfare than *Maus* received that same year, Last Gasp published Dori Seda's solo comics work, *Lonely Night Comics*, an unheralded work of female autobiography. The single issue takes up the themes and topics common to her earlier comics, including her pets, her sexual relationships, her drinking, and her partying. She often created comics about her relationship with her dog, Tona, under the title "Tona-Toons." These involved humorous incidences involving the dog's terrible hygiene and fascination with Dori's underwear. While Seda was not a prolific cartoonist, her unapologetically confessional comics had a profound influence on her contemporaries and the generation of female cartoonists who followed and engaged in similar subject matter: Phoebe Gloeckner, Julie Doucet, Mary Fleener, and others. Seda—who also had autobiographical stories that appeared in *Wimmen's Comix*, *Tits & Clits*, and *Weirdo* (where she debuted in 1981)—died from respiratory failure at the age of thirty-seven. Her comics were collected posthumously in *Dori Stories* (2000).

Queer comics and the underground

Another unheralded contributor to the tradition of autobiographical comics was Mary Wings (nom de plume for Mary Geller), creator of *Come Out Comix* (1973) and *Dyke Shorts* (1978). These works follow in the spirit of Justin Green's *Binky Brown* as long, sustained narratives following pseudonymous autobiographical characters. *Come Out Comix* follows "Maggi" (sometimes spelled "Maggie") from a failed heterosexual relationship through various tumultuous experiences with what she describes as the "lesbian community" until she ends up in a monogamous relationship with a woman named Dorothy. The final panel reads,

> What will happen next?? Will they live happily ever after?? Monogamously or polygamously? And how will they come out into the vast and varied lesbian community??? Well, there's only one way to find out, and you know what that is: come out and join the great adventure!!! (32)

Dyke Shorts, however, does not pick up this hanging narrative thread. Instead, the comic tells several different stories of other women told through the framing device of Mary's move to California. In both of these comics, Wings's style is expressive and experimental, using varied hand-lettering, borderless layouts, and shifting visual styles.

Howard Cruse established *Gay Comix*, published by Denis Kitchen's Kitchen Sink Press, in 1980, as the underground movement faded and the alternative comics movement was beginning. *Gay Comix* was Cruse's direct response to the early trends in gay comics, which focused more on erotica and bawdy humor, as was the case in Larry Fuller's anthology, *Gay Heartthrobs* (1976). Cruse hoped to use his series to offer more personal stories that explored the multifaceted queer community.

Gay Comix provided a venue and safe space for autobiographical stories that could not be found in mainstream comics or even in most undergrounds. An extraordinary example appears in issue 3 (1982): "I'm Me" by David Kottler. This three-page strip tells the story of David's development as a gay transsexual. Born Debbie Kottler, the cartoonist goes through "normal" heterosexual phases where she likes boys, even into her twenties. She dabbles in lesbianism, but finds that she doesn't agree politically with them, especially about men. She later gets married to Tom, and at twenty-seven discovers her "transsexual" identity. David takes hormones and wears men's clothes, but doesn't opt for surgery. Ultimately, David and Tom stay together as a gay couple. David realizes how his identity doesn't fit with any of society's expectations for gender or sexuality, nor do he and Tom clearly fit into either the heterosexual or homosexual communities. In a short space, Kottler reveals his experiences of being marginalized within a community that is already marginalized. This is a very positive, upbeat story about accepting one's identity, drawn in a cartoony style—a remarkable story that seems ahead of its time even today.

As with the earlier feminist comics, many of the stories in *Gay Comix* take the form of personal essays that offer a strong political or social message. *Gay Comix* 4 (1983) features the six-page story "Ready or not, here it comes ... Safe Sex" by Howard Cruse. As the story opens, "The artist embarks on a perilous voyage ...," where Cruse documents the social panic about AIDS that occurred within the gay community and in the public at large. Cruse uses his humorous cartooning style to depict the outrageousness of myths and urban legends about the contagiousness of HIV, like stories of sewer-dwelling, AIDS-carrying alligators who got sick from the blood of dead AIDS patients flushed into the city's sanitation system, or a secret plot to kill all of the gays. He also addresses the lengths to which gay men go to avoid the threat: even a masturbating man panics when he sees a blemish on a nude model's picture in a pornographic magazine. This story appeared quite early in the AIDS epidemic, and Cruse uses his autobiographical persona, his cartooning style, and his sense of humor to allay the fears and panic that had begun. Later creators would also take up their own personal stories of HIV/AIDS, including David Wojnarowicz's *7 Miles a Second* (with James Romberger, 1996), Judd Winick's *Pedro and Me* (2000), and the contributors to the *Strip AIDS USA* anthology (1988).

Cruse also included semi-autobiographical stories in *Gay Comix* that reflected his desire to offer comics that represented the realities of the gay experience at the time. Perhaps his most famous is "Billy Goes Out" from *Gay Comix* 1 (1980a), which takes place in "1980 in New York City: before the epidemic had reared its head" and shows the title character going out to a gay club, while a running interior monolog goes through various landmark experiences in his life, including facing discrimination, rejection, and guilt. In the second issue (1980b), Cruse published "Jerry Mack," a story about a Christian minister who recounts an adolescent homosexual experience with his friend Evan in their small Alabama hometown. Later, Jerry, who is now married with children, sees that Evan has grown up to be a cartoonist who creates comics about "gay liberation." Cruse identifies the story as fiction, but the Jerry character is based on his own first encounter with a gay man, and that person did go on to become a preacher. In addition, the Evan character clearly has parallels to Cruse. Though this story is loosely based on his own experiences, Cruse imagines them through the perspective of the closeted gay preacher who has suppressed his desires throughout his life. As a result, Cruse accomplishes an empathetic portrait of Jerry. This story is also notable because it anticipates Cruse's *Stuck Rubber Baby* (1995), his fictional graphic novel that mines his personal experiences growing up in a small Alabama town.

Alison Bechdel identifies the first issue of *Gay Comix*, which she found at New York City's Oscar Wilde Memorial Bookshop in 1981, as a watershed moment in her path toward becoming a cartoonist (Chute 2010: 24). In 1993, Bechdel would get her own dedicated issue of *Gay Comics* (after editor Andy Mangels changed the name in 1992). Issue 19, which declares "absolutely no *Dykes to Watch Out For*" on the cover, features autobiographical stories that anticipate *Fun Home*, including "Coming Out Story (1983)." Bechdel also contributed to *Wimmen's Comix*, most notably the autobiographical one-page story "The Mitt" in issue 15 (1989), which tells a story of a male cousin who exposed himself to Alison when they were children.

More recent works have explored and challenged the subject of normative gender identity in complex ways, especially for young girls. For example, Lynda Barry's "Girlness" in *One Hundred Demons* (2002) contrasts the lower-class tomboys of Lynda's neighborhood to the "girlish girls" of the higher-class neighborhood. Barry sees gender identity as enforced through mothers. Meanwhile, in *Fun Home*, Bechdel depicts her father as the one insistent on Alison following the norms of dress and hair that she resists. More recently, Liz Prince's *Tomboy* (2014b) documents her childhood resistance to socially constructed gender norms regarding clothing, toys, and play. Like *Tomboy* and *Fun Home*, much of the exploration of gender identity and sexuality appears in autobiographical comics about adolescence, including Maggie Thrash's *Honor Girl* (2015) and Ariel Schrag's high school memoirs (2008–9). Several contemporary works also address their creators' fluid sexuality, like Ellen Forney's *Marbles* (2012) and *I Love Led Zeppelin* (2006) and Marinaomi's *Kiss and Tell: A Romantic Resume, Ages 0 to 22* (2011), all of which describe the female authors' sexual encounters with men and women. By looking back to the early autobiographical stories that appeared in underground anthologies, we can see how these recent works capitalize on the inroads established by creators in the 1970s and 1980s.[11] Those anthologies offered venues for the earliest autobiographical work by some of the most significant creators in the genre, like Alison Bechdel, Trina Robbins, Mary Fleener, Dori Seda, Carol Tyler, Diane Noomin, Aline Kominsky-Crumb, Lynda Barry, Phoebe Gloeckner, Howard Cruse, and so on and so on.

Race and ethnicity

In addition to the many other ways in which Art Spiegelman's *Maus* has influenced autobiographical comics, it has also provided a model for dealing with issues of race and ethnicity. Specifically, Spiegelman's approach of exploring Jewish identity through a multi-generational narrative can be seen in works that address other racial and ethnic identities, including GB Tran's *Vietnamerica: A Family's Journey* (2010) and Jennifer Cruté's *Jennifer's Journal* (2015). Autobiographical creators also speak to their experiences with specific, significant historical events or periods, like Representative John Lewis's story of his struggles in the 1960s Civil Rights movement in the three-volume *March*, Lila Quintero Weaver's experience as a Latina teenager growing up in the US South during that same Civil Rights era in *Darkroom* (2012), Percy Carey's (aka MF Grimm) recounting of his role in the early 1980s hip-hop industry in *Sentences* (2007), Sarah Glidden's account of her evolving understanding of the Israeli–Palestinian conflict in *How to Understand Israel in 60 Days or Less* (2010), Riad Sattouf's life as the child of French and Arab parents living in the

Middle East during the late 1970s and early 1980s in *The Arab of the Future* (2015), and GB Tran's account of his family's experience during the Vietnam War and subsequent emigration to the United States in *Vietnamerica*.

John Lewis, Andrew Aydin, and Nate Powell's *March*

March covers Representative John Lewis's involvement in the Civil Rights movement of the 1950s and 1960s. Lewis is witness to several key events, most notably as a speaker at the 1963 March on Washington. He also documents his childhood experience with desegregation following the Supreme Court's *Brown v. Board of Education* of Topeka decision, his introduction as a teenager to the Reverend Martin Luther King, Jr., his involvement in student activism and nonviolent protest through his leadership role in the Student Nonviolent Coordinating Committee (SNCC), and his participation in the Freedom Rides. The work is framed by the 2009 inauguration of President Barack Obama, which gives the reader a profound sense of history and connection between the Civil Rights movement and contemporary United States. It also allows the series of graphic novels to end on a note of hopefulness for the future, but also with a sense that the battle for civil rights in ongoing.

March is aimed at young adult readers, though it doesn't flinch in its depiction of the violence and hatred aimed at protestors during these events. Civil rights activists, including Lewis, are severely beaten, verbally abused with racial slurs, and even attacked by dogs during their protests. The second volume ends with the bombing of the 16th Street Baptist Church in Birmingham, Alabama, in which four girls were killed and twenty-two other parishioners were injured. Powell depicts the bombing from inside the church, giving the reader some sense of being present at or even witness to this violent event.

As a youth, Lewis had read and been inspired by the comic *Martin Luther King and the Montgomery Story*, which had been published by the Fellowship of Reconciliation (FOR) as a means of spreading the word about nonviolent protest. Through that work, Lewis saw the value of comics as an educational tool, and this became the impetus for *March*. In addition, Andrew Aydin, Lewis's collaborator on this project as well as his advisor on media and public relations, had completed his master's thesis on the comic, its history, and production. *March*, then, serves not only as a graphic memoir of Lewis's experiences, but also as a lesson on the value of pacifism and nonviolent protest for a new generation of readers.

Jennifer Cruté's *Jennifer's Journal*

African-American artist Jennifer Cruté's autobiographical comic, *Jennifer's Journal: The Life of a SubUrban Girl* (2015), focuses on her childhood and family life growing up in a New York City suburb. The work is the first of what Cruté has promised to be a four-volume autobiography. Cruté's art and storytelling are deceptively simple. She uses what appears to be a cartoony, caricatured style, appropriate for a light-hearted humor strip. Her characters all have disproportionately large, circular heads, black dots for eyes, and small bodies. At first, this style is consistent with the book's tone. In the early strips, she deals with common experiences of a middle-class, suburban childhood, like sibling rivalry, goofy and embarrassing parents, and toys. The storytelling is episodic, though it builds a sense of the family dynamic through successive strips. As the comic progresses, however, it gradually shifts into more complex territory. She begins to detail encounters with her white classmates' casual racism, like the way in which they use the "n-word" in normal conversation (26–7). Cruté incorporates this account of racism into her childhood in such a way that it seems like a normal event. The way she deals with race then gets more complex as the comic goes along. For example, she describes herself as light-skinned, with freckles and red hair. When she was born, her relatives thought she was white, casting doubts on her paternity (34). Her story continues with more accounts of casual and not-so-casual racism, and the details of her family life become much less light-hearted. Her father goes from being a loveable goofball to a failed parent and husband who neglects to pay bills, spends recklessly, gambles, collects pornography, and sires several illegitimate children. Jennifer's parents ultimately divorce when she is eight years old. Cruté also explores her religious anxieties, which include dissatisfaction with the hypocrisy she sees in church leaders and members of the congregation, as well as her own guilt over masturbation.

Embedded within her own life story, Cruté also addresses her family's history, beginning with her great-grandmother Pearl, who leaves her Georgia home to elope in 1916. Then, Cruté tells of her maternal grandfather's abuse and neglect of his family. These stories give the reader a history of her family's experience not only with racism, but also with engrained cultural attitudes toward gender and family that have led to her own immediate family issues.

GB Tran's *Vietnamerica*

GB (Gia-Bao) Tran's *Vietnamerica* (2010) follows a complex narrative that covers his parents' lives growing up in Vietnam, their experience during the American war, and their emigration and subsequent adjustment to life in the United States. The story is framed by the separate funerals of Gia-Bao's grandparents, which result in flashbacks on each parent's past as well as his grandparents' own stories. The narrative contains frequent time shifts and movement between these different narrative levels. Occasionally, these time shifts will be cued by changes in lettering style or color scheme.

Gia-Bao is the first of his siblings born in the United States, and he grows up without much interest in the family's history. This disinterest is compounded by the family's silence. For example, Gia-Bao is a teenager before he finds out that his two older siblings have a different mother, and that his father was married to a French woman before the war. The narrative, then, follows Gia-Bao's growing interest in his family's history.

When the narrative shifts to the family's emigration to the United States, it begins to address their cultural struggles and experience with racism. For example, when the family first moves to South Carolina, a teacher explains to the parents about their daughter, Lisa: "although Lisa was excelling in her studies in Vietnam ... / We think it's best she starts a couple of grades lower here to give her English time to get more better" (112). The dig at the teacher here is not so subtle: Lisa is being held back not because of her intelligence or education level, but because the racist teacher assumes that her English language skills will not be as developed as they need to be (an issue that apparently does not affect the teacher). The move to the United States appears in a chapter titled "In a Foreign Culture Threatening Our Own." However, the title is laid out on a Scrabble board—a game the Tran children frequently play—which appears on a two-page spread. The words of the title can be read in a variety of ways. If one just focuses on the words on the first page of the spread, the title reads "In a Threatening Foreign Culture." The threat, then, is multi-leveled: it can be the threat of losing their own cultural identity in a new, dominant culture; the threat of inherent racism that sees them as inferior; and the threat of being seen as the Vietnamese enemy.

Vietnamerica tries to cover a lot of ground in its complex, layered narrative. The family's experience with racism in the US is only a small part of their overall story. However, the collective impact of the story reveals Gia-Bao's own growing interest in his family's history—what leads him to ultimately produce the work in the first place—and, by extension, his coming to grips with his own identity as the child and sibling of immigrants. To this extent, *Vietnamerica* has parallels to *Maus*: both deal with intergenerational conflict between parents and children, while also showing the son's interest in telling the family's story. However, while *Maus* shows Art in the process of producing the work through the interviews with his father and the appearance of Art at his drawing table, *Vietnamerica* concludes with Gia-Bao's first signs of interest in his family's story, when he agrees at the last minute to accompany the family to one of his grandparents' funerals.

Lila Quintero Weaver's *Darkroom: A Memoir in Black and White*

Some creators use the graphic memoir to tell stories that are often left out or otherwise elided from common narratives about race in the US. In *Darkroom* (2012), Lila Quintero Weaver's family leaves Argentina and emigrates to Marion, Alabama, during the Civil Rights movement of the 1960s. Weaver documents how her Latinx family occupies a liminal space between black and white—so much so that Lila feels marginalized from the movement that she actively supports. For example, Lila is ostracized from her white friends for her civil rights activism, yet her black friends have little sympathy for her social problems resulting from this position. Lila's father is a photojournalist documenting civil rights activities, but rather than simply republishing her father's photos, Weaver recreates them as drawings. This is a common strategy in graphic memoir—as we see to different degrees in Art Spiegelman's *Maus*, Nina Bunjevac's *Fatherland*, and many others—but none use the technique as extensively as Weaver does. As with the other examples, Weaver's recreated photos add a sense of authenticity to her work, documenting and verifying a Latinx experience that is often invisible in narratives of the Civil Rights movement. However, on a more personal level, the recreations also foster a connection between father and daughter through shared projects. (See Chapter 3 for more on photography and authenticity.)

Jewish identity

Jewish identity has been a significant topic in scholarship on autobiographical comics, much of it specifically focused on Art Spiegelman's *Maus* and other Holocaust graphic narratives, like Miriam Katin's. Much scholarship also fits Jewish autobiographical comics into the larger tradition of Jewish comic book creators, going back to early twentieth-century comic strips and Golden Age/World War II era superhero comics. An important bridge figure between these eras is Will Eisner, who created superhero comics like *The Spirit* in the Golden Age, but then produced more personal and autobiographical stories later in his career, many about Jewish life.[12]

Female creators have also been responsible for most of the autobiographical comics dealing with Jewish identity. Sarah Lightman's edited collection, *Graphic Details: Jewish Women's Confessional Comics in Essays and Interviews* (2014), based on Lightman's traveling exhibit of the same name, details this phenomenon through a series of scholarly essays and interviews with creators. Stephen Tabachnick (2014) compares several female Jewish creators—such as Aline Kominsky-Crumb, Diane Noomin, Vanessa Davis, and Miss Lasko-Gross—pointing out that their autobiographical stories embrace Jewish ethnic identity "while ignoring or even attacking religious belief" (157–8). Kominsky-Crumb's work is frequently discussed in terms of her use and complication of female Jewish stereotypes.[13] In *Make Me a Woman* (2010), Davis details her experience as a Jewish woman through several short stories, including ones on her bat mitzvah and her family's celebration of religious holidays. Like Kominsky-Crumb, she also addresses issues of body image and Jewish identity as well, including her experiences at a "fat camp." In the final story of the collection, Davis also acknowledges her debt to Kominsky-Crumb as a key influence on her work. Thus, the cycle of influence on autobiographical comics creators continues.

Davis's work occasionally engages with the politics of Jewish identity, especially in relation to Israel, but Sarah Glidden's *How to Understand Israel in 60 Days or Less* (2010) deals directly with the author's struggle to grasp the Israeli–Palestinian conflict (what she refers to as "The Situation") through the experience of her "Birthright Israel" tour. Sarah is critical of much of the information she gets on this tour, seeing it as largely pro-Israel propaganda. In the end, though, her opinion on "The Situation" becomes much more complex and ambivalent. During her final day in Israel, she gets into yet another political argument with her friend, Nadan. Here she has an epiphany about her need to have Nadan share her opinion: "Why does it matter what one Israeli guy thinks about my point of view? // Especially given the fact that I still don't really know what that point of view is yet, and that maybe I never will" (203).

Glidden struggles, then, to find her place in relation to her Jewish identity and to Jewish history and politics as well. Many of the autobiographical comics that deal with racial and ethnic identity also reveal the artists' struggles with their relationships to history and politics. Some, like Representative John Lewis and Miriam Katin, had direct, personal experiences with significant historical events, while others work through their family history, like Spiegelman and Crutè. Still other creators use graphic memoir to explore their own identity and intersections related to various marginalized groups and their roles in history. This is most evident, perhaps, in Cristy C. Road's *Spit and Passion* (2012). This memoir tells of Cristy's coming-of-age as a queer female Cuban American heavily involved in the 1990s Miami punk scene. Road's project explicitly seeks to expose the absence of people like her based on race, gender, and sexuality. She often finds her Cuban-American identity and gay identity at odds with one another, as homophobia is a strong force within her racial background. However, she navigates these roles through her immersion in punk culture, especially through the music of the band Green Day. In other words, by "punking" history, she is able to find a space for herself and others like her.

Graphic medicine

Comic creator and physician Ian Williams coined the term "graphic medicine" in his 2010 MA thesis as a sub-category within the field of medical humanities, where the concept of "narrative medicine" was already taking hold. In the *Graphic Medicine Manifesto* (2015), MK Czerwiec et al. define the concept as "the intersection of the medium of comics and the discourse of healthcare" (1). More specifically, "Graphic medicine combines the principles of narrative medicine with an exploration of the visual systems of comic art, interrogating the representation of physical and emotional signs and symptoms within the medium" (1). Graphic medicine is not limited to autobiographical comics: any representation of the medical profession, disease, or health-related topic can fall within its purview, whether fiction or nonfiction. Therefore, this could include superheroes or villains with secret identities as doctors, doctor/nurse romance comics, instructional and public health comics, and many other examples. Autobiographical comics, however, serve as a significant area of study within graphic medicine, as these stories of personal experience can reveal the true potential of graphic medicine. Czerwiec et al. (2015) see such works serving as valuable resources for medical professionals, sufferers, caregivers, and families. The potential for comics is that the medium can help overcome the dehumanizing effect of many medical experiences in which the sufferer is reduced to a disease or a series of symptoms. As Williams (2012) argues,

[C]omics and graphic novels can effectively relate the patient experience and, indeed, the experience of the carer or healthcare provider, and ... comics might have a particular role to play in the discussion of difficult, complex or ambiguous subject matter. (21)

Comics, in fact, have been used to depict a variety of diseases, both mental and physical: cancer, Parkinson's disease (Peter Dunlap-Shohl's *My Degeneration* [2015]), HIV (Frederik Peeters's *Blue Pills: A Positive Love Story* [2008] and Judd Winick's *Pedro and Me* [2000]), spina bifida (Al Davison's *The Spiral Cage* [1990]), epilepsy (David B.'s *Epileptic* [2006]), obsessive-compulsive disorder (Justin Green's *Binky Brown Meets the Holy Virgin Mary* [1972], Alison Bechdel's *Fun Home* [2006], and John Porcellino's *The Hospital Suite* [2014]), manic depression (Ellen Forney's *Marbles* [2012]), orthodontics (Raina Telgemeier's *Smile* [2010]), and so on. Some works also deal with end-of-life care, like Joyce Farmer's *Special Exits* (2014), Roz Chast's *Can't We Talk about Something More Pleasant?* (2014), and Aneurin Wright's *Things to Do in a Retirement Home Trailer Park … When You're 29 and Unemployed* (2015). Along with several humanities and medical professionals, Williams and Czerwiec have gone on to found the "Graphic Medicine" book series with Pennsylvania State University Press, which began publishing in 2015 and has since released Ian Williams's *Bad Doctor: The Troubled Life and Times of Dr. Iwan James*, Dana Walrath's *Aliceheimer's: Alzheimer's through the Looking Glass*, as well as the above mentioned books by Czerwiec et al., Peter Dunlap-Shohl, and Aneurin Wright. Graphic medicine has also become an emerging area of scholarship, including a 2014 special issue of the journal *Configurations*[14] (volume 22, issue 2) focused on the subject and edited by Susan Squier and J. Ryan Marks.

Comics form and graphic medicine

What can autobiographical comics reveal about medicine and disease that would be unique to the medium, as opposed to prose narratives or other forms of medical writing? As discussed in the section on "Trauma," comics is a fragmentary medium in which the reader must engage with the images and text in order to fill in the gaps between panels. This lends itself to the depiction of traumatic memories, which are often fragmentary and disconnected. As with trauma as well, comics renders the private and the personal as public and visible, allowing readers to connect with the depicted experiences. What is true for representations of trauma, therefore, can be true for representations of illness and other health-related issues. Williams (2012) explains:

> It seems that the comics medium, due to its unique and specific properties, is ideally suited to portraying the subjective experiences of the author with regard to illness and suffering and is furthermore ideally suited to the education of both the public and professionals and that published graphic memoirs of suffering may be of help to the similarly afflicted, or carers and family of the ill. (27)

As such, these graphic memoirs of illness can have a pedagogical function as tools for learning about illness. Hillary Chute (2007) also emphasizes the power of comics to "visually literalize metaphor" as one of the ways in which comics about illness can communicate in ways that other media cannot (419).

Scholars writing about disease in autobiographical comics often cite "embodiment" as one of the significant elements that sets such narratives in the medium apart. The artist, telling the story of his or her own personal experience with disease, must draw his or her body over and over again through the course of the work. Martha Stoddard Holmes (2014) coins the term "graphic body studies" to define scholarship concerned with the representations of bodies in comics:

> By graphic body studies, I mean a theory and analysis of graphic representations of embodied experiences and social identities, drawing on the work of disability studies and other body studies theories but attending to the specific attributes of a hybrid genre that draws words and writes pictures. (147–8)

For the creators, the act of drawing and redrawing their own bodies through the course of creating their works "provides the opportunity for them to engage explicitly with their own body images and with the sociocultural assumptions and values that render bodies meaningful," as Elisabeth El Refaie (2012a: 91) explains what she refers to as "pictorial embodiment" (51). El

Refaie specifically references Al Davison's *The Spiral Cage* (1990), about the artist's experience with a severe form of spina bifida from childhood to adulthood, stating, "Al's self-portraits in *The Spiral Cage* ... are a far cry from the images of disabled men we frequently see in media" (91). Therefore, for disability studies—another area of interdisciplinary academic interest that overlaps with graphic medicine—pictorial embodiment can serve as a particularly useful tool in resisting stereotypes and other assumptions about disability.

Holmes identifies challenges autobiography faces when dealing with illness: "While all life writing raises rich questions about narrative and truth, life writing about illness may bear a larger burden of assumed or implicit authenticity, at least if we look at the outcry against authors whose narratives of embodied trauma are later questioned" (149). Readers have an emotional investment in narratives of illness, especially if they or their loved ones have suffered from the represented illness, and, therefore, they are attuned to any sense of fabrication or inauthenticity in the narrative. For Holmes, this burden increases with comics, where an artist's style may offer a representation that is not "realistic" in a conventional sense of the term.

The influence of *Binky Brown*

If we trace autobiographical comics back to Justin Green's *Binky Brown Meets the Holy Virgin Mary*, then we can see that graphic medicine functions in the genre from the beginning. As discussed in Chapter 5, Green's narrative details his experience with obsessive-compulsive disorder, which manifested itself through his Catholic guilt and sexual obsession with images of the Virgin Mary. Williams (2012) explains the unique and continuing importance of *Binky Brown* as a medical narrative, beyond its role as a seminal text:

> Green was only diagnosed with obsessive-compulsive disorder after the comic was published, at the time the condition was ill understood and there was no ready treatment; now in an age when the causes of obsessive-compulsive disorder are better understood, this comic book still works brilliantly as an example of what it is like to suffer the mental torments of the condition.

This represents, then, a valuable document containing narrative untainted by memes or expectations of what it is to suffer this condition drawn from popular media or medical description. (22)

At the time of *Binky Brown*'s publication (1972), obsessive-compulsive disorder had not yet been fixed in the cultural consciousness, and stereotypes of the disorder had yet to develop or become entrenched. Since *Binky Brown*, other autobiographical comics creators have dealt with their own experiences with obsessive-compulsive disorder, including Alison Bechdel in *Fun Home* and John Porcellino in *The Hospital Suite*. However, neither of these creators uses the same techniques that Green does to imagine the visual representation of an unseen psychological condition. As a comic, *Binky Brown* allows Green to visualize the exact nature of his fears and obsessions: for example, we see his fingers literally become penises that shoot out blasphemous rays in all directions. Such imagery has an effect that goes beyond the potential of figurative language to define this experience. Chute (2007) explains:

> With Green's fascinating visualization of obsessive-compulsive imaginings, he makes public the visual perceptions that had so governed his private life and thus underlines how comics, as a form both verbal and visual, can capaciously present the consciousness of a person suffering from a mental disorder. (415)

Thus, Chute highlights how, from one of the earliest texts in the genre, Green exploits the unique potential of comics to represent the subjective experience of mental disease. Other creators would use such techniques to, for example, visualize themselves as physical embodiments of their diseases, as in Ken Dahl's *Monsters* (2009), where the artist depicts himself as a giant herpes virus emanating more viruses out of his body.

Style and graphic medicine

An artist's style can have an important impact on the way the reader relates to the medical condition or experience being depicted. A more detailed or photorealistic style can function with a strong sense of authenticity, suggesting the events being depicted are accurate representations of the particular medical experience. Other creators have used a more expressionistic style that offers more opportunities for allegorical representations, like David B.'s use of a snake as a visual metaphor for his brother's disorder in *Epileptic*. Additionally, an artist may use a simpler visual style to capture what Scott McCloud (1993) describes as "amplification through simplification" (30), where the reader supposedly can associate better with figures and images drawn in a simpler, more iconic style. However, such a style can also have a different effect, one which draws the reader into a greater sense of empathy and association with the subject. An extreme example of this is Miriam Engelberg's *Cancer Made Me a Shallower Person* (2006). Engelberg, who died in 2006 after experiencing metastatic breast cancer, did not have training or background in cartooning. She drew her comic in a style that one could describe as amateurish, with a sense that anyone could utilize such a style to draw their own comic. The style has the effect of universalizing Miriam's experience even more than a conventional iconic style might function. In a way, if anyone could draw like this, then anyone could experience this as well. Matt Freedman's journal of his cancer treatment experience, *Relatively Indolent but Relentless* (2014), utilizes a style with the simplicity of Engelberg's, but also with a sketchiness that evokes a sense of immediacy in each journal entry. Freedman's handwritten text also functions in this way: it becomes smaller and more cramped as it tries to fill available space on the page, indicating that Freedman had not planned in advance how much text would fit on the page. In Allie Brosh's web series and print graphic memoir *Hyperbole and a Half* (2013), Brosh uses the digital drawing software Paintbrush to draw simple, rudimentary figures that also create a sense of immediacy and anxiety as she details her own experience with depression.

Cancer narratives

Cancer is one of the predominant subjects in graphic medicine narratives.[15] In addition to Engelberg's book and Freedman's journal, Harvey Pekar, Joyce Brabner, and Frank Stack's *Our Cancer Year* (1994), Stan Mack's *Janet and Me: An Illustrated*

Story of Love and Loss (2004), Marisa Acocella Marchetto's
Cancer Vixen (2006), Brian Fies's *Mom's Cancer* (2006), David
Small's *Stitches* (2009), and Jennifer Hayden's *The Story of My Tits*
(2015),[16] among others, document the creators' varied experiences
with cancer, either as sufferers or caregivers.

All of these works resist a sense of victimization or idealization
of suffering with the disease. Engelberg's title—*Cancer Made Me a
Shallower Person*—offers an explicit expression of such resistance,
and Marchetto's *Cancer Vixen* plays on "cancer victim." Fies's
Mom's Cancer utilizes the narrative potential of web comics to
follow the mother's treatment for lung cancer and the family's
response to it in an approximation of "real time" (see the section
on "Self-publishing and web comics" for more on this narrative
potential). Fies originally published the comic anonymously,
beginning in 2004. Unlike other such narratives that originate in
print, the story had no form or conclusion when Fies began it.
In the end, he points out that he fully expected the narrative to
end in his mother's death, since her type of lung cancer is fatal
nineteen out of twenty times (102–4). However, she survives the
cancer, making this the sort of triumphalist narrative that, as Fies
acknowledges, does not line up with the statistics. (Fies's mother
died shortly before the print edition of the series came out, as a
result of complications from the medication she had taken during
her treatment.) Ultimately, Fies's work connected with readers who
were going or had gone through similar experiences. Stan Mack's
Janet and Me, also a narrative told by the caregiver—in this case,
the husband caring for his wife—sadly does not end with the
cancer sufferer beating the odds.

David B.'s *Epileptic*

Epileptic (2005) by David B. (born Pierre-Françoise Beauchard)
is one of the most celebrated graphic narratives of illness. A close
reading of several passages in *Epileptic* (originally published as
L'Ascension du Haut-Mal in France, 1996–2004) can reveal many
of the ways in which a creator can exploit the comics medium in
a graphic medicine narrative. Beauchard covers the impact, from
childhood to adulthood, of his brother's epilepsy on the family.
Nina Mickwitz (2016) explains that "The comic describes a

complex range of emotional responses and charts the impact of illness on the whole family in ways that reach far beyond the scope of medical discourse" (134). As with many other graphic medicine autobiographies, Beauchard does not idealize either the sufferer or his family. David's brother, Jean-Christophe, often comes across as violent and unpleasant, while David occasionally fantasizes about his brother's death to rid the family of its burden. Beauchard details the various experimental and alternative treatments the family pursues after rejecting those offered by conventional medicine, which has the effect of presenting the parents in an unfavorable light as well. The net result is a complex ambivalence toward everyone involved. The reader may be sympathetic to the Beauchard family even when the text is critical of them, as their exploration of alternative medicine is due to their efforts to exhaust every possible treatment; however, the unforeseen cumulative effect of these treatments is damaging to Jean-Christophe and the family as a whole.

Beauchard makes an interesting choice in the opening page of the book. The narrative begins in 1994, when the adult David is visiting his parents. While David is brushing his teeth in the bathroom, Jean-Christophe enters, though he is momentarily unrecognizable to David. The brother is overweight, slackjawed, and slow, with missing front teeth, scabs and scars on his body and face, and hair missing from the back of his head due to repeated falls. The narrative then moves to 1964 and the brothers' childhood. The reader's first impression of Jean-Christophe occurs in the relative present, where we see the ultimate toll that epilepsy has had on him. Therefore, Beauchard has removed all sense of drama from the remaining narrative: we know that any treatment Jean-Christophe receives will fail, and that any perceived improvement in his condition will be short-lived. Any desire on the reader's part for the type of triumphalist narrative common to many stories of disease and illness (graphic or otherwise) is quashed from the first page of the book. However, Stephen Tabachnick (2011) argues that *Epileptic* is an "autobiography of discovery" (102) for David, and so the dramatic tension is less about Jean-Christophe's recovery narrative and more about how David's feelings and beliefs resolve in the end. For Tabachnick, David B.'s conclusion, then, is "while psychological and spiritual obstacles can be defeated, such an outcome is far from certain" (103). This conclusion is tied to choices David makes in relation to his art, and so, in this sense,

Epileptic reads as much as a *Künstlerroman* as it does a graphic medicine narrative.

Epileptic depicts Jean-Christophe's seizures in detail, including the physical contortions, violent thrashing, frequent injuries, and other dangers. However, throughout *Epileptic*, Beauchard employs visual metaphors to convey in visible form the invisible or unseen aspects of the disease as well. One of Beauchard's prominent visual metaphors imagines Jean-Christophe's epilepsy as a snake or a dragon that also becomes part of the design element on some pages. The dragon entangles and contorts Jean-Christophe during his seizures, but it can also be seen connecting him to his other family members, symbolizing the way in which the disease affects everyone. Mickwitz (2016) explains the effect of these images: "David B.'s use of visual metaphor undoes the separation between felt and seen, interior and external" (136). For Mickwitz, this technique distinguishes Beauchard's work from conventional medical discourse in particular and documentary forms in other media in general.

Beauchard also reveals the social stigma attached to an illness like epilepsy, with a visible, public manifestation that creates discomfort, alarm, repulsion, and judgment with any witnesses. Mickwitz (2016) describes one instance where Jean-Christophe has a seizure on a public street, including "the gratuitous and judging stares and unhelpful comments of onlookers" who are depicted as "an amorphous dark shape from which disembodied staring eyeballs, chattering rows of teeth, and beak-like noses protrude" (133). Such an image is evidence of the effects that can be created from Beauchard's dark, expressionistic style.

Graphic medicine and education

In general, graphic medicine narratives have an educational function: to reveal the experience of illness on individuals and families to unfamiliar readers. In some cases, readers might feel that such medical challenges are inevitable, as in the case of caring for an elderly parent. Roz Chast's *Can't We Talk about Something More Pleasant?* intersperses often humorous and poignant short strips about her parents' declining years with information on topics like finances, nursing home and hospice care, dementia, sundowning, and other frustrations and challenges. Chast's style alternates between cartoons and strips, long handwritten prose passages, and occasional photographs to tell the story and convey its information.[17]

Many works of graphic medicine merge the personal and the pedagogical in more explicit ways, interrupting the autobiographical narrative in order to offer information and instruction to the reader. In *Marbles*, Ellen Forney narrates her experience with and treatment for manic depression, but she also cuts into the narrative with information on mental illness, treatment, medication, and so on. Jared Gardner (2015) describes Forney's strategy as one in which "she blends practical advice and a veteran's perspective with her own personal journey to a place where she was finally able to look in the mirror and say, 'I'm okay.'" Similarly, Carol Lay's *The Big Skinny* (2008) tells the story of the artist's battle with her weight, from numerous failed diets to a successful weight-loss and exercise regimen. But Lay also provides the readers with details for how they can follow the same regimen, including step-by-step exercise routines and healthy recipes. In *Cancer Vixen*, Marchetto draws the biopsy needle at actual size on the page, giving the reader a clear sense of what it must have felt like to experience the biopsy. As Chute (2007) explains about this particular image, "the presentation is not disruptive or didactically discordant here, but flows easily in the comics format" (417). As another example, Brian Fies provides a chart that explains how to read an x-ray. Chute's point is true, then, of other comics that insert informative visuals without breaking the flow of the narrative. The pedagogical power of comics has always been strong, and educators have long taken advantage of it. We can see with graphic medicine a further exploitation of this potential: comics can allow for a more seamless transition from one narrative mode to the next, especially, as is the case with Forney's work and others, when the narrator remains consistent throughout.

Censorship and controversy

In the past decade or so, autobiographical comics have received significant cultural attention through inclusion on course syllabi in both high schools and colleges, features in mainstream media, and appearances on bestseller lists. With this increased centrality, however, comes increased public scrutiny. This scrutiny is exacerbated by the stereotype of comics as prurient, subliterate work aimed at a juvenile audience, which dates back to the comics censorship crusades of the 1940s and 1950s, culminating in the creation of the Comics Code Authority. Comic books have almost always courted controversy and have been the target of censorship through much of the medium's history, so it probably comes as no surprise that this trend continues. But the canonization of works like Marjane Satrapi's *Persepolis* (2004, 2005) and Alison Bechdel's *Fun Home* (2006) in educational curricula have made them particularly large targets for new censorship crusades. In addition, autobiographical comics that graphically expose certain uncomfortable truths about human experiences, like the sexual abuse at the heart of Phoebe Gloeckner's work, run into controversy from conservative audiences who have difficulty aligning the subject matter with the stereotypical perception of comics as juvenile.

Elizabeth Marshall and Leigh Gilmore (2015) point out that "Phoebe Gloeckner's *A Child's Life and Other Stories* was removed from library shelves in Stockton, California, in 2004 after an eleven-year-old boy checked the book out from the library" (103). As discussed in Chapter 5 on Gloeckner, the innocuous titles *A Child's Life* (1998) and *Diary of a Teenage Girl* (2002) belie the books' graphic, unsettling content. Therefore, such controversy would, unfortunately, seem to be inevitable with these titles: someone was bound to be drawn in by their innocuousness and offended by the content therein. Gloeckner's works are necessarily confrontational—they uncompromisingly demand the exposure of traumatic experiences that are otherwise considered taboo topics, and the subsequent controversy only proves the point that rendering trauma unspeakable is harmful: "It is not only her content that is disturbing, Gloeckner argues, but also her refusal to represent rape as invisible. Gloeckner moves the sexual precarity of girls out of the gutter and into the drawn space" (Marshall and Gilmore 2015: 108). Gloeckner's work is also often designed to direct the reader's eye toward the more uncomfortable aspects of her images. That readers respond negatively to such images and demand censorship of them is a, perhaps, inevitable outcome of Gloeckner's project.

A *Child's Life* and *Diary of the Teenage Girl* have not received the mainstream cultural attention of other autobiographical works, despite the latter's adaptation as a critically acclaimed movie in 2015. However, two of the more canonical works in Comics Studies, Alison Bechdel's *Fun Home* and Marjane Satrapi's *Persepolis*, have been censored and courted controversy connected to their high-profile reputations. For example, *Fun Home* received national attention in 2013 and 2014 when the College of Charleston in South Carolina assigned the book as a part of "College Reads!," the summer reading program associated with the school's First-Year Experience for incoming freshmen. First conservative students and parents, and later politicians and national groups criticized the book as "pornographic," citing a single page in which Alison performs oral sex on her college girlfriend, Joan (214). The panel also contains a T-shirt and protest sign that read, respectively, "Lesbian Terrorist" and "Keep Your God Off My Body." Conservative Christian groups saw these slogans as specific attacks on their beliefs and claimed that the selection of the book was insensitive to Christian readers. The controversy escalated when the South Carolina House of Representatives Budget Committee voted to deduct $52,000 (the cost of College Reads!) from the school's budget; the South Carolina House then voted to approve the budget with the deduction. The money was later restored, but with the caveat that it be used for specific instruction regarding the United States Constitution and other founding documents. The controversy also led to a performance of the Broadway musical adaptation of *Fun Home* on the college campus, while the musical was still in production. The incident is just one part of a larger "Culture War" by conservative groups attacking what they see as a liberal bias on college campuses. In 2015, Duke University in North Carolina similarly assigned the book for its summer reading program, and conservative students protested the book for its graphic sexual content as well.

Marjane Satrapi's *Persepolis* has also been on the receiving end of calls for censorship, though none rising to the level of *Fun Home* in South Carolina. *Persepolis*'s immediate critical acclaim with its first English publication in 2004 led the book to be adopted in US elementary school, middle school, high school, and college classrooms. The book did not receive any challenges until 2013, when it was abruptly pulled from libraries and classrooms in the Chicago,

Illinois, public school system. School officials cited graphic images of torture as the cause, including a picture where a guard urinates on a prisoner. However, some conservative critics were concerned with *Persepolis*'s sympathetic portrayal of the Iranian people and Muslims in general as well as its criticism of the US's involvement with the Shah of Iran. The book later received challenges from schools elsewhere in Illinois, in Oregon, and in Texas, making it one of the most frequently challenged texts in US public schools.[18] However, *Persepolis* has also become a key book for many schools' adoptions of Common Core standards, especially those that involve reading world literature and analyzing diverse perspectives.

Other autobiographical comics, such as Craig Thompson's *Blankets* (2003) and Art Spiegelman's *Maus* (1986, 1991), have also been the targets of censorship in recent years. The profile of cases like these will likely increase, as national news media have shown an interest in such stories. In addition, the Comic Book Legal Defense Fund (CBLDF), a nonprofit organization founded in 1986 to combat comics censorship, continues to track the various efforts to challenge and ban comics. Autobiographical comics came about in the underground movement to give a voice to various groups, especially women and the LGBTQ community, whose stories were ignored in the mainstream media. Many of these stories were marginalized because they challenged the hegemony. As discussed in other sections of this book, those pioneering creators helped initiate a movement that has led to works being recognized and valued in the cultural mainstream, though not without resistance. However, as autobiographical comics continue to be published and welcomed among readers and even film producers, they will continue to receive public attention and meet resistance.

Self-publishing and web comics

In a May 19, 2012, panel interview with W. J. T. Mitchell (2014) at the University of Chicago's "Comics: Philosophy and Practice" conference, Art Spiegelman declared that "the history of comics has up to now been the history of printing" (30). This, he adds, explains "Xeroxed revolutions and minicomics" (30). The "up to now" moment that Spiegelman describes is the advent of the Internet as a means of production and distribution of comics outside of the limits of print. That Spiegelman ties the self-publishing opportunities of photocopying and minicomics with web comics shows a historical continuity between these avenues of publication. With self-publishing in minicomics or zine formats and web comics, creators are not limited by the editorial mandates and other restrictions of the mainstream publishing industry (or even the independent publishing industry, which does generally offer greater freedom than the mainstream). Though the economics of self-publishing differ greatly from that of mainstream publishing, the trade-off for creators is greater creative freedom and ownership rights. This can be especially appealing for autobiographical comics creators, who can use the freedoms accorded by self-publishing to tell intensely personal stories that may not have a "market" otherwise. However, because of these freedoms and widely available means of production, autobiographical minicomics and web comics are very difficult to catalog. Some may generate small local or niche followings, while a few gain word-of-mouth publicity and the potential for print publication by a mainstream or independent publisher (if that is something the creator desires). The latter group tends to get the most attention, naturally, even though some perfectly worthy comics never reach the audience they deserve.

The available means of production for comics has had a significant impact on the history and development of autobiographical comics. Roger Sabin (1993) cites the "new accessibility of offset litho printing" as a key contributing factor to the origin of underground comix in the late 1960s (37). While the underground movement opened up comics to more unfiltered, personal self-expression, the DIY movement within the punk subculture of the late 1970s expanded opportunities for young creators to find low-cost methods for creating and distributing their work. For a variety of reasons, autobiography appealed to many of these DIY, amateur comics creators, making it the dominant genre within this movement. Self-publishing options for creators ranged from Harvey Pekar self-financing professionally produced print runs of *American Splendor* to zines and minicomics produced on a copying machine and hand-stapled.[19]

As Sean Carney (2008) argues, comics have always cultivated a sense of the handmade as a way to appeal to readers. He gives one example in the prevalence of hand-lettering thr history of comics, with publishers even going so far a hand-lettering in computer fonts in order to retain that sense. Though Carney doesn't address the self-publishing and minicomics movement, its continued prevalence and popularity also show how the appeal of the handmade remains a strong tradition with fans of the medium.

Comics publishing and distribution

To understand the challenges of self-publishing and distribution, it is useful to know the traditional and conventional system for comics distribution. Though chain and independent book stores carry graphic novels and comic books, the vast majority of comic books in the United States are purchased through comic book stores. This has been the case since the collapse of the newsstand market and the rise of the comic book store in the mid-1980s.

Comic book store distribution, specifically, is dominated by a single entity: Diamond Comic Distributors. The process of gaining distribution through Diamond is complex and often onerous. If the creator's work is not released through an established publisher like DC, Marvel, Image, IDW, Fantagraphics, Top Shelf, or Drawn & Quarterly, but is instead self-published, then Diamond has a process by which a creator can submit a work to them for distribution and inclusion in their monthly *Previews* catalog. If Diamond selects the comics, they pay the creator 60–70 percent of the cover price (payable only after thirty days of receipt of the comic) and require a minimum of $2,500 in sales to distribute the book to comic stores. The cost of producing, printing, and shipping the comic to Diamond falls on the creator. Very few minicomics or self-published books can meet the $2,500 minimum alone, even if the creator could pay all of the other personal costs. Minicomics already operate on very low margins, and so Diamond's arrangements are often untenable. Therefore, self-distribution becomes a much more viable option: the creator must still shoulder the costs, including the cost of distribution, but the creator can also pocket 100 percent of the cover price.

So, without easy access to comic book store distribution, creators of minicomics and other self-published work often have limited options, and the struggles with getting work into the hands of readers actually become further material for the comics. In *A Mess of Everything* (2010), Miss Lasko-Gross illustrates the experience of finding comic shops and record stores to carry her minicomics series *AiM* on a consignment basis, in a story titled "Consignment." In the story, fifteen-year-old Miss meets with encouragement from one comic store owner, while finding the employees at Power Records to be sarcastic and patronizing, even though they do take five copies of her comic. The story ends with Miss at an independent record and comics store receiving discouraging looks from the workers there. Her final speech balloon trails off into an ellipsis, indicating that this "distribution system" of peddling her comics from store to store by hand will continue endlessly.

Other creators—like Julia Wertz, Dustin Harbin, Gabrielle Bell, and others—reveal the experience of attending comic conventions and small press expos to sell their wares. Julia Wertz (2015) demonstrates some of the dangers and awkward moments that can happen during the close interactions with fans who follow the creator's personal, intimate stories (63; see Fig. 4.3). In *The Voyeurs* (2012), Bell tells the story of how, when she was just starting out with minicomics in the late 1990s, she and a friend went to the San Diego Comic-Con and would temporarily set up and sell their comics at empty tables until the pros assigned to the tables would show up (120–1). This guerilla technique, known as "table-squatting," raised the ire of nearby pros, though convention staff condoned the activity because an occupied table looked better than an empty one. In retrospect, Bell sympathizes with the angry pro:

> I understand her frustration now. Here she'd spent years developing her craft and career, playing by the rules, and here was us: presumptuous, amateurish, jumping the line, using little more than our youthful charm to sell our xeroxed [*sic*] unprofessional first efforts. (121)

Such stories also reveal the importance of networking and word of mouth in the modes of alternative distribution. Minicomics practitioners trade comics with each other to further spread their work. In addition, creators also use mail-order distribution, either through their own websites, on platforms like Etsy, or with

FIGURE 4.3 *"Q&A @ SPX" from Julia Wertz's* Drinking at the Movies *(2015). © Julia Wertz. Used with permission.*

collectives, as is the case with Oily Comics (oilycomics.com), a minicomics subscription service.

Several significant autobiographical comics creators began their careers producing minicomics before getting picked up by larger publishers. As an extraordinary example, John Porcellino's *King-Cat Comics and Stories* began in 1989 and has had seventy-six issues as of this writing, while Porcellino has had other success with full-length autobiographical graphic novels, like *Perfect Example* (2005) and *The Hospital Suite* (2014), and a collection of the minicomics, *King-Cat Classix* (2007).

Self-publishing and materiality

In his discussion of Alison Bechdel's *Fun Home*, Aaron Kashtan (2013) calls for comics scholars to pay greater attention to issues of materiality and mediality, especially as they contribute to the meaning and experience of the text. This call would be particularly appropriate for self-publishing comics (especially minicomics) and web comics. Even if the ultimate end result of a creator's work is some widely distributed print publication (like a comic book listed in Diamond's catalog or a bound volume sold in book stores), the earlier self-published versions exist as separate texts with different meanings and experiences for the reader. The self-published comic is often a very different material object, usually with some kind of handmade quality. Knowing that a creator may have personally photocopied, folded, and stapled the comic you are reading, in addition to writing and drawing it, makes it feel unique and special, and that is different from reading a mass-produced comic or bound volume. For example, reading John Porcellino's *King-Cat Comics and Stories* in its self-published zine format is a different experience from reading the same stories in the collected *King-Cat Classix* (2007) published by Drawn & Quarterly. Porcellino's art still has its simple, authentic quality in each, but the creator's hand seems more evident in the zine. In some cases, there are also very significant material differences. In one of his earliest comics—issue 8 (1989)—Porcellino actually taped a lock of his hair onto the page as the reader's "souvenir" [*sic*] (though only for the first eighteen copies). That story is reprinted in *King-Cat Classix*, but without the hair (23).

In addition, the reader's experience in purchasing and reading that object affects its meaning as well. A reader who tracks down a minicomic by seeking out the creator at a convention or by ordering it directly from the creator's website has a different, unique experience with the text, partially through a greater sense of connection to the creator. When that comic is autobiographical, then that connection can become even more personal. Such a relationship between creator and reader can, of course, have significant dangers if the reader infers a personal connection that the creator neither wants nor intends, but, on the whole, the connection can enhance the reader's experience of the work. For creators, this connection may also provide an opportunity for quick feedback from readers, but, again, whether or not that feedback is useful, welcome, or desired by the creator is another matter (Julia Wertz's comic, Fig. 4.3, is also relevant here: some of that feedback may come in the form of personal advice to the creator).

Print publication can change the relationship between the work and the creator, at least in the minds of some fans. Fan culture, particularly comics fan culture, often puts a premium on a certain kind of authenticity that can come with self-publishing in relative obscurity. Once the creator achieves the markers of success that come with print publication and wider distribution, some fans may lose their proprietary sense of significance within the creator's circle of readers. This is the attitude that leads some fans to accuse creators of "selling out" or "betraying" their most dedicated readers.

I don't want to come across as too critical of fan culture in general or of comics fans in particular. Many creators find their positive interactions with fans to be valuable, encouraging, and motivational. Through the ubiquity of social media and the popularity of comic book conventions, readers have greater access to the creators behind the works they love. The implied intimacy of autobiography can potentially dissolve the barriers between readers and creators even further, in both welcome and unwelcome ways.

Web comics

In the world of self-publishing, the already low overhead of minicomics declined even further with the advent of web comics.

Costs for printing, photocopying, and supplies were replaced with costs related to hardware, software, servers, domain names, and Internet access. With web comics, readers can make regular, dedicated engagement with the work (and with something like James Kochalka's *American Elf* diary web comic, that engagement could be daily), where the reader has to make a concerted effort or even a regular appointment to keep up with the comic. This can also facilitate a sense of connection between creators and audience. In addition, web comics often have vibrant comments sections and message boards that allow readers to connect with creators and offer feedback. Like the potentially awkward personal encounters at conventions, however, the value of such tools for creators is heavily dependent on the behavior of fans.

Autobiographical comics on the web can take several forms. Some can take the form of self-contained, focused narratives, like Stuart Campbell's *These Memories Won't Last* (2015, discussed below), and *Carriers* by Lauren R. Weinstein (2014), about how Weinstein and her husband dealt with the fact that both were carriers for the cystic fibrosis gene, and what that meant for their unborn child. In one of the more notable examples, Raina Telgemeier began her autobiographical comic *Smile* as a weekly web comic in 2004, published on the website Girlamatic.com, before it was completed in print through Scholastic's Graphix imprint. Others can be a series of self-contained short stories (*Underwire* by Jennifer Hayden, 2008–10, originally published on Act-I-Vate and later collected by Top Shelf [2011]) or open-ended diary comics. Some take advantage of formal elements available with web publication, while others simply use the medium as a means of distribution for their otherwise traditional comic stories and strips.

The enormous popularity and democratic potential of web comics can be seen in two examples: Sarah C. Andersen's *Sarah's Scribbles* (begun in 2011) and Allie Brosh's *Hyperbole and a Half* (begun in 2009). Both series follow the "rage comics" phenomenon (discussed in the introduction), using crude and highly abstract illustration styles that include disproportionately large, round heads and eyes. *Sarah's Scribbles* is made up of single-page strips that highlight the common experiences of young people with anxieties about impending adulthood. Andersen began distributing the strip through various social media platforms, like Tumblr and

Facebook, and its popularity led to a print collection in 2016 titled *Adulthood Is a Myth*.

While *Sarah's Scribbles* follows a fairly traditional strip format, Allie Brosh's *Hyperbole and a Half* is a bit more free in its form, combining cartoon illustration and blog entries in a way that challenge common definitions of "comics." Brosh uses the digital drawing software Paintbrush to create a simple art style, slightly more complex than stick figures, which has facilitated significant reader engagement and accounts for much of the series' enormous popularity. Much of the series features observational humor related to common, daily activities, but Brosh's work probably became most noted and praised for its frank portrayal of depression. The web series was later collected, along with new material, in *Hyperbole and a Half: Unfortunate Situations, Flawed Coping Mechanisms, Mayhem, and Other Things that Happened* (2013), which went on to become a bestseller. Both *Sarah's Scribbles* and *Hyperbole and a Half* are deceptively simple looking: both creators have been able to connect with readers in profound ways through the articulation of shared experiences, and their viral success has attracted a broad audience that may not otherwise read comics.

Scott McCloud's "infinite canvas"

The "infinite canvas" is a concept originated by Scott McCloud in *Reinventing Comics* (2000) to describe the potential of web comics to take advantage of the medium and exploit its potential to tell unique stories different from those told within the physical limitations of print. McCloud proposes that creators think of the screen as a window, rather than an equivalent to a page in a print comic. The "infinite" part of the concept means that creators are also not bound by any length requirements, page shapes, or reading directions that limit print narratives. Creators could also control information flow and pacing in new ways, and they could incorporate elements like sound and animation to enhance the experience (though with the caution that the work must remain at its heart a sequential comics narrative).

Stuart Campbell's *These Memories Won't Last*

Stuart Campbell's (2015) *These Memories Won't Last* is an example of an autobiographical web comic that uses McCloud's concept of the "infinite canvas" and explores the unique potential of the medium for an unconventional comic story that include animation and sound. Campbell tells the story of his ninety-three-year-old grandfather's decline into dementia, a topic that other creators like Roz Chast and Joyce Farmer have covered (see the "Graphic medicine" section in this chapter). Campbell's work is a complex narrative and interactive experience. Readers are first introduced to a loading screen, where the question "When you look back on your life, what memories would you choose to share?" appears, each word in its own separate blue balloon that fades as the next comes into view. A red string creeps up the screen to indicate the comic is loading, and ethereal music can be heard in the background. Readers experiencing this comic for the first time will learn that the loading screen is essentially teaching us how to read the work: the images and text will be ephemeral, and readers will not be able to hang onto the page/screen in any kind of stable way. In fact, once scrolling commences, readers may find that they can't scroll back in the text to refresh their memory: the image and text will have faded away, unrecoverable.

The first image to appear is Campbell's grandfather, sitting in a chair and holding a rope that will become a motif throughout the story. Campbell's narration appears as part of the red string. Throughout the comic, almost all of the images and the grandfather's dialog are colored blue and the string and narration remain red. In addition, the red string and captions move from the bottom to the top of the screen, while the blue images and dialog move from the top, down. When scrolling, readers can essentially line up the text and image in different configurations, but the two do meet at a middle point on the screen. However, the image and text are also constantly in a kind of floating motion that the reader cannot entirely stabilize. Figure 4.4 shows what Campbell's art looks like if it were static in order to give a sense of his style and the work's vertical orientation.

The narrative follows the grandfather, who was born in Hungary in 1922, through his struggles with old age and dementia after his wife's death. Campbell points out that the grandfather's memory

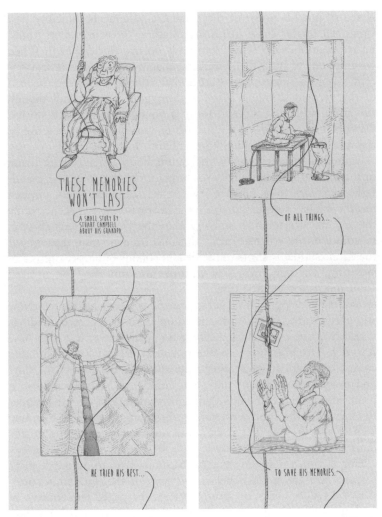

FIGURE 4.4 *Frames from Stuart Campbell's* These Memories Won't Last *(2015). © Stuart Campbell. Used with permission of the artist.*

is sharp, but his grasp of the present is where his difficulty lies. Campbell relates some of his grandfather's favorite stories about his experience in the Hungarian army during World War II. When we enter one of these memories, the images begin to scroll horizontally within a single panel border that appears on screen, instead of the vertical scrolling that has dominated so far. And though the grandfather is supposed to be a young man in these stories, Campbell draws him as a ninety-three-year-old, giving a sense of the way in which the grandfather inhabits his memory.

Campbell also represents his grandfather's difficulty with living in the present in a unique way. During a hospital stay, the grandfather becomes violent and believes he is back in the war. Campbell has the image's setting fade from the hospital to a war scene, while the grandfather remains stable within the changing background. In addition, the ethereal music that has been running throughout the comic suddenly shifts to the distant sounds of battle: sirens and shooting. The new images of wartime also mix the blue and red color motifs for the first time.

While the navigation of *These Memories Won't Last* is relatively straightforward, its narrative is complex, and repeated readings reveal that one could have a different experience with it each time it's read. Campbell exploits the potential of McCloud's "infinite canvas" concept to great effect: the space of the comic, the flow and movement of image and text, could not be duplicated in a print comic. The cumulative effect of the work allows the reader to experience the ephemeral nature of the present and the blending of past and present that is an approximation of the grandfather's daily existence.

For the most part, however, web comics tend to duplicate print formats like the multi-panel comic strip or the multipage comic where a reader clicks or scrolls to turn the page. The content of such works would tend to be largely duplicable from one medium to another.[20] For example, Dustin Harbin produces diary comics on his website (dharbin.com) and has collected them in print form as *Diary Comics* (2015) from Koyama Press. Many of his web comics follow a consistent four-panel grid and appear as such on the printed page as well.

Diary comics

Though diary comics did not originate on the web, the advent of the web comics medium has allowed for an expansion of the genre. Now, diary comics are the most popular form of autobiographical web comics. As Isaac Cates (2011) explains, "It would be difficult to overstate the ubiquity of diary comics among today's young cartoonists, particularly as a learning exercise or a temporary rite of passage for cartoonists in their teens or twenties" (210). With diary comics, creators could capture the details of their daily lives to an even greater extent than before, or, in some cases, simply use the format as a daily warm-up exercise, much like a sketchbook but more public. They could also follow a release schedule that suited their own personal levels of productivity, including anything from irregular schedules to experiments in daily or even hourly diaries. In the most ambitious example, James Kochalka produced his daily diary comic, *American Elf*, for fourteen years straight, beginning in 1998 and ending in 2012. There are way too many diary comics to list here, but some of the notable ones include *EmiTown* by Emi Lenox (daily from 2008 to 2011, published sporadically after that),[21] *DAR!* by Erika Moen (2003–9), *Ellerbisms* by Marc Ellerby (2007–10), *Dharbin* by Dustin Harbin (begun in 2010, but still published on an irregular schedule), and *Leslie's Diary Comics* by Leslie Stein, currently published on the VICE website. All of these diary comics have since seen print publication. Some other creators who have made the transition from web to print with their diary comics include Gabrielle Bell, Julia Wertz, and Liz Prince. The highly personal nature of diary comics combined with the accessibility of creators through comments sections and dedicated forums to create a highly motivated and dedicated fan base for many of these series.

Cates (2011) points out that diary comics challenge conventional notions of diaries and autobiographical comics. Diaries, he explains, are generally understood to be private (216), while diary comics are posted to the web for any reader to see. Autobiographical comics also tend to follow a narrative structure, focusing on particular relevant events that build upon each other as a story. Diary comics, on the other hand, are open-ended: the creator generally doesn't know where the diary will end up because he or she is creating it while living through the experiences: "Diary

strips cannot know the future of the 'story' in which they partic-
ipate" (211). Cates describes the overall effect of diary comics as
"accretive" (214): that is, the reader builds a sense of connection
to character and experience through the process of following the
comic over long terms.

The long-term dedication of a creator to a diary project
can often have pitfalls. Dustin Harbin's early strips occasionally
expressed his concern that his life wasn't interesting enough for
a diary comic, and that the work was an exercise in ego gratifi-
cation, before he later comes to the conclusion about the value of
self-observation and living in the moment that the diary promotes.
Another pitfall is what Elisabeth El Refaie (2012a) calls "premeditated commemoration": the idea that an autobiographical comics
creator would stage events in his or her life because they would
make for good stories (103). El Refaie uses the term in reference
to scenes in Ariel Schrag's work, where Ariel shows her work to
her friends in order to generate responses that would provide her
with more material for her comics. This issue comes up often in
diary comics, where a character in the comic will directly ask the
diarist something to the effect of "Are you doing this to make a
good story?"—thus challenging the authenticity of the creator's
work. In an *American Elf* strip called "The Set-Up" (originally
published January 15, 2004, reprinted in Kochalka [2007]), James
and his wife are discussing the sound that their baby, Eli, makes
when he coughs. James says that it "sounds like it's bubbling up
through a bowl of pudding," and then he asks his wife what she
thinks. She responds that it sounds like "a little monkey cough"
before she realizes what her husband is up to: "Hey! Are you just
trying to set me up to say something for your strip?" The fact that
it still becomes content for the strip, anyway, points to just one of
the ways in which these diary comics can become self-reflexive.[22]

Self-publishing and web comics remain some of the most vibrant
venues for autobiographical expression. Creators can use these
forms to experiment with new ways of telling stories and of giving
readers unique experiences with comics. However, the economics
of self-publishing and web comics make them challenges for
creators to sustain, despite the fact that they have lower overheads
than traditional print publication. In a 2010 strip titled "The
Comics of Business," included in *The Voyeurs* (2012), Gabrielle
Bell speaks to a class at the School of Visual Arts about "The

Business of Comics." In caption boxes, Bell explains her "business model": "My business model came from a quote I once read in an email that ended with 'decide what you want to do and the money will follow.' // Years later, I find this to be entirely untrue, unless what you want to do is investment banking, real estate speculation or maybe robbing banks" (141). When a student asks her, "Does it worry you that you're giving your comics away for free on the Internet?" she responds, "Well, free seems to be the going rate" (141). This darkly funny moment is critical of the expectation that many contemporary readers have regarding free access to all entertainment through the Internet. It also captures the essence of the dilemma that many creators who self-publish in print or on the web face, but which has also been a running concern throughout the history of art: the struggle between art and commerce.

Notes

1   Tom Hart's wife, cartoonist Leela Corman, has also documented her experience with the loss of Rosie in several short works, many of which have been collected in *We All Wish for Deadly Force* (2016).

2   Other than the "suburban" part, the author speaks from experience here.

3   For example, Earle (2014) analyzes Derf Backderf's memoir, *My Friend Dahmer*, as a *Bildungsroman*.

4   Joe Matt collects comics in *Fair Weather* (2002), but we get the sense that he is interested in comics more as an investment than as a vocation.

5   Also, on the trip, Raina brings Lynda Barry comics to read. This is the first nod we get to one of her influences.

6   Frank Bramlett (2015) argues that most comics deal to some degree with "elements of everyday practice," so the idea of the "quotidian" in comics needs to be extended from specifically "slice of life" comics to the majority of works in the medium. Bramlett concludes,

> Even though not every facet of every comic may help to construct the nexus of everydayness, all comics rely on readers' sense of the everyday, both their own "read world" quotidian and the recognition that the culture inside the comic rests on various nexus of practice and thus constitute the quotidian. (258)

This point is well taken; however, this section will focus on the
quotidian through the narrow slice of life subgenre.

7   In *The Comic Book Holocaust*, Johnny Ryan (2006) makes similar
points about the lurid, exhibitionistic, and solipsistic nature
of autobiographical comics with a one-page strip titled "Every
Auto-Bio Comic Ever Written." The unnamed protagonist of the
strip tries to show how edgy he is by masturbating and using a
dildo. He then goes on to prove what a sensitive artist he is by
emphasizing his flaws, bragging about his talent, and waxing
philosophically about art and life. Though Ryan's title generalizes
about autobiographical comics, he seems to be specifically targeting
the confessional group.

8   In the 1990s, Diane Noomin revived the name *Twisted Sisters*
for two anthologies and a miniseries, so this title also had a life
beyond its underground origins. In addition, *Wimmen's Comix*
ceased publication in 1977 with issue 7, but returned in 1983 with
issue 8.

9   Trina Robbins (1999), perhaps reductively, traces back the
influences on the female underground creators to earlier genre
comics that preceded the advent of autobiographical comics: "big
chunks of women's comix tend to be about the artist's dysfunctional
family, miserable childhood, fat thighs, and boyfriend problems,"
and despite its apparent underground origins, "the autobiographical
comic actually harkens back to the confessional style of mainstream
romance comics" (91).

10   Many stories in *Wimmen's Comix* and the other underground
anthologies are difficult to identify clearly as autobiographical. Trina
Robbins's "Sandy Comes Out" and Debbie Holland's "Fucked Up"
use the common convention of having the cartoonist sitting at her
drawing board and directly addressing the reader with the assurance
that the story is true. However, other stories use an unnamed
first-person narrator but will give few other hints that the story is
presenting the author's personal experience. In some cases, like Lee
Marrs's "All in a Day's Work" and other stories that she did in
the early issues of *Wimmen's Comix*, her cartoon avatar resembles
her enough for the reader to draw the conclusion that the story
is autobiographical. This means, though, that some assumptions
are made about stories based on their slim connections to generic
conventions. For such cases, I have relied on the phrase "personal
stories" for those that do not offer overwhelming evidence of their
genre identification.

11   The anthology *No Straight Lines: Four Decades of Queer Comics*

(2012), edited by Justin Hall, contains a mixture of fictional and autobiographical stories, but taken together, the works collected by Hall show the historical development of queer comics from the first strips appearing in gay newspapers through the influence of underground comix and on to contemporary independent creators.

12   Eisner's autobiographical stories, including *The Dreamer*, *To the Heart of the Storm*, and *The Name of the Game* have been collected in the volume *Life, in Pictures: Autobiographical Stories* (2007). See Dong (2011) for a discussion of these comics.

13   A summary of this scholarship can be found in the section on Aline Kominsky-Crumb and Robert Crumb in Chapter 5.

14   *Configurations*'s editorial statement notes that the journal focuses on "the multi-disciplinary study of the relations among literature and language, the arts, science, medicine, and technology" (qtd in Squier and Marks 2014: 149).

15   For overviews of graphic memoirs that deal with cancer, see Chute (2007), Holmes (2014), Miller (2014), Waples (2014).

16   See Appendix 2 for an extensive interview with Jennifer Hayden, where the comics creator talks at length about the creation process and the choices that went into making *The Story of my Tits*.

17   For a discussion of Chast's use of photography, see Chapter 3.

18   For a more detailed examination of the *Persepolis* controversy in the Chicago public schools, see McNicol (2015).

19   Isaac Cates (2011) defines "minicomics" (sometimes spelled with a hyphen) as "self-published and usually hand-assembled photocopied comics, made, sold, and traded by amateur cartoonists ... Although they are often smaller or shorter than standard comics, the prefix *mini-* is generally understood to refer to the size of the comic's print run, which is frequently only a few hundred" (224 n.3). Though Cates identifies "amateur cartoonists" as the creators of minicomics, many professional comics creators will continue to produce minicomics for their own personal projects, to sell at conventions, or as a lark.

20   I make this a highly qualified statement because advocates for studying mediality in comics, like Aaron Kashtan (2013), would warn against statements that a work has a kind of stable, Platonic content which remains consistent even if the work is adapted in different media (like a web comic adapted to print, or a print comic adapted into an eBook format), and that the medium impacts the meaning of the work in significant ways.

21 It is unclear as of this writing if Lenox is still publishing new *EmiTown* strips. The last entry was published in June 2015, which is almost a year ago as I write this.

22 Kochalka has admitted to forcing situations in his life in order to create material for the comic: "There have been occasions where I've said things to people, just to get reactions from them, so I could draw a strip about it. I've done that to my wife before. It's kind of a mean trick" (qtd in Chaney 2011a: 32).

5

Key Texts

Justin Green's *Binky Brown Meets the Holy Virgin Mary*

Justin Green's underground comic, published in 1972 by Last Gasp Eco-Funnies, is often cited as the first American autobiographical comic. While such declarations are often problematic, *Binky Brown*'s influence on later autobiographical comics is profound. Art Spiegelman (1995) boldly claims that *Maus* would not exist if it weren't for Green's groundbreaking work: "Without Binky Brown there would be no MAUS" (4). Reading *Binky Brown* served as Aline Kominsky-Crumb's inspiration for creating her own autobiographical comics. Also, Green's frank depiction of obsessive-compulsive disorder anticipates Alison Bechdel's own in *Fun Home*. In addition, Green's exploration of the struggles and anxieties of adolescent sexuality establishes a common theme that runs through the history of the genre in works by Jeffrey Brown, Chester Brown, Ariel Schrag, Marinaomi, Alison Bechdel, and many others. Charles Hatfield (2005) cites sales of around 50,000 copies for *Binky Brown*, which he explains is "an extra-ordinary figure for [underground] comix" (131). The work has been reprinted, in whole or in part, numerous times, including *Justin Green's Binky Brown Sampler* (1995), which includes several other Binky Brown stories, and a large, oversized hardcover edition (2009) that reprints the original art.

Young Binky Brown—a stand-in for Green[1]—conflates and compounds his growing adolescent confusion about his own sexual desires with the strict religious teachings of the nuns at his Catholic school, especially through the figure of the Holy Virgin Mary. Binky's sexual fantasies often lead to "impure" thoughts about the Virgin Mary, resulting in enormous guilt. His obsessive-compulsive disorder manifests itself as a means of driving out these troubling thoughts. As the disorder builds, he comes to believe that his penis emits a ray that could defile or even destroy any sacred object that it was pointed at, such as a church, an icon of the Virgin Mary, a rosary, or a crucifix. The range of these rays grows exponentially as Binky's obsession increases, from sacred objects in his visible range to a church that might intersect with one of his rays in any direction and at any distance. This then becomes an obsessive belief that all of his appendages are penises shooting out rays into infinity. Even inanimate objects become penis-shaped for Binky: tennis rackets, weather vanes, keys, shoes, toothbrushes, soda bottles, and chairs. Ultimately, this obsession leads to paralysis. Hatfield (2005) effectively sums up the work as "a fantastic, bleakly humorous mix of informed anti-Catholic polemic and self-scourging confessional. Over its forty pages, Green uncorks his psyche" (131).

On the inside front cover of the original comic, Green offers the following disclaimer:

It's not my fault if young Catholic children mistake this comic for Treasure Chest and then get fucked-up for life. Dealers are instructed, under pain of mortal sin, not to sell it to them. It's probably a venial sin even to sell this to adults.

Immediately, Green places the work in relation to a comics tradition—specifically, a tradition in which comics, such as Treasure Chest, were used by the Catholic Church to make the faith appealing to children. Green's work will also be dealing with issues of faith, but not in any way that the Catholic Church would approve. Therefore, Binky Brown serves as a kind of anti-Treasure Chest, subverting the Church's use of comics as religious propaganda by using a comic as anti-Catholic polemic.

Green frames Binky's story with his own first-person narration. In the opening splash page, "A Confession to my Readers," Justin appears suspended upside down over the drawing page, with his hands bound and a scythe pointed directly at his genitals (see Fig. 1.1). He holds a brush in his mouth to draw the comic that we are about to read. Justin explains the value of using comics, traditionally ghettoized as a children's medium, to tell his story and work through his traumatic childhood experiences. This bizarre scene parodies the conventional images of the cartoonist sitting at his drawing board, which were among the earliest depictions of the autobiographical mode in comics. Therefore, while *Binky Brown* is cited as the beginning of the autobiographical tradition in comics, it also closely follows the strands of that tradition laid out in much earlier comics.

Immediately, however, Green also establishes the value that autobiographical comics about trauma and mental disorders can have. He explains the purpose of this comic we are about to read:

> My justification for undertaking this task is that many others are slaves to their neuroses. Maybe if they read about one neurotic's dilemma in easy-to-understand comic-book format these tormented folks will no longer see themselves as mere food-tubes living in isolation. If all we neurotics were tied together we would entwine the globe many times over in a vast chain of common suffering.

The initial impetus for the book, then, is to use the comics medium in this special way, communicating more effectively through the form than might be done in other media. The book also has a special value for a narrower audience, one that may share experiences with Green. Gardner (2008) specifies the nature of this value:

> The question for the tradition of autography has long been, and remains, not whether the act of graphic memoir will set the autobiographical subject free (Green makes it very clear that it will not), but whether it will release him into a chain of common suffering, and whether that chain can be made to communicate, to bind one to the other. (10)

Gardner shows here that Green challenges one possible justification for confessional autobiography—a cathartic release for the artist—but instead builds empathy and creates a sense of shared experiences among readers.[2]

Prior to the publication of *Binky Brown Meets the Holy Virgin Mary*, Green had used the same avatar in shorter autobiographical works. His first Binky Brown story, "Confession of a School Boy," was published in a 1968 issue of the *Providence EXTRA!* This story begins to document his obsessive relation with Catholicism. In 1969, he published "Binky Brown Makes Up His Own Puberty Rites," a seven-page story in Print Mint's *Yellow Dog* 17. Green (1995) considers this "an embarrassing garage tape" (78), but it does contain some seeds for the larger Binky Brown story, especially in the way that it addresses the collision between adolescent sexual development and Catholic guilt. Then, in 1970, he did "The Agony of Binky Brown," a four-pager published in the 1971 anthology *Laff in the Dark*. Its positive reception inspired him to continue in autobiography and "explore the world of neurosis" (1995: 78). On several occasions, Green also published stories under the title "Justin Green's Theater of Cruelty," as in *Bijou Funnies* 6 (1971) and 7 (1972). These tend to be straighter, more realistic autobiographical stories, though the Green-like protagonist goes unnamed. Thus, Green toyed and experimented with autobiography for several years before embarking on the longer, more innovative story. Brown also returns in later short stories, some of which follow a more straight-forward, realistic narrative less focused on his interior life, as in "The Sweet Void of Youth with Binky Brown" (1976, reprinted in *Justin Green's Binky Brown Sampler* [1995]), which covers Binky's development as an artist from high school to college and beyond— parts of Green's life not addressed in the earlier work. However, other stories extend the allegorical elements of *Binky Brown*: in "Sweet Surrender" (1978, reprinted in *Justin Green's Binky Brown Sampler* [1995]), we get a return of the neurotic Binky, who is tied up and living in a shoe. A sadistic dog named Nostalgia wears an usher costume and forces Brown to watch movies of his childhood.

Sacred and Profane (1976) reprints the story "We Fellow Traveleers," which was originally serialized in the Marvel published *Comix Book* 1–3 (1974–5). "Traveleers" returns Green to the topics of guilt, Catholic faith, and mental illness, but this time in a deeper and more complex allegory. On the inside front cover, Green offers "A Toast," which explains not only the therapeutic value of using the comic form to work through his own issues with the Church, but also to possibly affect some change in the reader:

> Guilt, fear, sexual repression, and just plain morbidity are my habitual responses to the general idea of Christ impaled on

a cross ... If the curse to be levied on me for tampering with
sacred stuff is that all thoughts on the subject coming from my
blasphemous lips will register as babble in the ears of my fellow
humans, then may they gain knowledge through the inverse
method of dissecting the lies & fallacies I have manufactured in
my flight from a misplaced divinity which leads to idolatry and
superstition. I only wanted to undertake the responsibility of
using this mutant artform for an evolutionary motive, though
I've heard that "the road to hell is paved with good intentions."

"Traveleers" is a much more heavily allegorical work than *Binky
Brown*, with dense symbolism packed into every panel like the
"chicken fat" Bill Elder would use in old *Mad* comics. In the
story, an unnamed young man wearing a "Fighting Irish" shirt
has to carry around his "imaginary brother" named "Neurosis."
The protagonist and Neurosis end up at "The Saw-Church of
Profanity," where they meet a carpenter named Handy Jud who
tries to teach them that we all share the guilt for Christ's death.
This comic shows a trajectory for Green's work and the specific
ways in which he addresses the relation between faith and mental
illness. While *Binky Brown*, on the one hand, used vivid visual
symbolism to represent Binky's faith and obsessions, the narrative
remained grounded in a sense that the symbolism was attached to
Green's real experiences. "Traveleers," on the other hand, feels far
less grounded in lived experience, and the allegory is often difficult
to penetrate.

Much of the scholarship on *Binky Brown* deals with its
placement in and influence on the history of autobiographical
comics. For example, Elisabeth El Refaie (2012a) only references
it in terms of its historical importance (38). Joseph Witek (2011),
however, positions *Binky Brown* within the prior history of comics,
asking, "If the comics form is so thoroughly and fundamentally
suited to narrativize the self, why did it take so long for anyone
to notice, and how did Justin Green happen to be the one to do
it?" (228). Witek points out that Green relies on many tropes
and conventions from earlier comics: the nightmare landscapes of
Winsor McCay, superheroes' fragmented identities, and even "the
familiar comic book fight scene" as evinced in the comic's full title,
Binky Brown Meets the Holy Virgin Mary, which sounds like a sort
of superhero team-up (228).

Charles Hatfield (2005) uses *Binky Brown* to discuss the problems of "authenticity" in autobiographical comics. The separation of Justin the creator as narrator and Binky Brown as character, along with the various ways in which Binky is visualized, challenges notions of autobiographical objectivity:

> *Binky* ... demonstrates how the persona of the cartoonist is always inevitably in doubt—how a mocking visual self-reflexivity informs even the foundations of this genre. Indeed, radical subjectivity is the focus of *Binky*, and Green's cartoon world is as aggressively imaginative as Binky's own inner world is obsessive and guilt-wracked. (138)

From the earliest moments of confessional autobiography in comics, the power of comics to affect the genre in radically different ways from other media is starkly evident.

The importance, then, of *Binky Brown* has been not only to initiate a form of confessional autobiography in the comics medium, but also to take the potential of the underground movement to a more sophisticated level and make comics do something that other media either can't do or can't do as effectively. As we saw in Chapter 2, the initial impetus for the underground movement was a reaction against the restrictions of the Comics Code and the ghettoization of comics as a juvenile medium. The push into more adult content often meant political protest or challenging taboos regarding sexual or scatalogical humor. With *Binky Brown* and other important comics from 1972, like the first issue of *Wimmen's Comix* and Art Spiegelman's first "Maus" story, the maturation of comics took on greater potential. Green and others demonstrated that comics, when unencumbered by censorship or the juvenile stigma, could offer a venue for intensely personal, sophisticated storytelling. Green continued to push that potential in comics throughout the underground era with works like "Sweet Void of Youth," "Sweet Surrender," and "We Fellow Traveleers."

Robert Crumb and Aline Kominsky-Crumb

Separately and together, Robert Crumb and Aline Kominsky-Crumb[3] have had a profound influence on autobiographical comics ever since the autobiographical mode appeared in underground comix. Crumb's earliest autobiographical works, such as "The Confessions of R. Crumb" in *The People's Comics* (1972a) and "The Many Faces of R. Crumb" from *XYZ Comics* (1972b), roughly coincide with the appearance of Justin Green's *Binky Brown Meets the Holy Virgin Mary* in 1972.[4] Green has cited Crumb's work as the inspiration to move to California and create underground comix. Alternately, Aline Kominsky-Crumb claims *Binky Brown* as the source of inspiration for her own emigration to California and her decision to pursue autobiographical expression through comics. In "More of the Bunch" from *Twisted Sisters* 1 (1976a), she demonstrates this influence: Aline's alter ego, The Bunch, reads *Binky Brown* and declares, "Hey this is heavy shit. This kid's got problems ... and so do I!" Both Crumb and Kominsky-Crumb have created autobiographical personae that they use consistently in short stories that have appeared in anthologies and their own solo books. Beginning in 1974, the now married underground cartoonists have occasionally collaborated on a series of stories about their lives together, from life on a commune in California to their present existence as expatriates in France. In these stories, they each draw themselves, making for an interesting juxtaposition of styles. The series began with full-length stories in *Dirty Laundry Comics* 1 (1974) and 2 (1977) (collected by Last Gasp as *The Complete Dirty Laundry Comics* in 1993), followed by shorter pieces in the pages of *Best Buy Comics*, *Weirdo*, *Prime Cuts*, *Self-Loathing Comics*, and *The New Yorker*, among others. The collaborations were all collected in the volume *Drawn Together* (2012).

Robert Crumb

When he gained fame as an underground cartoonist, Crumb was primarily known for his humorous, taboo-challenging comics, often featuring characters like Mr. Natural, Fritz the Cat, and Angelfood McSpade. Crumb also became a recurring character in his own comics as he established his comic persona in the early 1970s: thin, gangly, abrasive, paranoid, anti-social, curmudgeonly, sex-obsessed, excessively nostalgic, self-loathing, and misogynistic. The earliest self-portraits appear in stories that are not so much narratives but extensive monologs, often directly addressing his critics. For example, in *Big Ass Comics* 2 (1971), he appears in a one-page story: "And Now, a Word to You Feminist Women," subtitled, "from that ol' Male-Chauvinist Pig, R. Crumb Himself!!" Sitting on a couch, he directly addresses the audience, especially critics of the way in which he depicts women in his comics: "I don't deny that my cartoons contain a great deal of hostile and ofttimes brutal acts against women! I'm well aware of this dark side of my ego!" He goes on to point out, "I think it's an oversimplification to say that a picture or drawing is promoting something just because it portrays it!" He denies any political content to his work and argues that such limitations demanded of artists are "pure totalitarianism!" and that he's defending "freedom of expression." As the strip goes along, his language becomes increasingly hostile, devolving into gender slurs. What starts out as a sincere defense of his work and a criticism of censorship devolves into a depiction of himself exactly as his critics imagine him to be. Many of his most famous self-portraits exhibit this same kind of ironic deconstruction. "The Many Faces of R. Crumb" (from *XYZ Comics*, 1972b) begins with the artist ejaculating out of a window while masturbating to his own comics: "Here's me 'hard' at work in my studio!" Crumb then follows this with a series of self-portraits in individual panels, ranging from "the long-suffering patient artist-saint" to "the misanthropic, reclusive crank" and the "wasted degenerate." As Charles Hatfield (2005) points out, "The very random, non-narrative quality of this series also testifies to the plasticity of the artist's self-image ... [I]f none of these images is adequate to unlock the 'real' Crumb, then all are nonetheless part of the way he sees himself" (120). This prismatic view of the artist's personae anticipates the way in which "pictorial embodiment" (El Refaie 2012a: 51) and other aspects of comic art challenge notions of a stable identity for the autobiographical subject. Aline Kominsky-Crumb also probes this stylistic technique even further.

Crumb's work for *Weirdo*—which he co-created, edited, and served as primary contributor—and later comics advance his exploration of the confessional mode from his earlier work and offer greater introspection. In "I Remember the Sixties" from *Weirdo* 4 (Winter 1981–2), Crumb reflects back on the 1960s while marking the changes he has noticed in himself and others from that period. In the 1960s, he hated cops and other authority figures, but now he finds himself relieved when he sees a cop car while walking around "negro youths." He is grateful to feminists for setting him straight on his sex-obsession. He also reflects on LSD trips, both good and bad, and comments generally on the loss of idealism in his generation. In all, this story reveals his ambivalence toward the counterculture movement in which he gained his fame.

His confessional mode is often self-critical and nakedly honest. "Memories Are Made of This!" (*Weirdo* 22, Spring 1988) has Crumb confessing to an infidelity in 1976, where he takes advantage of a drunk fan who was initially resistant to his advances. He concludes the story with "Why do I have this compulsion to confess?! / Guess it's my Catholic upbringing … ." This honesty and self-criticism would become the norm for the generation of autobiographical comics creators who followed Crumb. According to El Refaie (2012a), "Crumb's outrageous and sexually explicit confessional comics had a lasting effect on the autobiographical comics genre, particularly in the US, where many graphic memoirists cite his work as a huge influence on their own artistic endeavors" (37), including Alison Bechdel, Phoebe Gloeckner, Julie Doucet, Chester Brown, and Joe Matt.

Aline Kominsky-Crumb

Aline Kominsky-Crumb's autobiographical short stories have appeared in a variety of underground and independent comics, beginning with "Goldie: A Neurotic Woman" in *Wimmen's Comix* 1 (1972). Following the second Goldie story in *Wimmen's Comix* 2, Kominsky-Crumb had a falling-out with other members of the Wimmen's Comix Collective because she was "frustrated by what she perceived as an almost superhero-inflected glamorization of women under the auspices of feminism" (Chute 2010: 24). With fellow cartoonist Diane Noomin, she started *Twisted Sisters* in

1976, which featured the first appearance of her autobiographical persona, "The Bunch."[5] In addition to these series, she published her short stories featuring The Bunch in various other underground anthology series, as well as her own solo comic, *Power Pak* (two issues, 1979 and 1981). She also contributed to *Weirdo*, for which she later became editor from 1986 to 1993. Her Bunch stories have been collected in *Love That Bunch* (1990) and in *Need More Love: A Graphic Memoir* (2007), which includes comics stories, prose, photographs, and other media.

The first issue of *Twisted Sisters* (1976) features the oft-cited cover in which The Bunch is sitting on the toilet, grunting and anxious. Her thought balloons reveal her anxieties: "I look like a 50 yr. old businessman! / What if someone comes while I'm making?? / How many calories in a cheese enchilada?" Meanwhile, a calorie counter sits on a hamper and a cat is about to eat a partially chewed sandwich and pickle on the floor. Inside the issue, Kominsky-Crumb contributes two interlinked autobiographical stories: "The Young Bunch: An Unromantic Adventure Story" and "More of the Bunch." Taken together, the two stories cover her life from her teenage years to her earliest foray into underground comix with the creation of her first "Goldie" story that appeared in *Wimmen's Comix* 1 (1972). In fact, many of the events covered in "More of the Bunch" are also depicted in the earlier "Goldie" story. The *Twisted Sisters* stories also address key themes and experiences that recur throughout her career: rape, sex, abuse, ethnic identity, and body image.

"The Young Bunch" (1976b) is an episodic story that begins with the Bunch's first sexual experience: at the age of fourteen, she was date-raped by a classmate named Al. In the scene, Al has driven Aline to a secluded area in his car. He insists, "I won't do anything you don't want me to." However, when she asks him not to kiss her, he still does, and then he moves on to feel her breasts. Despite her continued protestations, Al thinks, "She's letting me feel her up." Al continues to force himself on her, and he eventually ejaculates inside her. Kominsky-Crumb draws Al's penis as an ugly, enormous monstrosity, with more detail than any other object in the comic. Later, after telling the story to her best friend, Carol, Aline fantasizes about Al's penis. The story demonstrates ambivalence about this first, non-consensual sexual experience. As Chute (2010) notes about much of Kominsky-Crumb's work, "It is important that Kominsky-Crumb acknowledges both enjoyment and shame; her work does not simply celebrate transgression" (30). Kominsky-Crumb never draws erotic or titillating sex scenes, but instead challenges readers' notions of how sex can be depicted: "Kominsky-Crumb's political project is to visualize how sexuality, even when disruptive, does not have to be turned over to the gaze of others" (Chute 2010: 30). This unglamorous, de-eroticized, and unapologetic representation of sexuality not only sets Kominsky-Crumb apart from other underground cartoonists, but also anticipates later autobiographical comics creators like Phoebe Gloeckner and Debbie Drechsler.

This story also shows the parental abuse she experienced from both her mother and father: the mother's (often referred to in the Bunch stories as "Blabette") abuse is usually emotional in nature, and the father combines physical abuse with demeaning language. When Bunch asks to go to the Museum of Modern Art, the father responds, "She ain't interested in no museum. She just wants to pick up some boys and fuck." She goes to the city, anyway, and ends up having forced oral sex with a member of the band The Fugs. She gets home late, and her father proceeds to choke her and slam her head into the wall. The mother screams, "Arnie don't kill her!" In the next story, "More of the Bunch," Aline, now in her twenties, associates her neuroses with her father's physical abuse, as she bangs her own head into the wall. In later stories, she comes to terms with her mother's emotional abuse, especially when she documents her own experiences with motherhood after her daughter, Sophie, is born, as in the story "Mommy Dearest Bunch" from *Wimmen's Comix* 9 (1984).

Body image is also a common topic in Kominsky-Crumb's work. She often depicts herself as exercise-obsessed, performing grueling aerobic routines. One of her more notable stories about body image is "Bunch Plays with Herself" from *Arcade* 3 (Fall 1975). The story challenges the reader's erotic expectations of the title: Bunch squeezes pimples, scratches her butt, smells her finger afterwards, picks her nose, and masturbates. She concludes the story by telling the reader, "My body is an endless source of entertainment." This focus on body image also extends to her art style: as Chute (2010) observes, "she frequently draws herself differently from panel to panel, even within the space of one story" (31). The effect of this "present[s] an unfixed, nonunitary, resolutely shifting female self" (31). This complicates El Refaie's (2012a) notion of "pictorial embodiment": the idea that autobiographical artists draw themselves again and again in the same way each time (51). Furthermore, Kominsky-Crumb admits that her self-portrait is less attractive than she is in real life, and than the way in which other creators have depicted her, including her husband. El Refaie (2012a) describes her as "a female comics artist taking complete control of her own pictorial embodiment, and rejecting any attempts by her husband, readers, other artists, or wider society to impose extraneous body images on her" (82). In fact, the *Dirty Laundry Comics* often show Aline resisting Robert's attempts to revise her art or change her style.

Her concern about body image also connects to another common topic in her work: Jewish identity. This subject has attracted the most critical attention for scholars, who look primarily at the way she both deploys and complicates Jewish female stereotypes (see Oksman [2007], Clementi [2013], and Precup [2015]). In "Nose Job" from *Wimmen's Comix* 15 (1989), Bunch, now forty years old, considers the possibility of plastic surgery as a solution to some of her many body image problems. However, she rejects this idea and then reflects on her teenage years when she and her Jewish friends resisted the WASPy beauty norms of straight hair and small noses, even though some of their Jewish peers were getting nose jobs, and her own mother put pressure on her to follow suit.

Dirty Laundry Comics

Dirty Laundry Comics and other collaborative works document the couple's unconventional relationship, including graphic details of their sex life, Robert's infidelities, Aline's body-image issues, parenthood, and their financial problems due to Robert's lawsuit over the rights to "Keep on Truckin'" and an IRS tax bill. For example, in "Aline 'n' Bob's Funtime Funnies," from *Dirty Laundry Comics* 1 (1974), Robert forces Aline to perform oral sex on him, causing her to throw up. He then shoves her face into the vomit while entering her from behind. During this scene, Aline confesses to liking the humiliation (1993: 21). However, elsewhere in the story, Aline also admits to making this story up. Such admissions call into question the veracity of this series as autobiography. Even more so, the series often diverges into unrealistic fantasy. Also in the first issue, Aline and Bob are kidnapped by aliens and rescued by a Flash Gordonesque Timothy Leary. Equally improbable, Aline and Bob get washed away in a flood, and Aline swims to shore carrying Bob and their cat on her back. Alternately, this early story also deals with the realities of their lives in the California commune and Crumb's long absences while on the road with his band, the Cheap Suit Serenaders, where he engages in infidelities with his fans. This contrast between fantasy and reality, or between fabrication and verifiability, challenges conventional notions of autobiography. Do the fantasy elements reveal truths about the nature of their relationship? Does the admission of fabrication call into question the veracity of other seemingly realistic elements of the stories?

Bob and Aline also frequently comment on the creation of the comic itself, including their admission to fabricating some details. At one point in the second issue, Aline calls attention to the fact that Bob is making the comic too grim. He responds that they are doing "confessional literature," which is "all the rage now'days!!" (1993: 68). This self-consciousness pokes fun at the nature of autobiographical comics as well as their own legacies as the genre innovators who were among those that established the confessional mode in the first place.

Harvey Pekar's *American Splendor*

Harvey Pekar began self-publishing *American Splendor* in 1976, with annual issues appearing through number 16 in 1991 (the only issue released through Tundra Publishing). Pekar put out subsequent volumes through Dark Horse (1993–2002) and DC Comics' Vertigo imprint (2006–8). In 1987, Pekar won an American Book Award for the first anthology collection, *American Splendor: The Life and Times of Harvey Pekar* (1986), which was published by Doubleday. He gained national notoriety for his multiple appearances on *Late Night with David Letterman* from 1987 to 1989, though the attention was due more to Pekar's eccentric personality than his comics. The series was adapted into several stage plays in the late 1980s and early 1990s, and it became the basis for a 2003 film

(*American Splendor*) by Shari Springer Berman and Robert Pulcini and starring Paul Giamatti as Harvey (though Pekar does appear as himself throughout the film). Pekar experienced three bouts of cancer later in life, including one documented in *Our Cancer Year* (Brabner et al. 1994), co-written with his wife, Joyce Brabner. Soon after a third cancer diagnosis, he died on July 12, 2010.

Joseph Witek (1989) summarizes *American Splendor* by observing that "Pekar writes stories about his own daily life, depicts anecdotes and conversations he has heard and overheard, dramatizes vignettes from his civil-service job in Cleveland, and presents his often glum ruminations about his career and his life in general" (121). Harvey usually appears as the central character in his stories, though he also often reports the stories of others. Even then, he remains at the periphery of the scene, sometimes as a silent, recording observer. Frequently, though not regularly, Pekar would use one of several personae in his comics, giving them such names as "Herschel," "Our Man," and "Jack the Bellboy." Even with these alternative names, artists drew the characters as Harvey Pekar.

Unlike his precursors as well as most of his followers, Pekar is not a "cartoonist" in that he does not draw his own stories. Instead, he relies on a stable of established underground and independent artists, such as Robert Crumb, Frank Stack, Dean Haspiel, Gary Dumm, Joe Sacco, Val Mayerik, Josh Neufeld, and many others. Pekar's frequently described creative process involves rough, stick-figure layouts that the artists then flesh out. This working relationship is among the key topics discussed by scholars when dealing with *American Splendor* because each artist's unique depiction of Harvey demonstrates the instability of the subject's identity in autobiographical comics, which is especially notable because readers of autobiography assume a consistent "I" that is the author/subject of the work. An oft-cited image from the story "A Marriage Album" in *American Splendor* 9 (1984a) drives this home: Harvey's future wife, Joyce Brabner, is flying to Cleveland to meet him for the first time after the two had exchanged letters. Joyce's familiarity with Harvey comes only from the comics, and this understanding is depicted as a thought balloon containing various images of Harvey drawn in the style of different artists on the series. As Hatfield notes, this panel "suggest[s] how Joyce's image of [Harvey] was influenced by his comics prior to their first face-to-face meeting" (126). The proliferation of images, Hatfield argues, highlights "our own participation in the author's self-construction" as well as the way in which autobiographical comics in general can reveal the multiplicity of identity (126). For Witek (1989), the stylistic diversity of this image reflects the general diversity of personae Pekar adopts and narratives he utilizes (139).

Following Pekar, a handful of other comics writers created collaborative autobiographical comics working with other artists. The most notable examples include Dennis Eichhorn, whose series *Real Stuff*, among others, contained short stories of his eventful experiences that often dealt with drugs, violence, and run-ins with the law. Eichhorn employed a variety of underground and independent artists, many of whom also collaborated with Pekar. Another notable example is comedian and actor Del Close, who wrote a series of autobiographical stories for DC Comics's horror anthology series, *Wasteland*.[6]

Hatfield (2005) describes Pekar's importance in the history of autobiographical comics, noting that he "brought a radical appreciation for the mundane" through "a defiantly working-class strain of autobiography" (111). Nina Mickwitz (2016) expands on this significance: "*American Splendor* portrays the ways in which triviality and profundity intertwine, as found in the attention to seemingly mundane and generally overlooked aspects of everyday life" (37). Pekar's significance stems not only from his subject matter, but also from his collaborative approach to autobiography and his efforts at self-publishing and distribution, which were relatively untested when he began *American Splendor* in 1976.

In *American Splendor* 4 (1979), Harvey explains the origin of his self-published comic, starting with "The Young Crumb Story," where Harvey tells of his first meeting with Robert Crumb in Cleveland in 1962 and their subsequent friendship. The two meet through a shared interest in record collecting, but Crumb also inspires Pekar's interest in comics. Crumb heads to San Francisco in 1967 to begin his career as an underground cartoonist, but the two maintain their friendship despite the distance, and Crumb makes occasional return visits to Cleveland. Pekar credits Crumb's success as an underground creator with his own inspiration for diving into his own autobiographical comics. During one of these visits, Harvey thinks about the potential for the medium and his own plans for doing something different with comics:

For a couple of years I had been thinking I could write comic book stories that were different from anything being done by both straight cartoonists and underground cartoonists like Crumb. / The guys who do that animal comic an' super-hero stuff for straight comics are really limited because they gotta try t' appeal to kids. Th' guys who do underground comics have really opened things up, but there are still plenty more things that can be done with 'em. They got great potential. You c'n do as much with comics as the novel or movies or plays or anything. Comics are words an' pictures; you c'n do anything with words an' pictures!

Michael G. Rhode (2008) points out that "Pekar was never really of the underground comix movement," in that he was not interested in depicting sex, drugs, and violence, which were such significant topics for underground creators (viii). Instead, Pekar saw in the underground revolution an opportunity for a kind of self-expression in comics that was not yet being exploited by creators like Crumb but followed in the experimental path paved by them. While quite a few creators had already engaged in autobiographical stories, none did so in the manner or depth that Pekar did. Pekar's stories were shocking in both their banality as well as their unflinching confessionalism. That confessional mode was already well established by Crumb, Justin Green, Aline Kominsky-Crumb, Spain Rodriguez, Art Spiegelman, and others. Pekar, however, extended this confessionalism to a much longer project. Perhaps the only comparable work could be found in Kominsky-Crumb's numerous Bunch stories, which have appeared since the early 1970s.

The typical Pekar story often involves Harvey observing or directly experiencing the mundane experiences of everyday life, or what he often referred to as "the quotidian." In a 1993 *Comics Journal* interview with Gary Groth, Pekar explains that "mundane events, because they occur so frequently, have a much greater influence on people's lives" than the type of fantasy normally represented in comics (38). Mickwitz (2016) argues that Pekar's authenticity comes from his "willingness to portray himself in less than flattering light" (43). In addition, "Other textual strategies, such as the attention to different patterns of speech accents, and colloquial phrases that are part of Pekar's observed everyday life, add to the apparent authenticity of [the story's] telling" (43). For example, in "Standing Behind Old Jewish Ladies in Supermarket Lines," from *American Splendor* 3 (1978; art by R. Crumb), Harvey complains that it's a bad idea to do what the title says. One time he gets out of line when an old Jewish woman starts complaining to the cashier. Instead, he gets in line with "some goyish looking people" and the line moves faster with a more efficient cashier. When he gets home, he realizes that he forgot something and has to go back to the store. He goes into the express line, but it's too slow, and he recognizes the cashier as a bad one who once gave him too much change. He's behind an old Jewish lady, but she kindly offers to let him get in line in front of her. He turns her down, but he's surprised how this woman bucks the stereotypes he has. The old woman even comes back to give the cashier the extra change she gave her. The story ends, "Anyway, that was one of the most interesting incidents that's ever happened to me in a supermarket ... maybe **the** most interesting, as a matter of fact ... ." The mundane experience here yields something more: a challenge to the ethnic stereotype that Harvey had previously endorsed. However, Pekar revisits similar perils in "Another Old Jewish Lady, Another Store" from issue 12 (1987; art by Joe Zabel and Gary Dumm). Here, Harvey silently observes a conflict between the title character and a young mother in a busy grocery store line. The mother claims that the older woman has cut in line in front of her. The story demonstrates Pekar's attention to dialect; for example, the old Jewish woman says to the mother, "No vun's on fire. I'm not een a hurry. Eef you vanted you could go ahead of me." After the mother leaves, the clerk realizes that she overcharged her for an item; the older woman responds vindictively, "Det's **good** for her!" The epiphany that Harvey experiences in the earlier story seems rolled back here—the stereotype is reinforced rather than challenged.

Other common Pekar stories are often relatively plotless, with Harvey monologing through his own thought balloons. Harvey doesn't always paint a pretty picture of himself. He's quick to lose his temper with co-workers, for example, and he thinks of himself as intellectually superior to everyone else. In many other stories, Harvey is not the protagonist, but instead a kind of dispassionate interlocutor who is listening and reproducing the thoughts, stories, opinions, and philosophies of his acquaintances. Often, these people have problematic opinions, for example about race and gender. Some of these characters recur throughout the series as friends, neighbors, and co-workers in his job at the Cleveland Veterans Administration hospital.

Because of repeated characters and settings, Witek (1989) explains, "reading *American Splendor* [is] a cumulative experience" (137). That is, narrative threads form over the course of the series, like those surrounding Pekar's job at the Veterans Administration and the lives of his co-workers. However, that cumulative experience does not conform to a preset narrative or plan that Pekar had been following throughout the series. Instead, it emerges organically over the thirty-plus years that Pekar produced the series. Mickwitz (2016) describes the effect of reading this series over the course of many years:

> *American Splendor* is an unfolding autobiographical work, and the cumulative way in which readers get to know Harvey through a patchwork of seemingly unconnected stories and incessantly shifting tones and registers, his observations in the present, remembered anecdotes, reflections, and emotional outbursts corresponds to subjectivity as a continuous process and self-narration. (43)

This is an important element of *American Splendor*'s periodical publication, and it anticipates the similar experience of reading works like Joe Matt's *Peepshow* and Dennis Eichhorn's *Real Stuff*, as well as the diary comics by James Kochalka, Dustin Harbin, Gabrielle Bell, and others.

Pekar's work is also important for its method of production and distribution. In the mid-1970s, self-publishing in the comics industry was rare; even the underground cartoonists went through publishing houses dedicated to comix, like Last Gasp, Rip-Off Press, Kitchen Sink, and so on. At the point that Pekar wanted to break into underground comix, however, the industry had hit a slump, and few of the surviving publishers were willing to take a chance on untested talent. In "How I Quit Collecting Records and Put Out a Comic Book with the Money I Saved," also from *American Splendor* 4 (1979), Harvey explains how he arrived at the decision to self-publish. As the title of the story suggests, because Harvey quit his expensive record collecting habit, he had some spare money to spend. His attempts to place his own stories with established publishers were meeting with little success. After checking into printing costs, he figured out that he could budget enough savings to put out one comic a year with a print run of 10,000 copies. Despite the fact that he often lost money, Pekar sustained the annual self-publishing schedule through issue 16 in 1991 (an issue co-published with Tundra).

Pekar gained mainstream notoriety during several appearances on David Letterman's talk show between 1987 and 1989, which he depicted in several comics stories, most notably in *American Splendor* 12, 13 (including "My Struggle with Corporate Corruption and Network Philistinism" [1988]), and 14 (dubbed the "David Letterman Exploitation Issue" on the cover). Pekar's behavior on the show made him something of a cult figure, but in his later appearances, his repeated challenges to corporate media and NBC owner General Electric's involvement in the defense industry conflicted too much with the loose, humorous style of Letterman.

American Splendor continued as a kind of brand name with the publisher Dark Horse in 1993. In this iteration of the title, Pekar expanded beyond his own life story while still keeping in the realm of nonfiction comics. He wrote biographical tales about British fan Colin Warneford's experience with Asperger's Syndrome (*American Splendor: Transatlantic Comics*, 1998, drawn by Warneford), co-worker Robert McNeill's military experience in the Vietnam War (*American Splendor: Unsung Hero*, 2002, drawn by David Collier), and the lives of musical legends (*American Splendor: Music Comics*, 1997, drawn by Joe Sacco). During this period, Pekar also produced *Our Cancer Year* (1994), his most ambitious and critically acclaimed work in collaboration with his wife, Joyce Brabner, and with art by Frank Stack.

In 2003, Pekar received more mainstream attention from the adaptation of *American Splendor* into a film, written and directed by Shari Springer Berman and Robert Pulcini, and starring Paul Giamatti as Harvey. The film combines dramatizations of scenes from the comic along with documentary footage of and commentary by Pekar and Joyce Brabner. Pekar and Brabner followed the film with *Our Movie Year* (2004), a collection of stories detailing their experience making and publicizing the movie.

At the time of his death in 2010, Pekar was well enough known to garner obituaries in the mainstream press, and his comics have remained in print. In all, Pekar's work has had a profound influence on future generations of autobiographical comics creators. Hatfield (2005) describes the trend in autobiographical comics that runs through Pekar as "reinvent[ing] the comic book hero" from the larger-than-life superheroes of mainstream comics to the celebration of the mundane and the "scarifying confessional" of contemporary alternative comics (111). The genealogical line from Pekar to future generations of autobiographical comics is clear and marked by creators acknowledging his importance to their work.

Keiji Nakazawa's *Barefoot Gen: A Cartoon Story of Hiroshima*

Keiji Nakazawa's ten-volume manga series *Barefoot Gen* [*Hadashi no Gen*] tells the semi-autobiographical story of Nakazawa's survival of the Hiroshima atomic bombing in 1945 and its aftermath through the character Gen Nakaoka. It covers Gen's life from the weeks before the bombing, when he was six years old, to his departure from Hiroshima to pursue his manga career in Tokyo. The original manga series was published in several different formats between 1972 and 1985, and was later adapted as a live-action film in three parts, from 1976 to 1980. That was followed by two anime adaptations (1983, 1986) and a live-action television series (2007). Nakazawa proffers a strong anti-war message that is critical of both Japan's militarism and nationalism that prolonged the war and the US's decision to drop the atomic bomb and then occupy Japan. As Jeff Adams (2008) explains, the Japanese and American actions "are critiqued by Nakazawa through his experience as a child, and it is the effect of [these] colossal national and global events upon children in first hand accounts that makes his documentary manga distinctive" (91).

The anti-war message begins early in *Barefoot Gen*, mainly through the voice of Gen's father, who is arrested, abused, threatened, and isolated for his vocal criticism of Japan's continued involvement in World War II. The family also suffers as a result of the father's position: their livelihood is threatened while the father is imprisoned and injured from the police's abuse; Gen and his younger brother are bullied and teased for having a father who is a "coward"; and Gen's older brother feels compelled to enlist in the air force in order to salvage the family's reputation. Despite these setbacks, the father sends a clear message to Gen and the other children that taking a strong moral position and standing up to authority are necessary and worthwhile. That message continues for Gen throughout the narrative. Even in the final volume, as Gen leaves Hiroshima for Tokyo, he hears his father's oft-repeated lesson about overcoming adversity through a metaphor about wheat growing stronger after being trampled down. Along the way, Gen continues to maintain a strong moral position and empathy for his fellow human beings, even though he must regularly face the inherent selfishness and abusive behavior of others. Gen's journey ultimately presents a triumph for the lessons his father instills in him.

The path toward that uplifting conclusion is filled with traumatic experiences. Nakazawa depicts the atomic bombing and its immediate aftermath in graphic detail. Gen survives the blast because his back is to a cement wall when the bomb hits, but the teacher to whom he is speaking literally melts before his eyes. Gen witnesses other survivors with liquefied skin melting off their bodies, wandering aimlessly like creatures from a horror movie. He sees others die painfully from radiation poisoning after vomiting and losing control of their bowels. In one of the more emotionally jarring scenes, Gen witnesses his father, sister, and younger brother burn to death in their collapsed home, while he stands helplessly by, failing in his efforts to save them. His father admonishes him to leave and survive so that he can take care of his pregnant mother, while the younger brother screams for Gen to help him. The pathos of such a scene has a direct impact on the reader, and other scenes of the suffering Gen and his family experience only extend the reader's empathy for the character.

Nakazawa uses a fairly traditional manga style, featuring exaggerated physical characteristics and occasional cartoonish violence. However, he also shows graphic images of the war's destruction—children on fire after US bombing raids, bodies of women and children crushed on rocks after committing suicide, in addition to the people with liquefied skin dripping off of them as a result of the Hiroshima nuclear blast. Such images become even more horrifying when contrasted with the innocent and comedic images of young Gen and his brother in the early scenes of volume one. Nakazawa also juxtaposes the cartoonish manga images with a more detailed and realistic style for backgrounds and military scenes. Such a juxtaposition is a common characteristic of manga style, but here, it heightens the sense that this story is taking place in the real world. The story of Gen's family intercuts with historical details of the development and deployment of the first atomic bomb, which are also drawn in a photo-realistic style. These parallel narrative lines show the inexorable momentum of history, against which the family is helpless.

Prior to creating *Barefoot Gen*, Nakazawa published the more directly autobiographical manga *I Saw It!* [*Ore wa Mita*], as a fifty-page story in the periodical anthology *Weekly Shonen Jump* in 1972. As such, it coincided with the publication of the earliest autobiographical comics coming out of the US through the underground movement, such as Justin Green's *Binky Brown Meets the Holy Virgin Mary*. *I Saw It!* is framed by scenes where an adult Keiji, living in Tokyo, reflects on the suffering his mother endured after surviving the Hiroshima bombing. Keiji unveils the rest of the narrative as a series of flashbacks. Some basic elements of the *Barefoot Gen* narrative appear here, but other elements show some differences between the two works. These differences highlight the ways in which Nakazawa developed *I Saw It!* into *Barefoot Gen*, especially to raise the emotional impact of Gen's story. As in *Barefoot Gen*, Keiji in *I Saw It!* is saved from the bomb blast by his proximity to a concrete wall at his school. His mother does give premature birth to his sister after the bombing, and the infant dies months later from malnutrition. Also, in the months following the war, Keiji and his family face some of the same discrimination that is evident with Gen. Nakazawa does depict his father as a clog painter, though, significantly, the father's anti-war position is not addressed in *I Saw It!*. In addition, Keiji does not see his father, younger brother, and sister die as they are trapped in their burning house. In the immediate aftermath of the bombing, Keiji gets a bald spot on his head where he suffered a burn that didn't heal properly, but all of his hair does not fall out, as it does for Gen. And unlike Gen, Keiji's older brother, Yasuto, does not volunteer for the Japanese air force; instead, he's drafted to serve as a welder in the shipyard. Yasuto is dismissed from this position in order to help his family recover, so Keiji is not alone in trying to help his mother and sister survive, the way that Gen is. Late in *I Saw It!*,

Keiji is exposed to the manga work of Osama Tezuka, and this inspires him to pursue a career as a comics artist. (Such influence can similarly be seen in Yoshihiro Tatsumi's *A Drifting Life* [2009], which also begins in 1945.) When Keiji's mother dies in 1966, her body is cremated, but her bones are so thoroughly degenerated by radiation poisoning that they burn to ash; whereas, some bones usually survive the cremation process. At this point, Keiji vows to make comics about the atomic bomb, exclaiming, "I'll fight it and destroy it through cartoons!!"

Beginning in 1976, an organization called Project Gen, made up of anti-nuclear activists from Japan and the US, began efforts to translate *Barefoot Gen* into English. The initial Anglophone publication appeared as *Gen of Hiroshima*, released by EduComics that year. This was, according to Adams (2008), "the first full-length translations of a manga series from Japanese into English to be published in the West" (92). The American publisher Leonard Rifas found the sales too low to continue publishing after the second issue, especially in light of added expenses for translating and reformatting the manga for Western audiences (Adams 2008: 94). The work may also have lost traction with US audiences who weren't prepared for some of the conventions of manga, such as the cartoonish violence shown between Gen's father and the children (95). Beginning in 1988, New Society Publishers released a new English translation of *Barefoot Gen* in separate graphic novel volumes. More recently, Last Gasp, one of the key underground publishers who survived the movement's collapse, put out all ten volumes in another new translation from 2004 to 2010. The series has been championed by Art Spiegelman, who claimed Nakazawa's work as an early influence on the creation of *Maus* and who wrote the introduction for the first two Last Gasp volumes.

Barefoot Gen is an important autobiographical comic due to its early appearance in the history of the genre as well as its influence on other genre pioneers, like Spiegelman. However, it is also significant because of the way in which it demonstrates the educational potential of autobiographical comics, especially when dealing with events of such historical importance as the bombing of Hiroshima. It has served as a tool for activism by providing a clear and effective anti-war message for readers. In both *I Saw It!* and *Barefoot Gen*, Nakazawa emphasizes his role as witness, not only to the Hiroshima bombing, but also to the inhumanity of his fellow citizens toward survivors. This role contributes to both works' sense of authenticity, even when Nakazawa's use of a typical manga style and manga conventions of humor and exaggerated violence may challenge the reader's sense of realism.

Art Spiegelman's *Maus: A Survivor's Tale* and *In the Shadow of No Towers*

Maus: A Survivor's Tale

Art Spiegelman's *Maus: A Survivor's Tale* was first serialized in the pages of *Raw*, the groundbreaking, experimental comics magazine co-founded by Spiegelman and his wife, Françoise Mouly. The serialization ran from the second issue (1980) to the final one (1991). The chapters were then collected into two volumes: *Maus I: My Father Bleeds History* (1986) and *Maus II: And Here My Troubles Began* (1991).[7] The first volume was nominated for the National Book Critics Circle award in biography, a first for a comic book. The second volume received a special Pulitzer Prize in 1992, also a first, marking an important turning point in the popular acceptance of comics as a literary form. It has since gone on to become one of the best known and most frequently studied graphic novels ever published. *Maus* is part memoir of Spiegelman's dysfunctional relationship with his father, Vladek, and part family history, recounting Vladek's experience as a Holocaust survivor, along with Spiegelman's mother, Anja. Its most significant feature is Spiegelman's inventive use of zoomorphism: Jews appear as mice and Nazis appear as cats. With this technique, Spiegelman relies on a history of anthropomorphic animals in comics, especially ones featuring "funny animals" like Mickey Mouse and Donald Duck, but Spiegelman places *Maus* in an ironic relationship to that tradition.

A proto-*Maus* story appeared in *Funny Aminals* (1972), the same year that Justin Green released *Binky Brown Meets the Holy Virgin Mary*. *Funny Aminals* was an underground comix parody of the funny animal tradition, though Spiegelman's three-page story is much more somber and dramatic than the other stories in the anthology. "Maus" establishes the mice/Jews allegory that

Spiegelman would exploit further, and it also uses sharp irony to create a dramatic, unsettling effect. The story opens with the narrator, Mickey, explaining, "When I was a young mouse in Rego Park, New York, my poppa used to tell me bedtime stories about life in the old country during the war ... ." The innocent "bedtime story" tone stands in sharp contrast to the Holocaust subject matter. Many of the plot details here also appear in the later work: Mickey's father and mother hide out in a secret attic room with a group of other mice; they are captured after another mouse informs on them; the informant is later murdered in the concentration camp, and so on. After a series of escapes and more hiding out, Mickey's father and mother are captured and sent to "Mauschwitz." The story ends, essentially, where *Maus I* ends as well, with the Spiegelmans' arrival at the concentration camp. A late panel shows a scene of mice loading dead, emaciated, naked mice onto a pile, and then the father can't go on with the story: "... And so it was ... I can tell you no more now ... / ... I can tell you no more ... It's time to go to sleep, Mickey!" Spiegelman aims for a tone of harsh, bitter irony at the end, while the later work would try for something more subtle in Art's ambivalent relationship with his father.

Many scholars and critics compare the ending of this story to the final scene of *Maus*, where a bedridden Vladek implores Art (whom he mistakenly calls "Richieu," the name of Art's older brother who died during the war) to stop recording and let him rest. This ending inverts the ending of the earlier story, where Spiegelman's stand-in, Mickey, is the one in bed. Vladek's narrative also ends with the post-war reunion of him and Anja, on which Vladek concludes, "More I don't need to tell you. We were both very happy, and lived happy, happy ever after" (136). We know that this invocation of a fairy tale ending is not true: Anja committed suicide in 1968, for one. Rosemary V. Hathaway (2011) specifically connects this "fairy tale rhetoric" to the bedtime story conceit used in the earlier story (264).

Maus is by far the most frequently discussed work in Comics Studies scholarship, with more than 150 hits appearing in a search of the Modern Language Association bibliography alone. Summarizing all of the approaches to this seminal work would be impossible in this brief section. Many scholars, like Hillary Chute (2008a) in her groundbreaking *PMLA* essay, "Comics as

176   AUTOBIOGRAPHICAL COMICS

Literature? Reading Graphic Narrative," treat it as a model for the analysis of the comics form and an explanation of comics' unique qualities that separate it from other media. In that, it serves as a strong example: Chute writes, "The study of one touchstone text, *Maus*, is developing into an area that investigates the potential of the form at large" (457). She goes on to explain more specifically that *Maus*, as well as works by Marjane Satrapi, Alison Bechdel, Lynda Barry, Phoebe Gloeckner, and Aline Kominsky-Crumb, "presents a traumatic side of history, but … refuse[s] to show it through the lens of unspeakability or invisibility, instead registering its difficulty through inventive (and various) textual practice" (459). The role of *Maus* in the representation of history and trauma has been the key set of lenses through which the work has been read. In going back to one of the earliest works of comics scholarship—Joseph Witek's *Comic Books as History: The Narrative Art of Jack Jackson, Art Spiegelman, and Harvey Pekar* (1989)—we can see the argument being made for *Maus*'s centrality and innovative position in comics history: Spiegelman "build[s] … on traditional approaches to comics in order to expand the possibilities of the comic-book medium; this is history with a difference" (4). Hathaway (2011), who argues for *Maus*'s generic classification as "postmodern ethnography" rather than autobiography or oral history, encapsulates what makes the work so rich for critical discussion: "*Maus* resists and actively challenges notions of objectivity, truth, and authenticity. Furthermore, the work actively calls attention to itself as an artificial construct and offers metacriticism about its own manufacture" (251). Because Spiegelman tackles such large philosophical issues as "objectivity, truth, and authenticity," it can affect readers' understanding of these ideas writ large, and therefore affect the way that they read other works. Scholars have used *Maus* to address such issues as the representation of trauma, the possibility (or impossibility) of mourning, Holocaust memorialization, Jewish identity, generational conflict, memory, and photography.

In many ways, *Maus* has had a profound influence on comics in general and autobiographical comics in particular. In the wake of *Maus*, many other creators have used the medium to tell stories of their parents' experience and the impact that experience had on later generations. Such works include Alison Bechdel's *Fun Home* (2006), Miriam Katin's *We Are on Our Own* (2006) and *Letting*

It Go (2013), GB Tran's *Vietnamerica: A Family's Journey* (2010), Nina Bunjevac's *Fatherland: A Family History* (2014), and Carol Tyler's *Soldier's Heart: The Campaign to Understand my WWII Father: A Daughter's Memoir* (2015)—the latter three focusing specifically on parents' experiences in wartime. Miriam Hirsch (2011) uses the term "postmemory" to describe the way in which the memories of a previous generation can impact later generations; it is, in a sense, the child's memory of his or her parent's memories. Hirsch explains that "Postmemory is a powerful and very particular form of memory precisely because its connection to its object or source is mediated not through recollection but through an imaginative investment and creation" (22). In addition, "Postmemory characterizes the experience of those who grow up dominated by narratives that preceded their birth, whose own belated stories are evacuated by the stories of the previous generation shaped by traumatic events that can be neither understood nor recreated" (22). Hirsch applies this term to *Maus* in particular, and to the children of Holocaust survivors in general, but we can also see how it applies to these other works as well. GB Tran negotiates his parents' memory of their experience in the Vietnam War and their subsequent escape from Vietnam, all taking place before he was born. Nina Bunjevac attempts to recreate her father's experience in Yugoslavia during the communist takeover of that country and later as an exiled Serbian nationalist living in Canada; in doing so, she must go back generations to understand Yugoslavian and Serbian history. "Postmemory," then, is a useful term in discussing autobiographical comics that attempt to tell multi-generational narratives.

Many conventions of later autobiographical comics are established with *Maus*. Spiegelman uses a nonlinear flashback structure, cutting between Vladek's memories and Art's interviews with his father. In part two, Spiegelman introduces another level of narrative time, which involves the public and critical reception of part one and the composition of the second volume. During the interview scenes, the nature of Art's project is often addressed. For example, early in part one, Vladek implores Art to exclude information about Lucia, an early girlfriend before Art's mother. Vladek explains his reasoning: "It has nothing to do with Hitler, with the Holocaust!" (23). Yet we know from the passages that we have just read that Spiegelman does include Lucia's story. Other creators address similar tensions between family members and the autographer over what details to include in the work. For example, David B. in *Epileptic* (2006) shows the creator arguing with his mother over the inclusion of the family's history of alcoholism, the mother's concerns being that readers will make an incorrect connection between that history and her son's epilepsy. Also, Miriam Katin in *Letting It Go* discusses with her son how she plans to leave out certain scenes from her trip to Germany. The son admonishes her to tell the truth, and, in fact, the narrative has already shown that the scenes were included. Moments like these also contribute to a work's sense of authenticity: despite or because of challenges from loved ones, the creator maintains a dedication to the truth of the story (see the discussion of *mise en abyme* in "Critical questions" for more on these examples).

In 2011, Spiegelman published *MetaMaus*, a large supplemental text and accompanying DVD. The book consists largely of a series of interviews with Spiegelman and his family, conducted by Hillary Chute. It also contains draft materials, various comics by Spiegelman, other Holocaust illustrations, and even a collection of rejection letters for *Maus*'s original publication. The DVD features a complete digital version of *Maus*, with hyperlinked annotations and supporting materials, audio recordings of Spiegelman's interviews with his father, and home movies of a research trip to Auschwitz in 1987, among many other items. With this publication, *Maus* clearly has one of the most thoroughly documented and archived creations in literature. Such documentation contributes to *Maus*'s sense of authenticity and accuracy as a work of history and autobiography. As Hathaway (2011) notes, with the materials available in *MetaMaus*, "there is very little about Spiegelman's process that is left to question" (263).[8]

In the Shadow of No Towers

In the Shadow of No Towers, Spiegelman's response to the September 11, 2001, terrorist attacks that destroyed the World Trade Center towers in New York City, originally appeared from 2002 to 2004 as ten one-page strips serialized in the German newspaper *Die Zeit*. Pantheon collected the series as an oversized board book in 2004, and Spiegelman also included several classic

Sunday comics from series like *The Kinder Kids*, *Foxy Grandpa*, *Happy Hooligan*, *Little Nemo in Slumberland*, and *Bringing Up Father* in the back half of the book, titled "The Comic Supplement." The ten separate strips document Spiegelman's experience on the day of the attack, his continuing return to the memory of the event, his disillusion with the public and political responses to it in the months and years following, and his solace in old comic strips. Since its publication, *In the Shadow of No Towers* has also generated considerable scholarly attention. Many critics focus on the book's unconventional format and materiality, Spiegelman's continued exploration of historical trauma and witnessing begun in *Maus*, and its use of comic strip history.

Many scholars approach *In the Shadow of No Towers* as an extension of Spiegelman's focus on historical trauma and the Holocaust begun in *Maus*. Julie Reiser (2014) cites how various critical responses to the book are "steeped in trauma theory"—"they are positively suffused with trauma-centric views that recapitulate most of trauma theory's core positions," like Cathy Caruth's work (4). These responses include Espiritu (2006), Versluys (2006), and Hirsch (2004).[9]

Unlike with *Maus*, however, Spiegelman himself is the witness, rather than the recorder and reporter of his father's witnessing. *In the Shadow of No Towers* lends itself to this reading: Spiegelman returns to his *Maus*-avatar in several of the strips, giving a sense of continuity from the earlier work. This visual reference, then, also reinforces the connection Spiegelman makes between the Holocaust and 9/11. Jenn Brandt (2014) explains that "Spiegelman is forced to come to terms with his own self-representation in relation to trauma. He also effectively, through visuals, relates the events of 9/11 to the Holocaust, a comparison he makes throughout *In the Shadow of No Towers*" (73). For example, the third strip shows Art and his wife, Françoise, rushing to collect their daughter from her school near Ground Zero, immediately after the attack. Interspersed with this narrative is a monolog of *Maus*-Art explaining the air quality after 9/11. He begins,

I remember my father trying to describe what the smoke in Auschwitz smelled like. // ... The closest he got was telling me it was ... "indescribable." // [*Art pauses to puff his cigarette*] //

... That's exactly what the air in Lower Manhattan smelled like after Sept. 11! (3)

Art draws an equivalence between the two odors as being the same, yet in this explanation, the only thing they have in common is that they defy description—they fall outside the realm of language to capture them. Ironically, throughout this scene, Art is smoking a cigarette.

Spiegelman also uses his *Maus* avatar to establish continuity with the history of comic strips that runs throughout this book. For example, strips 6 and 7 both end with panels reminiscent of Winsor McCay's *Little Nemo in Slumberland*. In that classic series, Little Nemo would suddenly wake up from his dream in the final panel of each strip, usually because some experience in his dream adventure would jar him. Spiegelman depicts a child version of his *Maus* persona in the style of McCay, even signing the panels "McSpiegelman." In strip 8, Spiegelman has this same persona interacting with George Herriman's Krazy Kat and Offisa Pup (Art apparently standing in for Ignatz Mouse). Elsewhere, Spiegelman depicts himself as other classic comic strip characters, including Happy Hooligan[10] and Jiggs from *Bringing Up Father*. By placing his own *Maus* character alongside, or even directly replacing, these historically significant characters, Spiegelman puts his own work in the same historical continuity, which also establishes a sense of historical stability: while massive architectural structures and democratic institutions crumble, these characters and this comic strip history forge on unabated.

Julie Reiser (2014) comments that "The Comic Supplement" section of the book has largely been ignored: "it has received very little airtime in critical accounts that, frankly, seem to have no idea what to do with it" (11). However, some have since addressed it. In the introduction to the section, Spiegelman explains his interest in old comic strips and their relation to 9/11:

The only cultural artifacts that could get past my defenses to flood my eyes and brain with something other than images of burning towers were old comic strips; vital, unpretentious ephemera from the optimistic dawn of the 20th century. That they were made with so much skill and verve but never intended to last past the day they appeared gave them poignancy.

Strips in the "Supplement" section of the book feature many of the characters that appear in the main strips, but Spiegelman also includes this selection because they all make some comment on the events of 9/11 or the political climate that followed. Brandt explains that "Spiegelman's use of images from comic strips from the turn of the twentieth century represent his conflation of images past and present in an effort to overcome his temporal fixation with 9/11" (77). That is, Spiegelman frequently returns to the idea that time somehow stopped on September 11, 2001, and this return to the past is actually an attempt to find a way forward. Nicole Stamant (2015) focuses on Spiegelman's reference to the early strips as "ephemera": "interrogating what constitutes ephemera at this precise historical moment is one of the projects that *No Towers* undertakes. What kinds of things are meant to last?" (73). Comic strips were ephemeral because they were not intended to last: despite the "skill and verve" that creators like McCay and Herriman put into their work, the strips were meant to be enjoyed in the moment and then thrown out with the rest of the Sunday paper. The survival of such ephemera, then, stands in sharp contrast to the things that didn't survive 9/11: the massive architectural structures of the Twin Towers; the democratic institutions trampled by the US government in the war fervor that followed the attacks, despite the fact that Iraq had nothing to do with the event. Stamant goes on to explain: "This particular collection of comic strips reflects Spiegelman's own mourning process after September 11" (78), and part of that mourning process involves creating a "structure" that's far from ephemeral: the book itself, with its thick, sturdy cardboard construction.

In this way, the format of the book also receives considerable comment, not only in its construction, but also in its design. The series of ten separate full-page strips do not lend themselves to narrative coherence, some argue. Katalin Orbán (2007), for example, contends that "*No Towers* stresses the tableau, investing in the image to the point of resisting narrative" (82). Orbán offers a way to think about the work as a series of individual pages, each meant to make an impact as a whole image. Throughout the ten strips, Spiegelman deploys a collage technique, often using different styles and media (pen and ink, paint, photographs, computer-generated imagery), as well as laying images on top of each other. However, certain narrative elements do emerge: strips

2–4, for example, tell the story of Art and Françoise's struggle to retrieve their daughter from her near-Ground Zero school. This story, however, is neither continuous nor uninterrupted in these pages. Other motifs provide structure and continuity between the strips. Besides the frequent references to old comic strips, the most significant repeated image in the book is the "glowing bones" image of the North Tower before its collapse. Spiegelman explains in his introduction to the book, "The Sky Is Falling!":

> The pivotal image from my 9/11 morning—one that didn't get photographed or videotaped into public memory but still remains burned onto the inside of my eyelids several years later—was the image of the looming north tower's glowing bones just before it vaporized.

He goes on to describe the failed process of trying to paint this image before he was able to render it digitally. Many read this repeated image as a return to or reliving of traumatic memory, especially because it persists for years after the event. It was an image that existed for almost no time at all, and Spiegelman stands as the sole witness of it. With his rendition of it, he is able to freeze this moment of time, immortalize it, and continue to bring it back again and again. The image represents the transitional moment from the tower being and then not being—the hinge-point upon which "before" and "after" connect. Therefore, it also represents the "temporal fixation" that Brandt (2014) describes: the idea that time stopped on 9/11.

Phoebe Gloeckner's *A Child's Life* and *The Diary of a Teenage Girl*

Phoebe Gloeckner is best known for two significant works of autobiography: *A Child's Life and Other Stories* (1998) and *The Diary of a Teenage Girl* (2002). *A Child's Life* collects various short stories previously published in *Weirdo*, *Twisted Sisters*, *Wimmen's Comix*, and other underground comix and anthologies. The book is divided into four sections: "A Child's Life," "Other Childish Stories," "Teen Stories," and "Grown-Up Stories." *Diary* is a hybrid text, made up mostly of prose diary entries, but also including comic pages and single-page illustrations with captions. *Diary* became a critically acclaimed film in 2015, bringing the work renewed attention.

Both books are innocuously titled and reveal little about their contents. Either could be easily positioned in the young adult section of a book store or library. The use of the indefinite article in each title is also telling—"a child" and "a teenage girl" imply that the stories within will have universal qualities. However, within each work, Gloeckner details traumatic childhood and adolescent sexual experiences. The relation of the titles to the contents immediately reveals the confrontational, ethical nature of these works: the reader must face the disturbing idea that such experiences are common in the lives of children and teenage girls.

Both works are subtitled "An Account in Words and Pictures." The word "account" makes for an interesting choice: it implies a true story being related by a person who experienced it; in other words, an autobiographical story. However, Gloeckner challenges strict boundaries of "autobiography" through the use of her protagonist, "Minnie." Minnie is and is not Gloeckner, and the artist can be cagey in interviews and other writings about the relationship between the two. Yet, as Hillary Chute (2010) explains, "The trauma her work returns to again and again—the rape of a teenage girl by a father figure; that girl's descent into psychic oblivion, which includes further rape—matches events in her own life" (66). Gloeckner highlights the ambivalence in her 2011 prose piece, "Autobiography: The Process Negates the Term," which combines two letters from Minnie to the reader, intercut with short paragraphs by Gloeckner. In the first letter, Minnie describes how she desires connection with an audience: "This impulse to connect with you has driven me to write books, to draw pictures, and, at times, even to sing" (178). And so, Minnie, it seems, is the creator. Yet, in that same letter, Minnie asserts, "The creation is not the creator" (178). Following the first letter, a passage by Gloeckner warns against connecting creator and creation too closely, even if the impulse to do so is understandable:

> When a character in a novel seems to strongly resemble the author, it would make sense to assume that such works must be autobiographical. When pictures are combined with text, as in

a graphic novel, this resemblance may be further reinforced and even offered as "proof" that the book is, without a doubt, an "autobiography." However, although the correlation between author and character may seem blatantly clear, it is unwise to jump to the conclusion that the work is the "story of the author's life," in full or in part. (179)

The next letter from Minnie begins with the confounding sentence, "I am not Minnie Goetze," yet it is signed, "Love, Minnie" (179). Within the letter, Minnie/Phoebe explains the difficulty in creating one of her works, that it requires her to eradicate her self: "I am not writing about myself—I am delivering myself of myself, and that is not what I'd call autobiography—it is, rather, a form of suicide" (179). She wants to achieve a universality with her characters so that readers can look past the individualized details of a single person's life to a kind of "emotional truth" that the reader connects to (179). Such a desire tracks with the titles of her works, especially the use of the indefinite article combined with generalized nouns. The essay concludes with two sentences, each with its own paragraph: "I AM AN AUTOBIOGRAPHICAL CARTOONIST. No I'm not" (179). This is not an easy concept to wrap one's head around because the either/or nature of the question seems pretty straightforward: is her work autobiography? How can she be both an autobiographical cartoonist and not one at the same time? By not giving a definitive answer, Gloeckner redirects the reader to think instead about the universality of Minnie's experiences as represented in the two works: "she must be all girls, anyone" (179). Whether or not she is Gloeckner matters less than that. However, from a critical standpoint, this makes it difficult to write about these works: how much separation is there between Minnie and Gloeckner?

Gloeckner offers one of the more complex examples of visual style in autobiographical comics. A trained medical illustrator, Gloeckner imbues her images with almost photorealistic detail. Yet her characters also feature grotesque exaggerations: disproportionately large heads on otherwise proportionate bodies and enormous male genitalia. Representations of childhood sexual abuse are disturbing no matter how they are depicted; Gloeckner's detailed yet exaggerated physiology renders the images even more challenging. One outcome of the large heads, according to

Marshall and Gilmore (2015), is that they allow Gloeckner to draw more expressive, detailed faces. Yet these images also have an uncanny quality to them, and Gloeckner moderates the reader's gaze by pairing these images with a large amount of text. To read the page, the reader has to linger on the disturbing and unsettling images. Therefore, Gloeckner moves these images from the unspeakable to the unavoidable and confrontational. Edward Said refers to a similar technique in Joe Sacco's work as the "power to detain" (qtd in Chute 2010: 238 n.24), and Chute connects it with Lynda Barry's use of handwritten script in *One Hundred Demons* (2002). In one particularly striking panel, from the story "Fun Things to Do with Little Girls" in *A Child's Life*, Gloeckner draws the first sexual encounter between Minnie and her mother's boyfriend. This rectangular panel shows Minnie lying naked across the bottom third, while her mother's boyfriend takes up most of the top two-thirds. His large head—almost the same size as his entire torso—is strained and sweating, and his eyes are closed. Minnie's impassive face is turned to the reader, with large eyes staring directly at us. A narrative caption on the upper left corner of the panel reads, "Years later, the first time I had sex was with my mother's boyfriend. I was eager to be sophisticated and wanted nothing more to please" (67). The positioning of this text directly over Minnie's head requires the reader to linger on her face, and the description in the text calls on the reader to search for signs of that eagerness, which are not evident in the blank expression.

"Fun Things" also features another important element of Gloeckner's work: the ambivalent approach to trauma. Her mother's boyfriend is raping Minnie, yet her retrospective narration explains that she was "eager" to look sophisticated and please him. This ambivalence doesn't allow for easy judgment, as Chute (2010) remarks: "Part of the ethical drive behind Gloeckner's ambivalent images is to highlight the confusion that sexual trauma may provoke" (78). Reading a Phoebe Gloeckner story is not an easy experience, but her work gives the purest sense of how the comics medium can be used to deal with such difficult subject matter.

In another shocking panel from "Minnie's 3rd Love, or, Nightmare on Polk Street," also in *A Child's Life*, Minnie is passed out on a bed, naked, while her friend Tabitha watches television with her drug dealer. A man is spreading Minnie's legs with his erect penis hovering over her vagina. He holds the used tampon he has just pulled out of Minnie. Dialog balloons in which he complains about the fact that Minnie has her period all have tails that point to him, but they also point to the suspended tampon, forcing the reader's gaze toward this part of the image. The erection also points at the object from the other direction. Meanwhile, on the left side of the page, caption boxes surround Minnie's head, drawing our eyes to her in a way similar to the image in "Fun Things." Minnie's face is also turned toward the reader, but this time, her eyes are closed, so we cannot meet her gaze. Much of the upper-left quadrant is densely taken up with dialog balloons from the drug dealer, the rapist, and Tabitha. The density of text in this panel requires the reader to linger over it for a considerable time, making it difficult to look away from the disturbing image it contains. These panels exemplify the confrontational quality of Gloeckner's work: she directs the reader's attention in order to face representations of traumatic experiences that are not at all comfortable, and she thus implicates us in the events. Chute (2010) explains:

> We recognize the sensationalism of the event for the child; if we feel implicated in becoming ourselves voyeurs then that does not yet obviate understanding the structures of injustice: instead, it points up exactly how widespread that injustice is, how endemic and culturally threaded. (79)

We should feel uncomfortable and guilty, but that discomfort should lead to an understanding of how widespread such traumatic experiences are.

In addition to being the document of childhood trauma, *The Diary of a Teenage Girl* is also a *Künstlerroman*, showing the development of the artist as autobiographical cartoonist.[11] Minnie is exposed to underground comix early, and these have a profound impact on her desire to become a cartoonist. She goes to a headshop for the first time and buys *Binky Brown* (Justin Green), *Dirty Laundry* (Robert Crumb and Aline Kominsky-Crumb), *Arcade* (edited by Art Spiegelman), *Big Ass* (Robert Crumb), and *Corn Fed* (Kim Deitch). Prior to this experience, she had read issues of *Zap!*, *Wimmin's Comix*,[12] and *Cheech Wizard*, but none of those had impressed her as much as her new purchases. With the exception of Deitch's work, these are all historical milestones in the formation of autobiographical comics, so it makes sense that this would be the path the artist would follow. She fantasizes about meeting Aline Kominsky-Crumb and Robert Crumb, imagining what that couple's relationship is like. Later, she writes a fan letter to Aline, who responds that this was her first fan letter from a girl. Minnie later gets to meet Crumb through a connection with her mother. As she works on her earliest comics, she seeks out an underground publisher for advice on how to get her comics published (the publisher is unidentified in the diary, but it's clearly Last Gasp). The publisher doesn't offer her any feedback on her comics, but he does advise her "to learn how to draw everything" (124). Another key moment in her artistic development occurs when she sees a sign painted on the window of Golden Boy Pizza and recognizes it as the work of Justin Green. Her aesthetic sensibilities have become more acute at this point, with the ability to pick out a specific artist's work in the wild. Finally, she does take the steps toward becoming a professional comics artist by bringing her work to one of the underground publishers. The genealogy of autobiographical comics is clear here, with a direct line running from Justin Green, Aline Kominsky-Crumb, and Robert Crumb to Phoebe Gloeckner. (See Appendix 1 for a panel discussion featuring these creators and Carol Tyler.)

Joe Matt, Chester Brown, and Seth

Joe Matt, Chester Brown, and Seth are often lumped together in discussions of second wave North American autobiographical comics. They began publishing their work at roughly the same time in the late 1980s and early 1990s—Matt and Seth through Drawn & Quarterly; Brown first through Vortex and later Drawn & Quarterly. Notably, Bart Beaty (2011) identifies the trio as a "Toronto School." This identification is reinforced by the ways in which the three cartoonists so often cite each other. Their comics memoirs form the autobiographical equivalent of a shared universe like those of Marvel and DC superheroes. That is, the three regularly appear in each other's comics, usually as a sounding board for each author's thoughts and ideas, especially about their works in progress. As such, these creators reward devoted readers who pick up on the references to earlier stories or recurring jokes. The three build on the characterizations of each other, emphasizing such characteristics as Seth's dissatisfaction with modern technology and design; Joe's constant masturbation, porn dubbing, and relationship problems; Chester's sexual interests; and all three's collecting obsessions. However, the three also have similar sensibilities and experimental approaches that challenge autobiographical conventions.

Joe Matt

Matt was the first to include the others in his comics. However, the first strips Matt published in Kitchen Sink's *Snarf*, beginning in 1988, and later in the *Drawn & Quarterly* anthology show his earlier friendship with fellow comics creators Matt Wagner and Bernie Mireault, and Joe's initial meetings with Seth and Chester occur later in the series. These early strips are collected in *Peepshow: The Cartoon Diary of Joe Matt* (1992). Matt continued *Peepshow* as a semi-regular periodical, which ran for fourteen issues from 1992 to 2006 and was published by Drawn & Quarterly. These issues were collected in three volumes: *The Poor Bastard* (1996), *Fair Weather* (2002), and *Spent* (2007). Matt's creative output has been notoriously sparse, often with more than a year between issues of *Peepshow* before the series ceased publication. In 2015, Drawn & Quarterly included eighteen pages of new Matt comics in the publisher's 25th anniversary collection, which amounted to the total comics output for Matt over the previous ten years. This lack of productivity often features as a subject of Matt's work. For example, one issue of *Peepshow* will contain as a plot point his friends' reactions to their depiction in a previous issue, or, as in *Spent*, Matt will show himself in the throes of writer's block and procrastination.

This presents one of the more significant ways in which Matt challenges conventional notions of autobiography, especially in terms of the narrative's veracity or relationship to the "truth." *Peepshow* appears as a comic in the diegetic world of *Peepshow*, yet it is not quite the same comic that we are reading. In one key scene from issue 6 (*The Poor Bastard* 156), Joe's friends Andy and Kim react strongly to the way they come off in issue 3. However, their characters in that diegetic comic are slightly altered and given new names: Randy and Kitty. Andy even holds up a copy of the issue in question, showing a page that's an analog of a page in issue 3 (*The Poor Bastard* 67), though Randy has dreadlocks instead of Andy's shaved head. The reader, then, understands that "Andy" and "Kim" are themselves altered versions of Matt's real acquaintances (see more on this scene in the discussion of *"mise en abyme"* in Chapter 3).[13] The scene also gives the sense that *Peepshow*, at least in this first story, is relatively unplanned, as the publication of an earlier chapter informs the events in a later one. In a 1996 *Comics Journal* interview, Matt described the production of *Peepshow*'s first six issues: "I didn't envision issue #6 when I started issue #1. That's no way to put a collection or a story together. It's not a story. It's a meandering thing" (Brayshaw 1996: 61). The following six issues of *Peepshow* were more clearly planned out as a complete story, resulting in the collection *Fair Weather*.

This scene in *The Poor Bastard* also highlights the difference between reading the *Peepshow* periodical comic and reading the collected issues in *The Poor Bastard*. For readers of the periodical comic, these moments help to bridge the gap in Joe's life between issues: like us, the characters in the comic have had time to read and digest *Peepshow* before the next issue has come out (and in the case of Matt's slow production schedule, that time between issues can be years). However, when reading the series in collected form, the publishing gaps between issues are no longer apparent. In this case, the introduction of the characters and then their response to that introduction appear in the same narrative work, thus losing the sense of Joe, his characters, and the readers naturally aging in the time between issues.

Matt also later admits to fabricating events in previous issues, which again challenges the truth claims of autobiography. In the final chapter of *Spent* (which was also the final published issue of *Peepshow*), Joe pulls the collected editions of his previous two books off his shelf. In looking through *The Poor Bastard*, he exclaims, "none of this stuff even happened the way I drew it! It's half fabrication!" (120). He specifically addresses how his depiction of giving his girlfriend Trish a black eye doesn't take into account the number of times she physically abused him. Most notably, though, Joe regrets including the *ménage a trois* scene that never actually occurred. At the time, he felt such a scene would provide appropriate closure for the book. The reader might question if this fabricated scene even provides some "emotional truth" about the earlier, factually inaccurate scenes, in the way that Phoebe Gloeckner describes her approach to truth and fabrication. Matt puts the reader in an unstable position relative to the autobiographical nature of the story. For dedicated readers, the confession requires them to rethink stories they had trusted as "true" for more than ten years.

The comic also takes a toll on Matt's romantic relationships. The earliest *Peepshow* strips show Joe's tumultuous, occasionally violent relationship with his long-term girlfriend, Trish. *The Poor Bastard* details the dissolution of this relationship, at least partially caused by the way in which Joe depicts her in his comics. Matt can often be self-lacerating in his comics, taking the blame for failed relationships or confessing his most private issues, like his addiction to pornography in *Spent*. For Matt, as long as he is hardest on himself, he feels he has license to depict others negatively as well, as he explains in the Brayshaw (1996) interview. This also holds true for his art: he uses a clean-line, cartoony, detailed style, though he often draws himself with grotesque, exaggerated features, especially when he is in a state of lust or intense masturbation.

Chester Brown

Chester Brown's periodical series *Yummy Fur* began mostly with fictional, absurdist short pieces and the serialized *Ed the Happy Clown* story, later also delving into Brown's adaptations of the New Testament Gospels. Later, though, Brown was influenced by Matt, as well as Harvey Pekar, Julie Doucet, and Colin Upton, to pursue autobiography as well. His autobiographical stories began in *Yummy Fur* 19 (January 1990) with "Helder," about a difficult and potentially dangerous neighbor Chester has in the rooming house where he lives. This was immediately followed in the next issue by "Showing Helder," which detailed the creation of the previous story.[14] The combination of "Helder" and "Showing Helder" offers an interesting meditation on the nature of autobiographical comics. The latter story exposes the conscious choices and influences that went into the former story's creation, revealing that some fabrications happened for the sake of the narrative structure or at the behest of people involved in the story, like Chester's friend, Kris. The foregrounding of the original story's constructed nature brings us back to Hatfield's (2005) concept of "ironic authentication" (125): Brown's claim to the truth is the acknowledgment that his story is not, in fact, completely true.

The act of revision Brown reveals in "Showing Helder" is consistent with his revision strategies for later works. Each of his autobiographical comics—*The Playboy* (1992), *I Never Liked You* (1994), and *Paying for It* (2011), along with the collection of both fictional and autobiographical short stories, *The Little Man* (1998)—contains an extensive notes section with Brown's comments. For the stories previously serialized in *Yummy Fur*, like *The Playboy* and *I Never Liked You* (originally titled "Fuck" in *Yummy Fur* 26–30), Brown details and rationalizes revisions that he made between the two versions. He also acknowledges places in which he made conscious changes to the facts as he knows them. In *Paying for It*, this annotation compulsion achieves a new level: in addition to the extensive appendices and notes, Brown also added a new set of notes for the 2013 edition, which includes notes on his 2011 notes. One appendix also includes Seth's notes on his own appearances in the book, indicating challenges to Brown's memories or depictions of specific events. By including a potentially endless series of notes for each work, Brown keeps the text's relation to truth-claims fluid while still maintaining a sense of "ironic authentication."

Brown gained considerable attention and notoriety when he released *Paying for It* (2011), subtitled *A Comic-Strip Memoir about Being a John*. The memoir details how Chester began frequenting prostitutes to the point that these encounters became his only sexual relationships, and he ultimately developed a monogamous relationship with one particular prostitute. In addition to being a personal memoir, the book also serves as a socio-political argument in favor of the sex-work trade, often challenging stereotypes of prostitutes and their work, such as the frequency of physical abuse and drug use. The production of this memoir also coincides with Brown's failed efforts to run for the Canadian Parliament on the Libertarian ticket in 2008 and 2011, and his argument in favor of legalized prostitution is consistent with his libertarian political beliefs. In the book, the ethical and political arguments are made through Chester's conversations with his friends, especially fellow creators Joe and Seth, as well as in an extensive twenty-three-part appendix. In support of *Paying for It*, Brown conducted several interviews, many focusing on his political argument rather than his comics career, as can be seen in the interviews collected in *Chester Brown: Conversations*, edited by Dominick Grace and Eric Hoffman (2013).

Elisabeth El Refaie (2012a) argues that Brown's work attempts to create "a sense of distance between the reader and the autobiographical subject" (197). She cites specific examples from *I Never Liked You* where Brown uses distant perspective, high visual angles, and blank facial expressions on characters to discourage reader association or emotional connection (2012a: 198–9). This analysis could apply to any of Brown's work, from the adolescent recollections in *The Playboy* and *I Never Liked You* to the depictions of his adult interactions with prostitutes in *Paying for It*. Brown's style, especially in depicting himself, involves a gaunt, disproportionately elongated face, limited details, blank expressions, and glasses that obscure the eyes. The style could be described as "iconic" in Scott McCloud's (1993) sense of the word (51–3), yet it doesn't carry with it the associative power that McCloud describes. Dominick Grace and Eric Hoffman (2013) describe the style in *Paying for It* similarly, as reflective of his own sense of self as well as his argument about prostitution: "Faces show no emotion ... underlining the unemotional nature of the john–prostitute relationships; to reinforce his lack of emotion, Brown's comic alter-ego is drawn eyeless, almost always wearing his glasses (even during sex)" (xxvii).

Seth

The first three issues of Seth's periodical series *Palookaville* (1991– present) contain short autobiographical stories of the creator's youth. In a sort of reversal of the semi-autobiographical persona used by creators like Justin Green and Phoebe Gloeckner, Seth uses his real name, Gregory Gallant, in these stories. Like his fellow Toronto cartoonists, Seth often shows himself in a negative light. In "Why?"—a two-page story from *Drawn & Quarterly* 4 (March 1991)—Seth tells of how, as a kid, he played with a neighbor named Gary Evans. Gary "was retarded or a slow learner or something" (4). They go up into Seth's tree fort, and while up there, Seth kicks away the ladder, swings down a branch, and then sets up rakes at the base of the tree so that Gary can't jump down. Seth leaves Gary up in the tree for hours, and Gary cries. Seth finally restores the ladder, and Gary runs away, still crying. An arrow pointing to young Seth says "proud of himself" (5). Narrator Seth closes the story by asking, "Why would I cold-bloodedly devise a plan to trap a poor retarded kid in a tree? ... / 'cause like most kids—I was a fucking cruel little monster" (5). Seth is unapologetic about his cruelty here. In later works, especially *It's a Good Life, if You Don't Weaken*, his ambivalence toward himself will give rise to more critical introspection.

It's a Good Life, if You Don't Weaken (1996), originally serialized in *Palookaville* 4–9, raises fundamental questions about the nature of autobiography and authenticity. In the book, Seth discovers an obscure panel cartoonist named Kalo, whose work appeared briefly in *The New Yorker* and a few obscure publications. Seth goes on a quest to find out more about Kalo, leading him to Kalo's hometown and few surviving relatives. However, there is a problem here: Kalo, the cartoonist that Seth obsesses over, in fact, does not exist, and Seth never went on the quest to research his life. The text itself does not reveal this fabrication, and so readers may not even know about it without some external research on the book.

Beaty (2011) argues that the way in which the Matt, Brown, and Seth depict each other mutually reinforces the veracity of each creator's autobiography, which, in turn, rewards reading their work collectively. For example, if Seth appears as obsessed with collecting ephemera from the past, especially old comic strips and magazine cartoons, in Joe Matt's comics, then his own depiction of his collecting habits and obsessions with the past in *It's a Good Life, if You Don't Weaken* come across as authentic. In addition, Seth frequently shares his thoughts on Kalo and the status of his quest with Chester in a way that we expect from previous comics. However, such an example becomes problematic when considering the fictional nature of *It's a Good Life*. These conversations never happened, yet they feel "true" because they resemble other conversations that faithful readers are familiar with. *It's a Good Life* deeply challenges conventional notions of autobiography and "truth," but the relationship between the three creators exacerbates that challenge even further. Faithful readers have built up an impression of Seth that is consistent with his self-depiction in *It's a Good Life*, but what do those readers do with that impression when they find out Seth fabricated much of that story? (For further discussion of *It's a Good Life* as a fabricated memoir, see Chapter 3.)

Seth, Matt, and Brown have all cited Harvey Pekar as an influence or inspiration to create their own autobiographical comics. The three follow Pekar's focus on the mundane events of everyday life with sharply confessional autobiographical stories that do not, by any means, glamorize their subjects. Their stories also serve as meditations on the nature of autobiography, experimenting with ways that truth and fiction merge in the genre. The three also mutually influence one another. In his notes to *The Little Man*, Brown explains how Matt's work inspired him to pursue autobiography:

> I'd seen autobiographical comics before, but the diary approach, combined with what seemed like an intrepid willingness to reveal *everything*, gave his work immediacy and impact. Those strips were a step forward for personal expression in cartooning. (169)

In a group interview with *The Comics Journal* (issue 162, October 1993), they all agree that their relationship is competitive, but in a way that inspires them to raise their respective games (Daly 1993: 55–6). While Matt's published work has trickled to a halt since the last published issue of *Peepshow* in 2006, Seth and Brown have continued to publish on a regular basis, though not exclusively in autobiography, with Brown producing graphic-novel-length works like the historical narrative *Louis Reil* (2004) and Seth converting *Palookaville* into a (roughly) annual hardcover book.

Lynda Barry's *One Hundred Demons*

Lynda Barry's *One Hundred Demons* (2002)[15] is structured as a series of nineteen hand-painted vignettes called "demons," referring to the zen art exercise of the title. The vignettes, as originally published as web comics on Slate.com, each consisted of twenty panels. However, in the print version, Barry revised the stories to eighteen panels. Each vignette covers a different theme or event in Barry's life, ranging from childhood to adulthood. The separate stories are unified by a framing device of Lynda at the drawing board, working on the book that we are reading. This technique identifies the adult cartoonist Lynda as the consistent narrator throughout the book.

Barry's unique style in this book combines painted art, hand lettering, and collage elements that include photographs. Her lettering style mixes capital, block letters with cursive, which creates a particular effect, as Hillary Chute (2010) explains: "Barry creates the textual unevenness as a way of slowing down the experience of reading" (111). Each of the vignettes is punctuated by collages that include drawn images from the story, handwritten text, and photos of physical objects from her past. Barry continues to use the collage style to an even greater degree in *What It Is* (2008), *Picture This* (2010), and *Syllabus* (2014). As Chute (2010) and Susan Kirtley (2012) have noted, this style lends a sense of authenticity to the work: real objects, with connections to the stories being told, contribute to the reader's impression that these stories are "true." In addition, Barry includes photographs of herself at work: these images resemble her comic self-portraits in such a way that contributes further to the sense of authenticity. The "real" Lynda Barry of the photographs is clearly the same person who narrates the stories we have read.

Barry refers to her work as "autobifictionalography," an intentionally difficult term that deconstructs the truth–fiction binary that artificially separates autobiography from fiction. Barry asks in subsequent panels of her introduction, "Is it autobiography if parts of it are not true? // Is it fiction if parts of it are?" (7). Susan Kirtley applies Hatfield's concept of "ironic authentication" to Barry: "Through her self-representation as unattractive and awkward (at all ages and to varying degrees), Barry's self-deprecation argues for such ironic authentication" (160). This is reinforced by images of Barry at the drawing board, working on the very text we are reading (see the discussion of *mise en abyme* in Chapter 3 for more on how this technique lends itself to authenticity). "Autobifictionalography" may be one of the best ways to understand "ironic authentication," the idea of making a truth-claim through the denial of the possibility of truth-telling (Hatfield

2005: 126). The tension between truth and fiction is evident in the first "demon" or vignette, "Head Lice and My Worst Boyfriend." As her boyfriend delivers one of his tiresome condescending monologs about Lynda's identity as a "little ghetto girl," Barry tags his word balloon with the phrase "actual dialog" (21). This gesture toward authenticity raises questions about the dialog in the rest of the book: is it all "actual" if it is not identified as such? In addition, the boyfriend delivers this dialog while reading "Lonely Genius Gazette," a magazine that doesn't likely exist but emphasizes his pretentiousness.

Hillary Chute (2010) identifies "memory" as the key theme of this book: specifically, "*One Hundred Demons* is about the process of accumulating and distilling memories as visual practice" (114). Most of the stories address issues of memory: the present Lynda as narrator is depicted at her drawing board, reflecting on the events of her childhood. This retrospective narrative voice then tells the subsequent stories through caption boxes that run across the tops of each panel and, in many instances, dominate the panel. Some of the stories deal with memory directly, like "Cicadas," where she is troubled by the fact that she cannot remember the face of a boy she knew who committed suicide. The unreliability of memory presents a direct challenge to the truth–fiction binary. Had Barry not foregrounded her memory problem, readers would not have been able to tell that the visual representation of the boy was in any way inaccurate.

Most notably, Barry alludes to trauma that is not directly depicted in the book, as is the case in "Resilience," where the final panel suggests Barry was raped as a child (72). Readers only see a partial view of the abuser, whose upper torso and head are cut off by the borders of the panel. The angle of the image puts us on the ground with the child in a sympathetic perspective that renders the adult abuser both unknowable and threatening. Barry leaves the actual experience of the abuse unrepresented, which forces the reader to imagine what follows. The abundance of text in the panel also functions to obscure the abuser, while the text itself explains how the older Lynda has tried to forget the childhood trauma in order to achieve a sense of "wholeness": "I became a teenager when I discovered how to give myself that feeling of wholeness, even if it lasted only for a moment, even if it got me into huge trouble, it was the closest I could come to ... to ... I don't remember" (72).

What she doesn't remember seems to be some kind of pre-traumatic identity. The final image of "Resilience," with the vulnerable child Lynda on the verge of traumatic abuse, resonates throughout the book, as most of the stories take place in her life after this event. This approach, obscuring the traumatic moment or rendering it as unrepresentable, stands in sharp contrast to choices made by Phoebe Gloeckner (1998, 2002) and Debbie Dreschler (2008) to confront readers directly with the unsettling images of abuse.

One Hundred Demons has attracted the most scholarly attention of Barry's works. Several of these critics focus on Barry's racial identity and how it manifests itself in the book (see especially De Jesús 2004a, 2004b). Barry's family is Filipina, but with her red hair and pale skin, Barry can pass for Caucasian. Her mother and grandmother have more clearly marked racial identities. Barry's confrontation with her Filipina identity is specifically addressed in "The Visitor." In this story, teenage Lynda goes to Seattle's Chinatown district with a boy after the two have dropped acid. The boy is unaware of Lynda's Filipina background until her mother drives by and swears at her. When Lynda comes clean about her ethnicity, the boy leaves. Lynda's ability to pass as white often protects her, but when her ethnic identity is exposed, she becomes alienated from both of the worlds that she limns. Melinda de Jesús (2004a) explains that "Whiteness distances Lynda from colorism and racism but also from her family and culture" (231). In discussing the story "Common Scents," Kirtley (2012) identifies two different versions of Lynda: "the white Lynda as perceived by the neighbor girl and the Filipina Lynda as understood by her family. Lynda assumes the white identity to bond with the other children and hide from her ethnic identity" (170). These two versions join the many other versions of Lynda that appear in the book: the retrospective narrator and the various ages of Lynda.

Craig Thompson's *Blankets*

As discussed in Chapter 2, the 2003 publication of Craig Thompson's *Blankets* was a watershed moment in the history of autobiographical comics. Through Top Shelf Productions, Thompson released *Blankets* in a single, 600-page volume, rather than serializing it first, as had been done with *Maus*, *Persepolis*, and *One Hundred Demons*; the works of Joe Matt, Chester Brown, and Seth; and most other long autobiographical comics up until that point (short, one-shot comics, such as *Binky Brown*, would be an exception to this, of course, as would Harvey Pekar, Joyce Brabner, and Frank Stack's *Our Cancer Year* [1994]). The publication format of *Blankets* alone makes it a significant work, but thematically the work also connects with other key texts in the genre. While *Blankets* has not received the scholarly attention that many other autobiographical comics have,[16] it addresses several topics common to some of the more widely covered works: childhood sexual trauma and abuse, coming-of-age, religious belief, family drama, and artistic development.

Blankets is a complicated narrative that belies easy summarization. At its heart, it is a coming-of-age story about teenage Craig as he struggles with his family's fundamentalist Christian faith and his first love with a young woman named Raina. During a two-week visit with Raina that makes up the bulk of the work, Craig also experiences the dissolution of Raina's parents' marriage and that family's difficulties with raising two children with special needs. While staying at Raina's house, Craig's faith and Christian prohibitions on sex conflict with both his and Raina's desires.

Another, though more subtle, element of the narrative is Craig's relationship with his younger brother, Phil. Due to the Thompson family's income status, Craig and Phil have to share a room and a bed well into their pre-teen years. Craig feels enormous guilt for his perceived failure to protect his younger brother, first from abuse at the hands of their father, who regularly locks Phil in a dirty, crowded cubby hole when the two brothers misbehave, and later from a teenage babysitter who sexually molests both boys.

Thompson's work receives only passing mention in studies of autobiographical comics, as is the case with Hatfield (2005) and the collection edited by Chaney (2011b), if it is mentioned at all, as with Chute (2010) and the collection edited by Tolmie (2013). When *Blankets* does come up, Thompson's inventive visual style is often the topic of discussion: both Versaci (2007: 60–4) and El Refaie (2012a: 93, 129) engage in close readings of single scenes in the comic. They choose separate scenes from *Blankets* to illustrate how graphic memoirs can connect past and present in unique ways. El Refaie returns frequently to a single image from *Blankets* where

Craig has just been chastised by a teacher for writing a story in which all of his enemies are forced to eat excrement (*Blankets* 32). In shame, Craig cries and hides his head under the lid of his desk. This leads to a flashback where Craig remembers the abuse at the hands of his babysitter, who is one of the people Craig imagines eating excrement. The flashback ends with a striking image: the babysitter leads the unsuspecting brother into another room in a panel surrounded by a black shadow that blends in with a shadow surrounding Craig with his head in his desk. For El Refaie (2012a), this page serves as a primary example of how comics can visually depict the impact of the traumatic past on the present, what Hatfield (2005) refers to as an "impossible and provocative at-onceness" (51, qtd in El Refaie 2012a: 129). As with this page, comics can "capture the unique qualities of traumatic memory, which involves the intrusion of the past into the present in the form of repeated flashbacks, hallucinations, and dreams" (El Refaie 2012a: 129). The technique Thompson uses here is striking: the page consists ostensibly of two panels, yet the artist eschews traditional panel borders and replaces them with a dark shadow that blends present and past, showing how Craig's present shame is informed by the guilt he feels over his failure to protect his brother. Present and past exist simultaneously on the page.

This attention to Thompson's visual representation of traumatic memory indicates that *Blankets* can serve as an interesting companion piece to other representations of trauma, like Lynda Barry's *One Hundred Demons* (2002) and Phoebe Gloeckner's work (1998, 2002), both discussed elsewhere in this chapter. Gloeckner's visual representations of traumatic experience force the reader to confront them directly. Barry, on the other end of the spectrum, only hints at the trauma she experienced, more through the text even than the image. Thompson's work functions somewhere between these two examples. The first images of the abuse the brothers suffered at the hands of their babysitter only suggest the traumatic experiences that take place behind the closed door. For Gloeckner, the face of her abuser, Monroe, is large, detailed, and expressive. Barry's abuser is barely a body— just two legs and feet looming menacingly over the young Lynda. Thompson's babysitter is a large, imposing body, but the face is always partially obscured: his back is to the reader, his head is just outside of the panel border, or, most tellingly, his eyes are covered up by the label "babysitter" (29), which demonstrates Thompson's willful refusal to identify his abuser. A reader may be able to piece together an image of the babysitter's face from the parts shown in various panels, but a full, composite image remains elusive. Later in the narrative, Thompson returns to this memory with more detail, but it never achieves the level of explicitness shown by Gloeckner.

After hearing a story of how Raina defended her mentally handicapped brother, Craig feels guilty for his failure to protect his own brother from the abusive babysitter. Here, however, Craig is imagining his brother's experience, as he was outside of the closed door when the abuse happened. He imagines the babysitter pulling down Phil's pants as well as extreme close-ups of details on the babysitter's face (acne, tufts of adolescent facial hair). A final image shows the entire naked body of the babysitter pulled down into hell, a demonic hand clawing the face and obscuring it one last time. Even the text is slightly disconnected from the images. Craig is narrating how his younger self imagined what the physical body of a "high schooler" might be like, "with their LUMBERING, awkward FLESH, / body odors and foul mouths, / curdled ACNE, / first sproutings of facial hair, / and swollen sex organs" (292). This juxtaposition of image and text implies that the young Craig's entire frame of reference for adolescent physicality was colored by his exposure to the babysitter's body.

Blankets also compares interestingly with other coming-of-age graphic autobiographies. For example, its emphasis on Craig's sexuality and the way it is informed by his family parallels that of Alison Bechdel in *Fun Home* (2006) while offering a contrasting heterosexual narrative (one which, perhaps unsurprisingly, has not received the same level of controversy).

In addition, the narrative traces Craig's development as an artist. As kids, Craig and his brother draw adventure stories on the backs of used dot matrix printer paper, which provides an escape from their shared childhood traumas. However, as a teenager, Craig finds his art in conflict with his faith, and as a result, he burns all of his childhood work. As the story progresses, Craig continues to experience ambivalence about his artistic ambitions. While with Raina, they share creative time together where he draws and she writes poetry, and she asks him to paint a picture directly on her bedroom wall. Craig chooses an image of the two sitting on the branch of a bare tree, and this image repeatedly returns in the narrative as a motif representing both the relationship and the memory of the relationship. Finally, Craig embraces his artistic talent. The narrative ends with an adult Craig running through the snow during a return visit to his family's Wisconsin home. The narration reads, "How satisfying it is to leave a mark on a blank surface. / To make a map of my movement — / no matter how temporary" (581–2). Benjamin Stevens (2009) describes this final scene as an example of "metanarration" in which the narration comments on the nature of comics (para. 2). The parallels between the character's steps in the white snow and the artist's marks on the blank page invite the reader to see *Blankets* as a *Künstlerroman*, where the various experiences presented in the narrative funnel into Craig's development as an artist (for more on the *Künstlerroman*, see the "Adolescence" section in Chapter 4).

Marjane Satrapi's *Persepolis*

The history of *Persepolis*'s publication is an interesting phenomenon on its own. Like many graphic novels, it was serialized on first publication: in France as four books published by L'Association, and in the US in two volumes, *The Story of a Childhood* (2004) and *The Story of a Return* (2005), by Pantheon. Pantheon also released a single-volume collection, *The Complete Persepolis*, in 2007.[17] However, Pantheon still keeps the two separate volumes in print, giving readers and teachers different options. This publication strategy may not be interesting in and of itself (Pantheon has done something similar with Art Spiegelman's *Maus*), but more so in terms of how these various volumes sell. In comic store owner Brian Hibbs's (2015) annual analysis of graphic novel sales through Bookscan figures, *Persepolis: The Story of a Childhood* continues to be one of the bestselling graphic novels as of 2014, with regular growth from year to year. *The Story of a Return*, however, sells less than 10 percent of the first volume (Hibbs admits that the sales numbers he offers are not wholly reliable, but sales position and comparisons are more accurate). One possible way to account for this difference is that teachers include *The Story of a Childhood* in their classes significantly more often than they include the second part. Part one ends on a bit of a cliffhanger—Marji's mother has fainted at the airport when Marji leaves Iraq for school in Austria, leaving the reader to wonder about her parent's fate and Marji's potential return to her homeland. However, *The Story of a Childhood* is also a complete coming-of-age story leading to her adolescence, as the subtitle suggests.

The two volumes of *Persepolis* divide between Marji's childhood in part one and her adolescence and young adulthood in part two, culminating in her departure from Iran for a final time in 1994. In *The Story of a Childhood*, young Marji becomes aware of Iranian history, politics, and religion, and tries to establish her place in that culture. However, for a child, this usually takes an egoistic form— in relation to religion, she imagines herself as a prophet who can speak directly to God; historically, she traces her family connec- tions back to Iranian royalty; politically, she becomes excited about stories of family members who have suffered tremendously as political prisoners. Part of her motivation for finding these connec- tions lies in the social caché they provide—she likes to brag to her friends about how important her family, and by extension she, is. She doesn't seem to be interested in learning about her culture in order to develop a greater understanding of it, but instead to place herself in the upper echelons of that society. However, she also feels the cultural pull of the West as a form of rebellion, which manifests itself through fashion and music: jeans, Nike shoes, Kim Wilde's "Kids in America," Iron Maiden, and Michael Jackson. Much of Marji's childhood involves navigating this ambivalence toward her Iranian identity.

As a teenager, Marji expatriates to Vienna, where she attends high school. She struggles to maintain a connection to her Iranian identity, especially in a Western culture where news from inside Iran is unavailable. Once she does return to Iran, this struggle continues, especially as she deals with tensions created by the fundamentalist Islamic government and Iran's ongoing war with Iraq. Later, the cultural tension manifests itself in Marjane's art school education and her participation in the design of a theme park based on Persian mythology. The focus on her artistic training in Iran also gives the second volume elements of the *Künstlerroman*, or novel of artistic development.[18]

Many readers look to the opening images of part one as examples of Scott McCloud's (1993) "iconic abstraction"—the "amplification through simplification" (30) that can create a sense of connection, and even empathy, between a reader and the simplified, iconic figure in a comic. Satrapi's style certainly falls on the iconic end of McCloud's "picture plane" (51). As read through McCloud, then, the opening image of ten-year-old Marji, wearing a hijab and staring impassively at the reader, is undetailed and abstract enough to draw the reader in and begin the process of empathizing with her.

However, Joseph Darda (2013) argues something of the opposite. Rather than seeing shared similarities with the autobiographical subject, the reader sees "the protagonist as complex" and different from the reader (38). That involves, then, seeing this opening figure as a unique individual rather than as one who is just like the reader. Gillian Whitlock (2006) reinforces this reading and addresses the value of beginning *Persepolis* with the "The Veil": "The veil is, after all, one of the most intractable symbols of cultural difference between Muslim societies and the West" (974). Whitlock argues that Satrapi challenges the stereotype of the veiled Muslim woman by making the veil itself a part of the figure's individuality. The opening scene of *Persepolis* can seem deceptive at first—Marji's self-portrait and the subsequent images of other Muslim girls seem initially interchangeable, but more careful examination reveals each girl's subtle individuality:

> Satrapi subverts the tendency of "the other ones" [non-Muslim, Western readers] to dehumanize veiled women as massed figures indistinguishable one from the other. The art is to read for small difference. Satrapi's comics insist on it. (Whitlock 2006: 975)

Therefore, "The Veil" not only teaches the reader to see the subtle individuality of the young girls in these successive images, but also instructs on how to read the entire work more carefully and attentively to the smallest details. This development of reader awareness early in the text, combined with Satrapi's iconic style, then leads to an emotional connection with the reader: "Satrapi's cartoon drawing sustains the individuality and agency of her autobiographical avatar and friends vividly, and with compassion" (Whitlock 2006: 977).

In *Persepolis*, Satrapi expresses an overtly didactic purpose. She wants to humanize the Iranian people for Western readers, to counter the dehumanizing invisibility of Iranians in Western media, where, as Satrapi (2004) writes in her introduction, Iran "has been discussed mostly in connection with fundamentalism, fanaticism, and terrorism." Babak Elahi (2007) explains this didactic project: "Satrapi uses the frame of the comic panel to redirect the gaze of Western European and North American readers toward the individual life and the complex identity of her own narrative and autobiographical persona" (313).

As evident in the discussions of *Persepolis*'s opening panels, Satrapi's style is a common topic in scholarship on the comic. In addition to descriptions of her style as "iconic," Hillary Chute (2010) refers to it as "expressionistic and minimalist" (135) and "monochromatic … flat black and white" (144). Such a style, then, "suggests that the historically traumatic does not have to be visually traumatic" (135). The style is also consistent with Persian art, thus situating *Persepolis* within a culturally specific tradition (144). Therefore, readers may find Satrapi's style to be simplistic, but it is deceptively so, and is a conscious choice rather than a reflection of a lack of skill.

The expressionistic style can often be evocative and effective in representing the traumatic images that run through the text. When depicting an event in which 400 victims burned to death in a locked movie theater that was set on fire, Satrapi draws spectral flaming figures floating in the air (15). Similar expressionistic images appear throughout the narrative, often to depict scenes of warfare that Marji does not witness directly, such as the image of young soldiers in silhouette being blown up in a minefield with "keys to paradise" around their necks (102).

As with *Maus* and *Fun Home*, scholars often engage with *Persepolis* as an exemplar of the genre—a work that demonstrates autobiographical comics' potential. Darda (2013), for example, uses *Persepolis* to demonstrate how ethical engagement functions in graphic memoirs. Rocío Davis (2005) proposes a new way of reading autobiographical comics through *Persepolis*:

> [T]o engage these narratives effectively, we must move beyond an analytical model of merely reading the surface of texts for potential meanings and attend to the cultural and generic codes addressed by the authors to unravel what the texts execute within the contexts of larger questions of cultural and political mobilization. (265)

Therefore, *Persepolis*'s canonical status in Comics Studies stems partially from such readings that use it as a model for the analysis of graphic narratives. This modeling also demonstrates *Persepolis*'s value in the classroom. It serves as an entry-point into the discussion of the medium's powers and effects on the reader, while also standing on its own merits as a literary work that encourages readers (especially Western readers) to empathize with or understand a culture that is otherwise generally closed off and inaccessible.

In the years since its original publication, *Persepolis* has attained a high cultural status, crossing over with readers who may not normally seek out comic books. That status has increased since 2007, when Satrapi and co-director Vincent Paronnaud adapted the graphic memoir into a popular and critically acclaimed animated film, which duplicates Satrapi's iconic black-and-white art style. In addition, *Persepolis* has launched a cottage industry of autobiographical comics about adolescence in Iran and the experience of emigration, including Afschineh Latifi's *Even After All This Time: A Story of Love, Revolution, and Leaving Iran* (2005), Azadeh Moaveni's *Lipstick Jihad* (2005), and Parsua Bashi's *Nylon Road: A Graphic Memoir of Coming of Age in Iran* (2009). Meanwhile, *Persepolis* has a kind of underground status in Satrapi's native Iran. The book, which has not received an official translation into Farsi, is banned in Iran, but illegally imported editions sell on the black market.

Alison Bechdel's *Fun Home*

Alison Bechdel's *Fun Home: A Family Tragicomic* (2006) documents the difficult relationship that Bechdel had with her father, Bruce, who, as the book reveals, lived his adult life as a closeted gay man. The graphic memoir became an almost immediate critical sensation, generating considerable scholarly attention and appearing on class syllabi.[19] She had earlier gained attention for her long-running fictional comic strip, *Dykes to Watch Out For* (1983–2008), which ran in several independent newspapers and resulted in a dozen collected editions. She also created short comic stories for such series as *Wimmen's Comix*, *Gay Comix*, and others. She followed up *Fun Home* with *Are You My Mother?* (2012), a companion to *Fun Home* about, as the title suggests, her mother, but more about her struggle to find a way to talk about her mother. In 2014, Bechdel was awarded the prestigious MacArthur Fellowship, joining Ben Katchor as one of only two graphic novelists to receive the honor (Gene Luen Yang later received the fellowship in 2016). *Fun Home* was also adapted into a highly successful Broadway musical, which one five Tony Awards in 2015, including Best Musical.

Fun Home serves as a kind of investigation into the death of Alison Bechdel's father, as well as a memoir of her own coming out as a lesbian while in college. Bruce Bechdel's death is ruled an accident—he is hit by a Sunbeam bread truck while he disposes of yard waste in a ditch across from an old house he is restoring—but Alison and her family strongly suspect that he committed suicide. He does not, however, leave the normal indications of suicide, like a note or any sense that he was trying to put his affairs in order. Instead, Bechdel looks for clues that might indicate his mood in the last months of his life, and those days were eventful. During that time, Alison had written home to reveal that she was a lesbian, her mother in return revealed that Alison's father was a closeted gay man, and furthermore her mother had asked her husband for a divorce. Other, smaller clues emerge as well, such as the annotated copy of Albert Camus's *A Happy Death* which Bruce had been reading just before he died. As the narrative progresses, she also pulls at the strands of their strained relationship to reveal the family's difficult history. Bechdel follows a non-chronological narrative that flashes back and forward in time as she makes connections between events or as one memory triggers another.

Bechdel seeks evidence for her father's suicide and his secret life, so much of the narrative involves piecing together information from the past. However, she also often uses a kind of foreshadowing in her narrative that takes advantage of the comics form, especially its visual elements. While this is a common literary device for fictional works, it takes on the form of fate and inevitability in autobiography. In other words, foreshadowing is a fictional construction, and in the case of *Fun Home*, it indicates some greater force pushing Bruce Bechdel to his inevitable death. For example, in the first page of the book, Alison recalls playing "airplane" with her father: young Alison balances on her father's feet while he lays on the floor with his legs in the air. Next to Bruce is a copy of Leo

Tolstoy's *Anna Karenina*. As Kelley (2014) explains, "its presence subtly foreshadows Bruce's own demise—he was also killed by a large vehicle, probably of his own volition" (44). Kelley refers here to Anna Karenina's suicide, where she throws herself in front of a moving train. In one of the more overt examples of foreshadowing, Bechdel includes a loaf of Sunbeam bread among the provisions that the family takes on a camping trip (112). The bread appears again in a scene in the family kitchen, when Alison has the first frank talk with her mother about her father's sexuality, the strains on the family and the marriage, and the impending divorce (217). The only other time we see the Sunbeam logo is on the truck that kills Alison's father. The inclusion of the bread loaf in the camping scene and the kitchen conversation contributes to a sense of inevitability in Bruce's death, as if the bread truck is hurtling through history to arrive at the fated moment. But it's also an artificial construct, created by Bechdel to provide order and make sense of her father's death. She returns to the Sunbeam bread truck in the opening pages of *Are You My Mother?* (2012). On her way to visit her mother and tell her that she was in the process of creating *Fun Home*, Alison is in a near accident with a semi. As she pulls up alongside the truck, she is shocked to see the Sunbeam bread logo on the side. The symbolism here is obvious: her father's death and its accompanying trauma are coming back in her anticipation of the uncomfortable conversation she is about to have with her mother.

Throughout *Fun Home*, Bechdel deploys several strategies to bring order to her father's story, as well as her own. In many instances, Bechdel visualizes imagined scenes or fantasies that offer her some sense of wish fulfillment. Early on, Alison remembers that her father offered her his copy of Albert Camus's *The Myth of Sisyphus*, which is required reading for a Philosophy class Alison takes in college. She turns down the offer, but, in her efforts to retrospectively seek out signs of her father's suicidal thoughts, she wishes that she had the copy, and that her father had underlined a key passage about suicide as "a solution to the absurd" (qtd in 47). This annotation, which could have functioned as a suicide note of sorts, does not exist, but Bechdel creates it in her text, as if to fulfill her desire for its existence. She enacts these sorts of fantasies elsewhere as well, as when she imagines what it would be like to tell the truth about her father at his funeral (125). Perhaps the most poignant of these fantasies, however, occurs early in the book. Alison has speculated that by coming out to her parents, she may have contributed to her father's suicide. A caption reads, "If I had not felt compelled to share my little sexual discovery, perhaps the semi would have passed without incident four months later" (59). Beneath the caption appears a wide panel in which her father dumps yard waste into a ditch, unaware of the Sunbeam bread truck that has passed behind him. The comics form has given Bechdel this opportunity to draw an alternate history, even if just for a panel, where her father survives. But that survival only happens, she imagines, if she does not come out to her parents.

Frequently in *Fun Home* Bechdel imposes a sense of literariness on her father's death and uses literature to try to understand it. Much of the scholarship on *Fun Home* addresses the literary references that run through the book and connects those references to Bechdel's larger goals. For example, Annette Fantasia (2011) places *Fun Home* within the tradition of the *Bildungsroman*; Ariela Freedman (2009) demonstrates how modernism functions in the work, especially the references to Joyce; and Fiorenzo Iuliano (2015) identifies the narrative as "a complex experiment in rewriting Proust's *In Search of Lost Time*" (287). More literary allusions come from F. Scott Fitzgerald, Oscar Wilde, Henry James, the aforementioned Albert Camus, and others. Early in the narrative, Alison states that "my parents are most real to me in fictional terms" (67), as she describes their shared interest in F. Scott Fitzgerald that emerged during their courtship. So, she again attempts through these literary references, especially those drawn from the works that her father loved and pushed her to read, to bring order to her experience. In a larger sense, though, they also reveal Bechdel's literary ambitions for *Fun Home* by making a direct connection between this work and literary modernism, as Freedman (2009) argues.

Like Satrapi, Spiegelman, and others, Bechdel blends personal history with cultural history. Kelley (2014) shows how LGBTQ history functions in Bechdel's narrative: Bruce Bechdel realizes his own homosexuality some time in the late 1950s, when he is nineteen or twenty, and Alison makes her discovery at the same age, around 1979 or 1980. Thus, each of these experiences occurs ten years on either side of the monumental 1969 Stonewall riots. Additionally, the family's fateful trip to the Jersey Shore— where, as Alison finds out later, Bruce had an affair with Roy, the family's babysitter—occurs within weeks of the riots. Kelley (2014) describes the riots as both a "temporal fulcrum" and "a *sociopolitical* fulcrum" (45–6), meaning that the reader gets to see the lives of gay men and women in both the pre-Stonewall and post-Stonewall eras, the societal changes that occurred in the wake of Stonewall, and the different sets of choices that Bruce and Alison had in speaking of their identities. Bechdel doesn't idealize the historical moment in which Alison comes out as some perfect era of acceptance for homosexuals, as Kelley (2014) acknowledges (47). Instead, Bechdel contrasts the opportunities available to her with the silence and prejudice that her father knew in the 1950s. For example, while reimagining her family's trip to New York City during the Jersey Shore vacation, Bechdel has her retrospective narrator imagining what it was like to be gay in the 1950s, moving through the same space that her father had lived in during his youth (105–8). Through this, she develops a sense of empathy for him.

Perhaps one of the most extensive and complex uses of photography in graphic memoir appears in Alison Bechdel's *Fun Home*. Redrawn photographs appear throughout the book, especially on each chapter title page. For these pictures, Bechdel also uses cross-hatching, shading, and scalloped borders to distinguish the photos from a normal comics panel. Not all photos in the narrative are rendered this way, but many are. Most notable, though, is the two-page spread located near the center of the book. While going through a box of family pictures, Alison finds a previously unknown picture of Roy, her teenage babysitter, that was taken during the family trip to the Jersey Shore. In the picture, Roy lies on a bed in his underwear, "gilded with morning seaside light" (100). Alison sees this photo as evidence of her father's homosexuality, but she finds it odd that her father, so protective of his secret, private life, would leave this picture mixed in with other family photos of the vacation. This photo appears almost in the center of the book, and Bechdel emphasizes its importance to her investigation of her father's life in a couple of other ways. For one, it is the only double-page spread in the entire book. Also, it is the only time that Bechdel allows the gray-green monochromatic color to bleed out to the edges of the page; every other page has a traditional white border. Because of the bleed, a reader can close the book and still identify the center spread as the only thin gray-green line visible in the book.[20]

More significant, however, is the fact that the entirety of *Fun Home* is a series of duplicated photographs, in the sense that Bechdel used photo-references for every single image in the book. As Chute (2010) explains,

> for every pose of every panel in the entire book—which comes out to roughly one thousand panels—Bechdel ... created a reference shot by posing herself for each person in the frame with her digital camera, [even if] she already had a photographic reference shot from her parent's collection. (200)

This means that she had to inhabit the bodies of all of her characters, including her parents, even going so far as to photograph herself at the exact location of her father's death. This intensive creative process allows Bechdel to embody her parents, with "embodiment" being a significant theme throughout *Fun Home*, according to Chute (2010: 200).[21]

The intensity and detail of Bechdel's creative process is evident in other ways as well. In addition to recreating family photographs and her own photo references, she also painstakingly recreates original documents from her childhood. She creates a handwritten equivalent to the typeset fonts of books that she read, including the dictionary and literary sources; she duplicates her own childhood handwriting in her journal entries; she mimics both her father's and her mother's handwriting; and she also fabricates important documents, like the court papers related to her father's arrest for offering alcohol to a minor.[22] As she explains in an interview with Hillary Chute (2006), "That was one of the crazier rabbit holes I went down into on this project—reproducing my childhood diary entries and my dad's handwritten letters. It's all very carefully traced and redrawn" (1007).

Are You My Mother? (2012) further problematizes the relationship between photography and comics. In an early scene, Alison finds a series of photographs of her as a toddler with her mother. They depict her mother making faces and bouncing toddler Alison on her lap, the child's face in various states of joy. These pictures "had been scattered about in different albums and boxes" (31). That means she does not know the actual temporal sequence of these photographs, so she has to invent her own, thus creating a comic strip out of them. The idea that Alison has to impose an order on these sequential photographs mirrors her struggle to impose a narrative structure on her maternal relationship. But, despite the fact that Bechdel has redrawn these photographs in the manner of the earlier book, the pictures are not comics and were never intended to be, hence the fact that they were scattered in different locations before Alison brings them together. Because Alison's relationship with her mother does not have the clearly definable (though still artificial) narrative organization of her father's story, which Alison structures as a mystery about his death, this scene serves as a metaphor for the entire project, and the book becomes about the struggle to find an appropriate structure. In a sense, *Are You My Mother?* is a metanarrative about a work that doesn't exist: a narratively coherent, linear history of this relationship. In fact, after reading drafts of the first four chapters, Alison's mother refers to it as a "metabook" (286).

Fun Home follows in the tradition of Justin Green's *Binky Brown* (1972) by detailing the creator's battles with obsessive-compulsive disorder. While Green uses fantastical images and visual metaphors to capture the nature of his obsessions, Bechdel renders her experience more literally. Young Alison goes through a variety of rituals like lining up her shoes at night, counting floor tiles, and reciting an incantation in order to penetrate the invisible substance that prevents her from moving through doorways. With the latter, Green's technique would have involved drawing the substance to give the reader a visual sense of the particular obsession. Bechdel, however, does not offer this kind of visual representation: we know that Alison's obsessions aren't real, even if they were real to her. Bechdel explains her childhood OCD as an attempt to stem "life's attendant chaos" (149) by imposing a false order on it.

Bechdel represents her OCD, then, as a way of ordering her life at a young age, as she was sensing the chaos at the heart of her family. And though Alison overcomes the obsessive-compulsive behaviors of her youth, so much of *Fun Home* deals with Bechdel's attempts to impose order on her own chaotic life experiences and her father's own narrative. She uses literature, history, photography, and her own art and narrative choices to achieve this sense of order. However, she also acknowledges the artificiality of the ways in which she seeks order. She reveals that she can only think of her parents "in literary terms" (67), and, when connecting her father's story to the history of HIV/AIDS, she confesses, "maybe I'm trying to render my senseless personal loss meaningful by linking it, however posthumously, to a more coherent narrative" (196). She also admits when some of her images don't align with the facts (like when she draws a milkman rescuing her toddler father from the muddy field, instead of the mailman, as her grandmother told the story [41])[23] or when her images represent some kind of wish fulfillment (like when she imagines what it would have been like to tell the truth about her father at his funeral [125]). The literary references, the attempts at historical connections, the photographic performance, the visualized wish-fulfillment: all represent fabrications of order, and in acknowledging them as such, she draws her "curvy circumflex"—the sign she used in her childhood journal to obsessively question the validity of even her most mundane observations (142)—over the entire book.

Notes

1   In *The Binky Brown Sampler* (1995), Green explains that "Binky" was a nickname given to him as a child by his Uncle Joe (78). "Brown" is then meant to correspond with his own colorful surname.

2   Alternately, Charles Hatfield (2005) sees "the creation of *Binky Brown* [as] an elaborate act of penance" and "a purgative ritual" which we can see in the way that Green foregrounds the act of creation in the story in panels where the bound narrator creates the pages that we read (135).

3   There is some inconsistency about the way in which Aline Kominsky-Crumb's name is formatted. In *Need More Love* (2007), her name is not hyphenated, so scholarly works that focus on this book tend to also leave the name unhyphenated (see Oksman [2007] and Clementi [2013]). Most of the time, though, she does hyphenate the name, so that is the version that I'm going to go with. Also, to avoid confusion, I will refer to her throughout by her married name, even when discussing works that preceded her marriage to Robert Crumb.

4   As mentioned in the "History" chapter, Jared Gardner (2012) has identified self-portraiture and other autobiographical elements in Crumb's earlier work, even dating back to his 1950s juvenilia.

5   The nickname "The Bunch" comes from Crumb's character

"Honeybunch Kaminski." As Kominsky-Crumb explains, the character precedes her first meeting with Crumb, but friends in the underground comix community gave her the nickname "Honeybunch" (which she later shortened to "Bunch") because of the similarity between her last name and the character's (see Chute [2010]: 38–9).

6 Close also co-wrote a sharp parody of Pekar's work, titled "American Squalor," with collaborator John Ostrander and artist Don Simpson in *Wasteland* 3 (February 1988).

7 The second volume of *Maus* contains five chapters: four were previously published in *Raw*, and the final chapter was created for the volume.

8 More discussion of *Maus* can be found in other sections of this book, including the section on "Trauma" in Chapter 4 and throughout Chapter 3.

9 Reiser (2014) places *In the Shadow of No Towers* in continuity with Spiegelman's *Breakdowns* rather than with *Maus*, especially through Spiegelman's theory of comics form and aesthetics that is articulated in *Breakdowns* and realized in *No Towers*.

10 The transformation of Art to Happy Hooligan is worth noting here because it recalls an earlier Spiegelman strip from his underground days. In *Short Order Comix* 1 (1973b), Spiegelman contributed a one-page story, "Skeeter Grant by Skeeter Grant" (the name being an early pseudonym Spiegelman used for some of his stories, including some autobiographical ones). The strip describes a dream that Skeeter had in 1969, "after an evening of browsing through a pile of musty, old comic strips." He has transformed into Happy Hooligan. Not only that, but he has also entered a world that follows comic book logic: he disappears when moving from one panel to the next, his head comes off his neck when he tries to take the tin-can hat off of his head, and he complains that "It's hard to get used to having a balloon come out of your mouth whenever you talk!" When he relates his experience to a passerby, the stranger responds, "Relax, buddy boy ... / ... It's just the style you're drawn in!" The idea here of the fluidity between comics and the real world is consistent with Spiegelman's work on *In the Shadow of No Towers*. In addition, *Short Order Comix* 1 also features Spiegelman's "Prisoner on the Hell Planet," which figures significantly in *Maus*. It's curious that both of Spiegelman's major works call back to this specific underground comic.

11 See the section on "Adolescence" in Chapter 4 for more on autobiographical comics as *Bildungsroman* and *Künstlerroman*.

12   Though the title is spelled this way in the book, the series would
     have been known as *Wimmen's Comix* at the time this story takes
     place, in 1976.

13   Likely referring to such scenes, Charles Hatfield (2005) observes that
     "*Peepshow* often serves as a passive-aggressive intervention in his
     own real-life relationships" (126).

14   Both "Helder" and "Showing Helder" are reprinted in *The Little
     Man: Short Strips, 1980–1995* (1998). All citations for these stories
     will come from that collection and not the original *Yummy Fur*
     publication. See the "Critical questions" chapter for more on these
     stories.

15   *One Hundred Demons* has several different ways in which its title
     can be presented because it appears in multiple different forms on
     the title page. As such, scholars and critics make different choices
     when they reference the book: *One Hundred Demons!* and *One!
     Hundred! Demons!* being the most common alternatives. I will be
     sticking with the unpunctuated title, which seems to be the most
     common.

16   Perhaps one reason for the paucity of scholarship on *Blankets* lies
     in Douglas Wolk's (2007) criticism of Thompson's "sentimentality"
     and his failure to realize the interiority of other characters
     besides himself. The latter point, however, may be read as part of
     Craig's development in the narrative as he tries to overcome his
     egocentrism, especially in bonding with his brother at the end of
     the book. Wolk also criticizes Thompson for being more style than
     substance, though this may also be a difficult critique to measure.
     Thompson's visual style is certainly an important element of the
     work's overall success. See "Craig Thompson and James Kochalka:
     Craft Versus Cuteness" in Wolk (2007), 207–10.

17   In this section, all quotes and references to *Persepolis* come from
     The Complete Persepolis (2007) in order to avoid the confusion of
     switching between volumes.

18   The *Künstlerroman* is discussed at greater length in the section on
     "Adolescence" in Chapter 4.

19   *Fun Home* has also been the source of considerable controversy
     when used in the classroom or other educational settings. See the
     section on "Censorship and controversy" in the "Social and cultural
     impact" chapter for more information on these contentious issues.

20   The book's limited color scheme is also a frequent topic in
     scholarship on *Fun Home*. In the interview with Chute (2006),
     Bechdel explains,

At first I was resistant to the idea to using color at all, because one whole theme of the book is how my dad was such a crazy color freak and how I became a cartoonist because it was a black and white world where I didn't ever have to think about color. (1011)

But later, after reading Dan Clowes's *Ghost World*, she decided to use a similarly limited color palate.

21 In addition to Chute (2010), Watson (2008) also discusses the role of photography in *Fun Home*.

22 For more on Bechdel's recreation of archival documents, see Rohy (2010).

23 This scene is discussed in greater length in the Introduction.

Appendix 1: Panel Discussion—Comics and Autobiography

Phoebe Gloeckner, Justin Green, Aline Kominsky-Crumb, Carol Tyler

Moderated by Deborah Nelson
May 19, 2012

This panel discussion, held during the "Comics: Philosophy and Practice" conference at the University of Chicago, covers a wide variety of topics addressed elsewhere in this book: the origin and history of autobiographical comics, the creator's impetus for telling personal stories, the notion of "truth" in the genre, the effect of public exposure on those represented in the stories, and influences (comics and otherwise). Speaking here are four creators who have been making autobiographical comics since the 1970s and 1980s: Justin Green, Aline Kominsky-Crumb, Phoebe Gloeckner, and Carol Tyler (Robert Crumb, who was in the audience during this discussion, makes a contribution as well). This collection of four creators, all of whom share a system of influence with one another, offers a unique opportunity to see creators in conversation, talking about their craft.

Deborah Nelson, from the University of Chicago's Department of English, moderates the panel. This excerpt, which originally appeared in the special issue on "Comics and Media" of *Critical Inquiry* (Spring 2014, edited by Hillary Chute and Patrick Jagoda), contains the entire panel proper, but does not include the Q&A session that followed.

Deborah Nelson: *In what I've read from many of you, if not all of you, when you started doing autobiographical work, you had a strong sense of your own anonymity, in the sense that no one will ever see this.*
Aline Kominsky-Crumb: We were right.

DN: That clearly has disappeared if today's event is any proof of that. Can you talk a little bit about the origins of the work? When that anonymity changed, how that might have changed your relationship to your work, what you chose to write about, and what you plan on writing about?
Justin Green: Everyone I knew knew at least someone that was killed in Vietnam. And a couple people that were injured. And there was a feeling of a real collision, not quite like the intramural sport going on down by our hotel [over NATO]. I had terrible survivor guilt. I felt that what I was doing was very trivial, and I needed to wage my own war. And so I looked within and I don't know if this means anonymity, but I didn't want to present myself as a hero, but rather as a specimen. So the comic form gives you a multifaceted view of doing that. I don't know if you noticed, but old Superman comics have little panels at the top that say later, or soon, next day. Well, I turned that into the narrative voice where I would stack several lines of copy. But then I realized, I'm hiding up there. That's my voice, but I can show something below that either contradicts it or amplifies it. And on top of that, not only do I get to put balloons into the character's mouths, but there are thought balloons. So there is a multidimensional way of being anonymous yet at the same time pushing the story forward. But I never thought—I just thought it would, I guess, biodegrade. [*laughter*] It's a newsprint. It's been following me around for decades now.
Phoebe Gloeckner: When I was very young, I wanted to write about things that had happened to me, but I felt like

I wasn't supposed to. I was just compelled. I had to do it. And I think because I was so afraid of doing it, that I started separating a little and seeing myself as a character. Which actually allowed me to have more empathy for that character because I really, you know, couldn't stand myself, especially as a teenager. So you get this kind of schizophrenic thing, which I actually think is normal. You have to do that because, you know, comics are a narrative form, they have a narrative structure, which is all artifice. Life isn't like that. So you have to do so much manipulation of any set of facts or experiences to make them interesting or to make sense even to yourself. What you're after is not a set of true facts. You're after some sort of emotional truth, at least I guess I was, or just truth about what it is to be alive at whatever point. But I'm working on this project in Mexico in Juárez at the border, and it was supposed to be something that was done in a matter of months and then I was out of there. And I've been going back there for eight years and getting to know a few people very, very well. I think what I'm doing, although I didn't know it at first, is that I have to be in the story. I'm not an outsider reflecting things because I know it's my eyes. It means nothing to me if I'm just reflecting. I can't reflect something that I know little about. I have to, like, feel it and for me that meant going back repeatedly, suffering in a sense with those people that I was writing about. I had to muddy the mix or it wasn't even real.[1]

JG: So you are shifting your viewpoint as you become enveloped in the story.

PG: Oh, yes, I'm changing just immensely. The creation is a destructive process in a sense. You kind of destroy yourself and then rebuild it. And it's painful.

AK-C: It's dangerous what you're doing, too. Isn't it?

PG: Two of my friends got death threats and they were at my house for nearly six months because I had gotten a lawyer at the University of Michigan[2] to take their case pro bono. We just found out a week and a half ago that they did finally get asylum. It has been such a long process. It is like I'm so involved somehow.

Carol Tyler: I'm just amazed at what she just said. When I

started out as a painter, I just couldn't, like, say it all. And then what it was that I had to say was usually rooted in injustices, or personal slights, or how awkward I always feel. But since I've been doing this, gosh, since forever, especially with [my last project],[3] I'm so sick of talking about myself. Because I've grown into bigger, more important things. But yet I agree, I feel like I only know what I have gone through. And I trust my emotions and my instincts. So to make a fantasy character or something like that just seems ... what is that? When in fact the real, emotionally breathing thing that I feel is important.

So it is interesting how you start out telling stories about, oh, something that happened in, you know, in your twenties or thirties, things that mattered then, and now as I'm sixty, I feel like my subject matter is just changing. So much more intense. But at the same time I just want to say, oh, fuck it and do a page for *Weirdo* now and then. [*laughter*]

AK-C: I'm the grandmother or great grandmother of autobiographical comics. Justin is the great grandfather, but I started—

JG: We've entered a new generation now?

AK-C: I'm waiting for my grandchildren to announce what they're going to do. When I saw Justin's work it gave me permission to or a way to find my voice to talk about my own life, and I was motivated by rage at my mother. I could only talk about my mother all the time. Everything was in reference to my mother because she was so—such a monster. So seeing Justin's work gave me a way to combine my alienation from art school with the rage at my mother. For years, my motivating factor was to draw the meanest, most grotesque images of my mother. Now I feel really guilty because she's a nice old lady. I'm going to see her tomorrow in Miami. [*laughter*]

I really thought she would never see my work, and I don't think she would have if it wasn't for several factors. One was Terry Zwigoff's film [*Crumb*] in the 1990s. I thought his film would either never get finished or just show in some arty theaters that my mother would never go to. I was really honest in the film and I hold up these drawings of my mother, saying, yeah, I drew this of her, ha ha look at her, she really is like that, she's even worse than that, she's just a monster. I couldn't ever even capture what a monster she really is but I'm trying. I keep trying different ways to show more aspects of her monsterhood. So Terry said, aren't you scared your mother is going to see this? I said, no, she would only see it if it came to the shopping mall behind her condo. But it did! [*laughter*] And she called me up and said, well, you know, I saw the film and I am very hurt. She didn't talk to me for three months and then we never talked about it again. You know, since then, now that I'm a grandmother and a mother and my daughter has a lot of issues with me, you know, I feel sorry for my mother. I feel completely caught in between all of those things.

I still find that my relation with my family and the people close to me is what constantly feeds me because that's what I know the best and on a daily basis that's what irritates me the most, what moves me the most, what, you know, colors everything, are those immediate relationships. I don't even know how to get beyond that. I wouldn't know how to make a political comic or make any kind of social commentary beyond what I immediately know, what's in front of me and what I experience on the most direct level. And Justin, his comics showed me a way to access that voice and so that's a great gift, you know? I don't know what would have happened to me otherwise.

DN: *You've all made reference to Justin. Can you talk about influences both within the field of comics but also in art forms outside and around?*
CT: We have all kind of bounced off and influenced each other.
AK-C: Stand-up Jewish comics. Nature.
CT: Plants and stuff. [*laughter*]
AK-C: Don Rickles and Frida Kahlo. [*laughter*]
PG: I get really interested in self-published memoirists.

DN: *Like out of the back of their car, that kind of thing?*
PG: No, like the vanity presses. Now it is all on the Internet. You can easily do it POD.[4] Like Ira Lunan Ferguson. He was a psychologist who wrote thirty books, some of them as long as like 1,500 pages, all published by himself. And

one of them was a trilogy of books called *I Dug Graves at Night to go to College by Day.* [*laughter*] And then there was a subtitle, *Autobiography of a Half-Blind West Indian Immigrant.* He was this black man who had been rejected from Howard University, which had been his lifelong goal. And then he had a chip on his shoulder and got ten degrees and started writing about himself.

AK-C: It's like not being allowed in Israel or something.

PG: Exactly. When you read his words, it's so hard to get the story because he's just, like, saying anything. He's not doing what these guys do, which is processing it and turning it into something else. So it's a totally different kind of experience to read it. But yet it's fascinating.

JG: I remember being very attracted to the Ash Can school of painting and also to social realism. At the Art Institute— it is probably in the basement now, but *The Rock* by Peter Blume is this luxurious image of a future world of devastation with these distended characters. And I used to stand in front of it, hoping that, by osmosis, the meaning of the painting would come into me. And now it is my—what do you call it? Screen saver? [*laughter*] And it still has a resonance for me. But I remember in 1967, my privileged ass was in Rome. And it was there that I was working on my conscientious objector statement. And I was constantly shuttled off to these museums to see the works of the Renaissance. And I even went to St. Peter's, I saw the Pietà. And then I saw a little fragment of an underground paper with an R. Crumb drawing. I don't even remember which one it was. I just saw the line and it was like a call to action. It brought my own culture back to me in a sea of unfamiliar and oppressive images. And I'm not alone in this. I was talking to a man who must be twenty years my junior last night at dinner. He had the same thing with Mr. Natural. Instant recognition. And so I'd always been a closeted cartoonist. It was looked askance at RISD,[5] where I went. But it just came out whenever I—odd moments. But then I started to pursue it in earnest, and I saw that my efforts were turgid. They didn't have a zen-like mark.

There was an artist who somehow—he is obscure now, but his name was Ben Shahn. You see his influence in all these record covers from the 1950s, where guys would try to get his chops of that line; it had a scimitar-like application. Andy Warhol found an ingenious way of replicating that by inking something and then slapping something on top of it and then the result would look like he had the chops, but he didn't. [*laughter*] And he was a good artist, too. But he didn't have that, what I saw in Crumb. And then I was in Philadelphia and I was crashing on a pile of coats in a commune. I was laid out like a corpse. This scrawny little guy came in with a sketchbook and he started drawing me. And I was really pissed but I was so tired I couldn't say anything. [*laughter*] When I met Crumb a few years later, I realized he was that guy. [*laughter*]

PG: It's so funny you meet the people you need to meet.

DN: *Can you tell a story about that? How do you meet the people you need to meet?*

AK-C: It's a finite group for one thing.

PG: I've said this a million times, but—

AK-C: Don't say it.

PG: Quickly. I was fourteen or fifteen. My parents read *Zap Comix*. They had them wedged under their mattress and we weren't allowed to read them. But we read them, of course. Same thing, when I saw *Zap*, I think it was the first time I had ever seen a depiction of sex. I was at the point where I didn't really believe that sex was real, or [I believed that] someone made that idea up. [*laughter*] Like it couldn't really happen. Then I saw [Crumb's] Joe Blow. I don't know. It just—it was so beautiful. I mean I'm not even talking about the story. So beautiful, the drawing. And then I was obsessed with Janis Joplin and I saw the album; R. Crumb drew the picture on that. I had this feeling, like, oh, my God! It almost made me cry. And then I got *Twisted Sisters* because I used to go into head shops and sneak in there and feel weird and buy comics. And when I got *Twisted Sisters*— it was Diane Noomin and Aline Kominsky—I memorized that comic. I mean, I never read any other comics but underground comics.

AK-C: It was deeply disturbing that you were so into that work.

PG: You don't know how into it! I read it so many times and every time I would get something more out of it.

AK-C: She wanted to come and, like, Robert and I would be her parents. She had this fantasy that we would be nice parents—she told me that later. Oh my God, you were so twisted! Horrible! What an idea. Ask our daughter about it. Really. [*laughter*] It's not a good idea.

DN: So I had a slide up here which was Aline on the cover,[6] sitting on the toilet, for which she was roundly criticized. It was revolutionary. And there is also one of Justin from *Binky Brown* in there. I wanted you to talk a little bit about, you know, just the way that—the sex and the scatology of the work is so important to its charge. It was so controversial. It still retains a certain kind of charge, although obviously it changes over time. Can you talk a little bit about how you deal with that? When you want to do that, what are you thinking about? And also is that a distancing effect? Or a way to create proximity with your own sort of really intense bodily experiences? Or personal experiences? Phoebe, you draw very graphically, you draw very explicitly and very anatomically pristine images of sex, even if what's going on is far from that. So I just wonder if you could talk in general about some of those intensely private bodily components of the work.

PG: But don't you feel like, you know, the more—the less you hide certain things, the less personal, in a sense, your work becomes? Because everyone has experienced the same things or felt the same things. Everyone has gone to the bathroom for Christ's sake.

DN: Right. Sure.

PG: So even if it's autobiographical, the kind of truer it is, the more it becomes everybody.

JG: So in a sense it is like the continuation of Kurtzman to reality. I should have said *Mad Magazine* was a big influence. But what Phoebe was saying reminded me of that—that it's a way of undercutting so-called reality.

CT: I've never drawn explicit stuff. I am a little after you guys, you know? I didn't really start drawing or get published until the late '80s, so it just wasn't my subject matter. But I've not shied away from other emotionally charged subjects; I wanted to stab my daughter to death and stuff like that. [*laughter*] I had postpartum psychosis and I had this episode where I just, the knives were laying there, and I thought, oh yeah, I could just get her and then get me. It was horrible. What is the most horrible thing you can think of? Killing your kid, right? I thought, now do I draw that? Yes, I do, because the truth is, people have horrible, horrific thoughts and things happen. And I've had so many women come up to me and say, thank you, because you know what? I thought I was at my wit's end with my kid and I thought about how you sort of just ran from that and that's the same thing I did. That's good. So for whatever reason we go to these horrible things, but ... people love it. [*laughter*]

AK-C: I have to go back to the image of myself on the toilet. When I drew it I didn't even think anything of it because I think I always did my best thinking on the toilet. So it was obvious to draw myself thinking on the toilet because that's where I was mostly. And also I think I was interested in drawing underground comics because I thought they were things you read in the toilet and I was so sick of fine arts and thinking of putting stuff in galleries and trying to improve yourself and sell yourself and make yourself better than you are. So I was trying to go down into the gutter, and that's where I was. I didn't think anything of drawing myself on the toilet. And then Peter Bagge said to me, oh my God, you drew yourself on the toilet on the cover of a comic. I thought, yeah, that is really disturbing. Especially for a woman. It's so unfeminine, and so disgusting, it's such a turnoff, and I think that, all the sex I always did in my comics is the most unerotic thing that you could ever imagine. I think it's the opposite of erotic art, I think it's like ecch. Who would want to go near her? It's so horrible! And all the disgusting substances and bodily fluids and noises, and hideous sex organs looking like plucked chickens and things like that. I had to confront that in my work. That's how I see it now. But at the time I had no idea why I did anything. [*laughter*] Completely uncontrollable.

CT: [Justin,] will you please talk about the dick rays [in *Binky Brown*]?[7]

JG: Well, the rays, sadly, no more veer to Iowa. Or in this case I think Michigan, but no, they only go about half a city block.

AK-C: They're getting weaker with age?

JG: Yes, I'm afraid so.

CT: There are streets he can go down now in Cincinnati he couldn't go down.

JG: It is like having an annoying relative that you want to hit with a ball-peen hammer. You're tired of it. And besides, OCD, one of the few behavioral disorders that makes the world a better place [*laughter*]—has a component of detachment that knows that this can't be right. And so it is recording and it is having an active dialogue that says, stop it, what are you doing? This is ridiculous. But then the more primitive side has to go back and check the story regardless. So perspective is vital to my orientation to drawing and to understanding how a ray can function. But in a way it's such a bombastic view of the universe. And learning Photoshop is a gift. [*laughter*] Because I realized there's no ultimate line. You know, you can draw something in complete control. Your very best work. And you blow it up to four hundred percent and you see this sea of pixels that render your work a tar brush. And so that inexactitude is freeing, in a way. It means you can float anywhere.

Robert Crumb: Are there any medications for OCD?

JG: Of course there are.

RC: Do they work? If he took medications maybe he wouldn't have done those great comics.

Tyler: That's what Bill Griffith [of *Zippy the Pinhead*] said. He told me, Carol, never give him drugs.

AK-C: When I met Justin, I asked if drawing comics helped with the rays. I thought maybe that would be therapeutic to write about the stuff. He said, no, it made no difference whatsoever.

PG: Art is not therapy. It just makes you feel more connected to the world, perhaps, if you're lucky.

RC: You foist it on the public.

AK-C: Yeah, you foist it on the public but it doesn't take [the OCD] away. It's still there, it maybe even gets stronger the more you focus on it.

Tyler: OCD is an isolating syndrome and it is perfect for a cartoonist. Because you are in your studio and you can control your world.

JG: Would you want your traffic controller to have OCD? [*laughter*] The pharmacist?

PG: You remember those two frames from *Binky Brown*? It had the girl's bathing suit and a little hair was peeking out and then the nun's hat. A little strand of hair. That's so beautiful. That's so beautiful.

Notes

1   As of this writing, Gloeckner's multimedia Juarez project continues to be a work-in-progress.

2   Gloeckner is Associate Professor in the School of Art and Design at the University of Michigan.

3   The "last project" Tyler refers to here is *You'll Never Know*, the three-volume memoir of her father's experience in World War II, which was collected into a single volume titled *Soldier's Heart: The Campaign to Understand my WWII Veteran Father: A Daughter's Memoir* (2015).

4   Print-on-demand.

5   Green attended college at the Rhode Island School of Design.

6   The cover shown here is for *Twisted Sisters* 1 (1976), which is described below and also discussed in the section on Robert Crumb and Aline Kominsky-Crumb in Chapter 5.

7   In *Binky Brown Meets the Holy Virgin Mary*, the protagonist develops an Obsessive Compulsive Disorder in which he imagines that many phallic objects of all different kinds emit "penis rays" to be avoided.—HLC (Original note from co-editor Hillary L. Chute. See the section on *Binky Brown* in Chapter 5 for more on the penis rays.)

Appendix 2: Interview with Jennifer Hayden

The following excerpt comes from an interview with Jennifer Hayden, creator of *The Story of My Tits* (2015). The interview, conducted by Derek Parker Royal, was released as an episode of the *Comics Alternative* podcast on November 20, 2015. In the interview, Hayden discusses her experience creating the book, her influences, her reasons for choosing the comics medium, her decision on the book's title, and the book's reception by critics, readers, and her family. We also get to see a creator speak frankly about her philosophy of autobiographical comics, especially in the choices made for how to depict family members. In addition to *The Story of My Tits*, the interview also briefly covers her other autobiographical work, *Underwire*, which originally appeared as a series of web comics that were part of the Act-I-Vate "webcomix collective" begun by Dean Haspiel. *Underwire* was later collected in a print volume by Top Shelf (2011).

FIGURE A.2 *The cover to Jennifer Hayden's* The Story of My Tits *(2015). © Jennifer Hayden. Used with permission.*

Derek Royal: *A lot of people know about* The Story of My Tits, *but for those who are not in the know: how would you describe this to those who aren't familiar with the book?*

Jennifer Hayden: Well, you know, the elevator pitch is it's the story of my life and my experience with breast cancer. It's really more about my life than it is about breast cancer but it's sort of looking at my life through the prism of that experience.

DR: *But it's more than just about your experiences with breast cancer.*

JH: Yeah, I mean, the way I explain it, actually there's an

image in the book—one of the later chapter headings that
has a picture of the goddess image that evolves in the book
to have some importance and her breasts have eyes instead
of nipples on them and I always think of that as a perfect
image for what the book is. It's as if I saw my life more
clearly having had breast cancer and I was looking back at
it through my breasts.

DR: *I kind of broke [the memoir] up into three sections: that
the first third of the book is basically your relationship with
your body, specifically your breasts, growing up. Because
it's not just the cancer who defined who you are, but "what
am I supposed to have, as a woman, growing up? When are
they going to start showing? What is this going to mean for
me, myself, my identity, my sense of sexual being?" That
second third is not so much about you and your relationship
with your breasts, but with your family and cancer. Then we
get to that last third, and that's where we get to the story of
you discovering you had it, you had to have the operation,
the surgery. So there's much more to this than just a cancer
survivor story, which I really love about this book. In
fact, one could even call it a larger memoir than a targeted
memoir.*

JH: Thank you, thank you. It was hard to make the whole
book deal with my breasts, but the experience I wanted to
give the reader was the same experience I had had when I
got diagnosed, which was suddenly all the things in my past
that were the big stories that had to do with my relatives—
the family I married into and my own family—I wanted
the reader to have that same feeling of "oh my god, check
this out, she's getting diagnosed and her mother had breast
cancer and her parents' marriage fell apart around the time
her mother-in-law had lung cancer and ... [etc. noises]" I
didn't want to do it in flashbacks because it would have
been dull to do it that way, I wanted the reader to feel the
same impact I had.

So when I realized I wanted to do it that way, I realized I
had to put in all of that stuff in the middle and flesh out all
those relationships so that that part of my breast cancer—I
mean my breast cancer would not have had the significance
that it—a breast cancer story is not interesting, essentially,

except to the person going through it, except when you look at all the lives around them and you see it in context. So, when I started the book blithely not know what I was doing—because this is my first graphic novel, really, ever—it was about my breasts. It was about growing a pair. And then I realized, "now I have to make the setting to put the stone into, like a ring, and now I've got to build all this stuff around it so that the reader gets that same exact emotional impact that I had." That was what the second part of the book was, I was setting that up. And I did cheap shots like someone saying "Hey, nice tits" when I was getting drunk, to keep the tits rolling. I nursed my babies, they were in there, they were on me, they're in there. But you're right, they were not the focus.

Really I didn't spend as much time on nursing as I had wanted to, but in the end I thought that might not be as universal as the other illness and marriage stories were. What you really want to be doing is raising this to the level of art. The reasons for the middle of the book being less about my breasts and more about the life that went on that period of my life was to set things up for the reader for the third part of the book that was about the breast cancer. I sort of wished I had spent more time on nursing, but there were times I realized this was a women's story and times I realized it was much more universal than that. Everybody could relate to the dirt that was in my family, the skeletons in my closet, the pain and the agony—we all go through this. That was part of why I didn't feel more private about writing about it, because I thought, "This is going to help everybody who has gone through this stuff."

DR: *One of the things that strikes me that really comes out of that second part is your relationship with your now husband, Jim. It does set his character up in such a way that it has a big impact on that last third.*

JH: Yeah, yeah. And to see us go all the way through that time together, it makes the way we dealt with the stresses on us (when I went through the breast cancer) it gives it more significance, it gives it more meaning. You can enjoy having seen what troubles we had, you can have more fun looking at how we got through things. I have to add:

everyone thinks my husband's real name is Jim. There
are fictionalized things in the book and one of them is his
name—his name is Steve. In fact, a local reporter didn't ask
me and assumed, as you would, that his name is Jim, so
everyone thinks I'm sleeping with a guy named Jim now!
[*laughs*] Nevermind!

I changed names of family members, not pets, and I
also combined my brothers. I have two brothers and I
combined them into one person because I just had too many
characters, it was getting out of hand. Both of our families
are just too huge and I couldn't put them all in. It was
novelized a tiny bit.

I was thinking of it in those terms, how to turn it into
a book that was as satisfying as the novels I have read my
whole life and loved: Charles Dickens, Nabokov, Eudora
Welty's short stories. I wanted to be a writer for years
and I read so much fiction and literature. I really wanted
to construct this not like a memoir—this happened, then
this happened, then this happened—but so that it was a
dramatic construct. It had tragedy, it had comedy, it had
suspense, it had climaxes, it had arcs. Each chapter had an
arc! All these things I had learned but had not been able to
do in my own writing I felt able to do in a graphic novel,
bring all of those techniques to bear a bit.

DR: *Let's talk a bit about your writing background, because
this is something you mentioned several times in the new
book. This also occasionally comes up in* Underwire,
*that you started off wanting to become a writer and you
felt yourself—I can't remember where this comes up in*
Underwire, *maybe in the afterword or some place, where
you thought of yourself as kind of a failed writer?*

JH: Oh yeah!

DR: *Yeah, so how did your experience as a writer (failed or
otherwise) lead you to your work, let's say Act-I-Vate or to
start to publish books like the resulting* Underwire, *or the
more recent one?*

JH: It didn't lead to it! Having drawn when I was young and
obviously having an ability for it I turned my back on art
when I went to college because I went to a college that was
dreadful at teaching Studio Art. I majored instead in Art

History and sort of minored on my own in English and read every book I could get my hands on. When I got out of college I decided to become a writer and earned money as a public relations writer and I wrote fiction. I wrote really long, impossible, horrible novels. They never got published. I *suuuuuuuucked* so bad! Part of it I was young and I was insecure and I hadn't seen much of the world and I didn't know what I thought of life.

It was a stupid time for me to try and write about life. And I was lonely and depressed even though I was living with my husband. I didn't have very many friends at the time. I knew I was waiting for life to be all around me and once that happened my voice would come out but I was in a horrible fairytale where I was silent and I had no voice because this magic hadn't happened to me. I was bewitched.

When my kids were born, I kept trying to write when my son was born, then when my daughter came along all I wanted to give myself as a reward for squirting her out was a rapidograph pen. Totally, totally true, I went out and bought myself a rapidograph pen and regained that incredible pleasure of just drawing across the page and making a black line on a Bristol pad. I thought, "Oh, I have to do this, I have to do this!" I explained this in the book, basically!

The next step, I thought, because one of the things I'd always loved to draw was children, I should do children's books! I got to children's books tewnty-five years too late. They didn't want pen and ink anymore. They were like "Are you kidding me? You have to do this in color, we have this really nice cheap color reproduction!" Which wasn't available when I was growing up in the '70s. I fell in love with Maurice Sendak's early pen and ink work—I always loved it more than his later watercolors, which I thought was always a huge loss of his incredible talent as an ink guy. I loved the guy who did Eloise—Hilary Knight! And Aubrey Beardsley, and all of these people. I thought I wanted to do children's books, I thought they would love the pen and ink I did and they didn't. I went through this horrible time of trying to figure out how to paint. Again, I had ruined another art form for myself, yaaaay. Way to go!

The next thing that happens is I get breast cancer. I was in the middle of illustrating a children's book at the time. I had not ever heard of graphic novels. I had read comics when I was young, I had read the *Archies* and *Asterix and Obelix* and *Doonesbury*. As I'm recuperating from breast cancer I buy a stack of books I had read about in the *New York Times*, if you can believe it, and I'm reading Lynda Barry, Julie Doucet, Jeffrey Brown, Marjane Satrapi. I open these books up and my life is changed in an instant. I said, "Oh my god, where has this stuff been all my life? This is the most expressive stuff I've ever seen. I don't ever want to stop looking at this! I want to do this."

I knew the minute I'd gone through the breast cancer and been declared clean and, y'know, fixed, that I wanted to talk about the experience and share it with other women who were going to go through it. I thought, "Well, that was really awful, but maybe I could make it better for somebody." Since I saw the graphic novels, I realized this was how I had to tell this story. I spent a year reading the best I could get my hands on. I would seriously pick up a graphic novel, go "this is shit," throw it across the room, pick up another, "this is shit," pick up another: "Oh my god, this is incredible!" I'd read all of it, then read it two more times.

I studied and studied and studied. I read old Will Eisners (not *The Spirit*, but his graphic novel stuff), and *Maus*, and every masterpiece I could find. I internalized it, what I liked, what I didn't like, what I thought was a mistake, where it sped up, where it slowed down, where it was well-constructed, what had great impact. I went through it in my mind, like an English student! After one year went by I said, "Now, you go." And I started going and started this book.

DR: *Over what period of time were you working on* The Story of My Tits? *How long did it take from the time that you decided, as you mentioned, "I'm gonna do this book," until it got to a form where you can go "I can now get it published?"*

JH: It took eight years. I sat down and started it one year after my surgery, maybe a year and a couple of months:

November of '05. I sat down and I drew the first images that are still in the book. I threw out images if they weren't psychologically on the mark, if the emotion wasn't right in them. But I wrote this book in ink, panel by panel, and I never looked back. I never rewrote, I never restructured, because I had done so much of that in my writing that I knew I would never get this finished. I always assumed Top Shelf would ask for another draft (although I really hoped they wouldn't because I had done it in ink). I have to do things in ink because to me the minute you do pencils you lose the life, the life just goes right out of the picture for me.

That was eight years for all those pictures to get drawn, but I took breaks to do other work, I took breaks to live my life, to react to the emotions if it was too powerful, and now and then I would throw out a picture I had spent all day drawing because I realized, "y'know, that's not the right expression on his face" or whatever.

DR: *You mentioned your style of creation. One of the things Dean Haspiel says in the introduction to* Underwire *is that he couldn't believe that you didn't use pencils, that you went straight to pen. That seemed to amaze him more than anything.*

JH: He and I have such different places that our work is coming from and going to. It isn't so unusual for someone—I don't think Lynda Barry uses pencils, I've never asked her. I think there's a wild school of drawing in independent comics where it's assumed you don't use pencils. You can get away with it a lot better now that there's Photoshop, I've gotten very sneaky about making fixes in Photoshop and not sacrificing a drawing. It took me years to learn that.

By the time I got back to this in my adulthood I had been burned by illustration, I had been burned by fiction, and I was damned if I was going to be burned again. I was going to give myself everything I needed and forget about money and forget about deadlines and schedules and any rules at all! I didn't even read Scott McCloud! I tried to read his books about comics but I could feel that same sort of hand reaching out around my throat, making me do things someone else's way and I stopped reading it. I knew I knew

what to do and I knew I had to be free to do it. It was a
risk! I could have wasted the eight years completely. But I
had a feelings.

I think Dean is more impressed than he should be by that.
He does a perfect page, whereas I do one square at a time,
then I scan them and arrange them as a page in Photoshop.
I'm getting away with murder!

DR: *You mentioned that your goal was to be very personal
here, and that's one of the takeaways from not only* The
Story of My Tits *but also* Underwire. *I think—and maybe
I'm off base—but I get a sense that someone reading these
books comes away with probably a pretty good sense of the
kind of person that you are because you don't seem to mask
or to mislead or to be abstract in anyway. What we get in*
The Story of My Tits, *what we get in* Underwire, *is at least
who you appear to be and there's something very genuine
that comes out of that writing. I can't say that about
all graphic memoirs but I do get that sense. But there's
something very personable about your persona that comes
out of your writing.*

JH: That's just it, that the leap I was able to make from writing
to graphic novels. When I saw comics, autobiographical
comics, indie comics, I realized that the voice, my
beer-drinking voice, that I was never able to put down
on paper just in words. It was able to come out when I
was a full-fledged character. Part of it was I was doing
autobiographical so I wasn't trying to be anyone else, it was
just me. The other thing was I was able to combine all at
the same time the different facets of my personality. Yes I'm
being facetious, yes I'm being silly, yes I'm being ironic, now
I'm going to be deep, I'm going to stick it to you, now I'm
gonna gross you out: all these things in one beer.

Also that feeling of sitting around the kitchen table and
talking with women friends, which I had been doing as
a mother for years, and it had become its own artform. I
think conversation is a wonderful art form and it's being
lost now, largely. I hate going to someone's house and
there's no talking happening! It's an art that my family
loved, you sat down after dinner and you talked and there
were people at the table and the conversation went in

various ways. I think tapping into the conversational aspect of words was really important to me and only possible for me somehow in comics.

The other thing I love about conversation is this swirl of emotion that can happen. To me, it can happen so much faster as you're chatting away. That's how I wanted to transmit my ideas, my story. That's how I wanted to do it, always, and it just never clicked until I was doing it on comics.

DR: *A part of this conversational tone, and I would even call it vernacular as well, is embedded in the title itself:* The Story of My Tits. *I'm wondering, since the book's release, and it's been getting quite a bit of attention, have you gotten much of any pushback from any avenue of the reading public on that title?*

JH: Much more I've had people say, "Oh, that's such a great title. That's exactly right." Those tend to be women. Now and then a guy will say "What's going on?" and I'll say "Read the back, read the blurb. It's not a porn book, I promise you. I know you'd LIKE it to be, but it isn't." It's possible that it's kept me off things like radio, although maybe I'm just not a radio personality that they're all just dying to interview. I think that on the air this is going to be a deterrent but I think I can live with that. I'm sure it's not getting displayed prominently where kids can see it, but I don't think people are THAT conservative. They're more conservative in America than in other countries in the publishing business and in the artworld. But I don't think the word "tits" is going to kill it.

I thought long and hard about it, and when I was shopping the book to a few other places other than Top Shelf I had some pushback and they were like "Wellllll we might have to make it a working title and change it later." Yet another aspect of Top Shelf I just adored was Chris [Staros, Top Shelf publisher,] saying "I don't see any reason to change the title, just go for it man, whatever! This is the title!" That's how I felt. I didn't want any of this to be dishonest. I couldn't bear it, it was too important to me. This is the honest title. I haven't really felt much pushback at all.

DR: *You know, what I was thinking about in asking you that is not so much the general media reaction, but maybe in the line of where this book may be placed in libraries. It strikes me that what this book is about is perfect for libraries: public and otherwise. I could see a librarian looking at this title, even knowing the content, and having second thoughts about ordering it for their library just because of the potential issues that could arise with their patrons should they see this. Maybe this is too much of an assumption on my part. Have you heard anything like that from educators like "Oh this is a great book, I'd like to use it in the library or in the classroom, however ..."*

JH: No. When we introduced the book at BEA, Book Expo [America] in New York, librarians are a huge part of who goes to Book Expo and they were drooling over this book. They were coming up and buying them by the truckload! I really dig librarians and, you know, the female librarians—sure they look buttoned up to the average Joe, but they are not! They are cool people. They are well read and wide ranging in their tastes and understandings of the world, at least the ones I know. They all just loved—*Underwire* was a favorite with the librarians I knew! They couldn't wait for *The Story of My Tits*! I also think they've had harder books to put on the shelf. Indie graphic novels are often toeing the line between vulgarity and porn and literature. That's part of the fun! It's like being part of a punk band. It's part throwing up and part singing. I think they expect graphic novels to be a little bit on the edge. I haven't had any sense—I'm sure it varies from region to region of the United States, but the northeastern librarians I know have been very receptive to it.

I haven't done a tour of libraries to see who's got it. Most libraries are separating their graphic novels into the adults' section and the kids' section so they can keep kids out of the stuff they shouldn't be looking at. Although I think my book is perfectly safe for kids! As long as they know where they came from and how they were nursed, nothing will shock them!

DR: *That makes sense, you know, given the content of not only* The Story of My Tits *but also* Underwire *because*

*one of the things that comes out in both of those texts is
you and your husband's very open relationship with your
children.*

JH: It's gone in and out of being okay. My son seems to have
emerged unscathed by being raised by two weird parents.
We were bound to be weird parents: my husband's a
musician and composer, I was a writer and artist and now
I do comics. The point of our lives was art. It was never
house and family. Of course we were going to be odd
parents. My daughter has gone in and out of being bummed
out at what I do. I think she's now leading a double life
and half of her heart is supporting me and proud of me and
impressed and half of it is mortified and wishes I'd never
done it and wants to change her name.

DR: *You mean particularly this book,* The Story of My Tits?

JH: *Underwire* was an easier ride, and she was the star of a lot
of the stories, and she liked that attention. Then sometimes
it would make her upset because she would say, "you took
that story" or I ruined it. I illustrated one that she had
written and I illustrated it pretty graphically. It was about a
made-up goddess and the goddess gave birth and I had the
goddess actually giving birth with the blood and everything.
Charlotte was crying, "That's not how that story went,
Mom!" She wrote it when she was eight. I felt a little guilty,
maybe I shouldn't have done that but on the other hand I'm
here to tell the truth. After having cancer, I'm not gonna not
tell the truth ever again! I thought, "She's gotta grow," and
part of the problem was I couldn't keep the work separate,
in a studio, away from the house. I couldn't pay for a studio
if I wasn't doing children's book illustration anymore so I
moved into a bedroom at home. She walked in to see what
I was working on. Part of me was like "don't look, don't
look, don't look, you'll be happier if you don't look!" But
she always looked.

   Recently she said, "That was a weird way to grow up!
That probably wasn't a great idea." I apologized and said,
"When you have a mother who's an artist, it's gonna be a
bumpy ride." We get along beautifully, at least in that sense
it's been smooth. I am who I am, out there, visible to them.
The funny thing is they didn't have rough teenagehoods. I

think everyone in the family was allowed to be themselves. There was no rebellion around this house. The parents were too busy rebelling. The kids were just allowed to become who they were. Unfortunately, I was also writing down how they became who they were because I loved watching it. I'm kind of about everyone getting the space they need to be who they gotta be. Everybody's gotta be like that in my house.

DR: *Much of your writing is autobiographic in nature. You were just mentioning your daughter's reaction to some of the ways that her work had been represented in* Underwire, *and you mentioned earlier that you fictionalized some family information. Do you feel like you need to walk a fine line in representing other members of your family and friends when you're doing your narrative?*

JH: I heard someone said this who did do autobiographical work: you can always set up screens that nobody will notice. You can do it visually and you can do it in what you decide to touch on and you can always bleep over something you feel is too private or would give away too much about a person, and you don't want to do that to them. I've always tried to keep the story sacred. The story is uppermost. What I learned that I have to impart in the story. Because of that, if you're using autobiographical material, you don't have to tell the story like a journalist would, and include every ugly detail. You really can pick and choose and soften this and keep that real and as long as the story and the spirit of the story is honest. There's an art to that, the art of fiction. It's funny, I worked unsuccessfully in fiction all these years, but I began to see where I could use what I learned there in autobiography to keep from dragging anybody through the mud.

Yes, I am telling family stories and I got pretty nitty gritty about the stuff about my parents' marriage. I felt a little guilty later because they had aged so much while I had done the book that I felt like I wish I hadn't been as rough on them. I ran it by Chris Staros, who is a publisher with a lot of heart. I said, "Please read this, and tell me if you think I need to soften things." He said no. You gotta break a few eggs to tell a good story. You cannot leave the eggs intact, you cannot screen things. You see things in people's beginning autobiography. You see a frog and bug telling the story and you'll be like, "those are your parents, right?" You gotta make them people. It's just not coming across, the frog and bug aren't doing it.

You as the narrator and the core of the autobiography and the person who is perceiving always has to come off worse than all the other characters. That's another strong rule I have. I will never make more fun—an autobiography is not a place to vent spleen about what happened to you, and how everyone's responsible for your shitty life. You owe it to your art to be seeing clearly and see your own faults almost more clearly than the faults of those around you.

DR: *You've mentioned examples of autobiographic or memoir comics that you've read. What about prose autobiography? Are there any works that you feel are classic, that you are particularly drawn to, or that served as models for you in your own autobiographic work?*

JH: I did not read autobiographies in my twenties and thirties when I was reading a ton of literature. I would read letters that famous authors had written. I loved Virginia Woolf's letters. I think I read letters by Nabokov, a few other people. I was reading fiction then. The funny thing is, fiction is autobiography. What is really the difference unless you're writing pulp fiction? I loved *A Movable Feast* by Hemingway, I *loved* that book, I read it so many times. That's autobiography but it's set out in a bunch of essays that take you back to a period of time. He's really describing a time and a place more than he's telling his story.

I was talking to a friend recently, we just read *M Train*, Patti Smith's book. I was realizing that I love it when communication has a reason to exist, when writing is specifically written to an audience that inspires the writer to unburden themselves and to really express something. I think that's why I love letters. I'm afraid autobiography in the past seemed to me to be fake. It's seemed to be too much posing and too much screening. If I read autobiography the people were uncomfortable in some way doing it. It just didn't come off as authentic. I read diaries, I did read diaries. I was searching for someone who could write comfortably about their experience and not blame themselves and not blame the people around them and just be dispassionate. It was a rare book that did that.

Appendix 3: "Everybody Gets It Wrong!"—David Chelsea

These two pages come from David Chelsea's comic "Everybody Gets It Wrong!" originally published in *24x2* (2008). Chelsea addresses the central problem of focalization in autobiographical comics: how do artists visually represent their own points of view and subjectivity in comics form? Chelsea argues that the only true first-person narration in comics would be to render all images from the autobiographical subject's visual perspective. While a handful of creators have experimented with this perspective (Dan Clowes [1990], Danny Gregory [2003]), it is not a practical approach for the majority of autobiographical stories. Chelsea concludes with an explanation for the value of the objective perspective.

Scholars, especially those engaged in narrative theory, debate issues of focalization in comics, as discussed in Chapter 3, but here we see a comics creator—and one who was also a practitioner of autobiographical comics with *David Chelsea in Love* (1993)—wrestling with this idea.

FIGURE A.3 *Pages from David Chelsea's "Everybody Gets It Wrong!"* *(2008). © David Chelsea. Used with permission.*

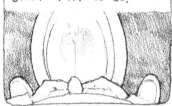

②

Appendix 4: *Autobiographical Conversations*—Ryan Claytor

The following pages come from Ryan Claytor's *Autobiographical Conversations* (2013), a graphic narrative of Claytor's conversations with Dr. Harry Polkinhorn, an English professor at San Diego State University, where he teaches a class on the personal essay. Throughout the book, Claytor and Polkinhorn discuss various philosophical and literary concepts related to autobiography and comics. Claytor's use of the comics form to discuss autobiographical comics allows him to visualize some of the concepts raised in ways that prose scholarship can't. In these pages, Claytor brings up David Chelsea's ideas about visual perspective and autobiography. Therefore, this selection is in dialog with the Chelsea pages from Appendix 3. Together, they offer insights into ways in which autobiographical comics creators think about issues like focalization, which is also a concern for scholars.

Autobiographical Conversations is a companion book to Claytor's autobiographical diary comic series, *And Then One Day* (2004–7). As part of that series, Claytor also produced an "autobiographical documentary" in comics form (2007). This work experiments with the issue of subjectivity in autobiography. For that book, Claytor interviewed family and friends and asked them questions about himself. He recorded their responses and then created a series of "talking head" strips based on them.

FIGURE A.4 *Pages from Ryan Claytor and Henry Polkinborn's Autobiographical Conversations (2013).* © *Ryan Claytor. Used with permission.*

GLOSSARY

The glossary provides definitions of many key terms and phrases that are used in the discussion of comics in general and autobiographical comics in particular. Some of these terms are neologisms or unique phrases created by scholars or creators to explain certain phenomena in autobiographical comics.

Autobifictionalography A neologism created by Lynda Barry to describe her approach to *One Hundred Demons* (2002), where the construction of her stories filtered through her memory automatically blurs the lines between truth and fiction.

Autobiographical pact From Philip Lejeune (1989), an understanding on the part of the reader that the author, narrator, and protagonist of an autobiography are all the same person (22).

Autobiographix Mary Fleener's term for the type of autobiographical comics that she does. The "x" shows the historical connection to the underground comix creators who pioneered confessional autobiographical comics, like Justin Green, Robert Crumb, and Aline Kominsky-Crumb.

Autobiography The life story of an individual, told by the person who experienced the events being recounted. According to Philip Lejeune (1989), "Retrospective prose narrative written by a real person concerning his own experience, where the focus is his individual life, in particular the story of his personality" (4).

Autographics/Autography Gillian Whitlock's (2006) neologism for autobiographical comics or graphic memoir. With this term, Whitlock "mean[s] to draw attention to the specific conjunctions of visual and verbal text in this genre of autobiography, and also to the subject positions that narrators negotiate in and through comics" (966).

Avatar In comics, the artist's drawn version of his or her self. That is, the figure that represents the creator in an autobiographical comic.

Bildungsroman A German term for the genre of novel that deals with a young person's education, spiritual development, or general coming-of-age.

Biocularity Marianne Hirsch's (2004) term for the image/text or verbal/
visual nature of comics.

Canon Those works accepted by scholars as being the most important
or meaningful. Within Comics Studies, the canon would be those
works that have received the most attention in terms of scholarship
and classroom use. Many scholars, however, reject the notion of
canon because of its implied exclusivity.

Closure Scott McCloud's (1993) term for the reader's role in creating
meaning within a comics narrative. As the reader transitions from one
panel to the next, he or she imagines the action that fills in the gap
created by the gutter between panels. This makes comics reading an
active, rather than passive, experience (60–93).

Diary comics Autobiographical comics that are produced on a regular
schedule, such as daily, weekly, or monthly, that document the regular
life of the cartoonist. They can be short, like the four-panel comics
of James Kochalka's *American Elf* or Dustin Harbin's *Dharbin*, or
they can be longer narratives of a specific event in the particular time
period covered. They differ from other autobiographical comics in that
they are produced roughly "in the moment" and, therefore, are not
meant to form a coherent, collective narrative when taken together.

Direct sales/direct market The distribution system for comics in which
the comics go from the publisher to the distributor (usually Diamond
Comics) to the comic book store.

DIY An acronym for "do-it-yourself," it emerged in the punk movement
of the 1970s as a form of resistance to corporate culture, especially in
the areas of music and publishing. With comics, it meant that creators
could produce and distribute their own comics without going through
the proposal, acceptance, and editorial processes of the publishing
industry. See also "minicomics."

Focalization In Narrative Theory, this is the consciousness through
which the narrative is filtered; this can have either a verbal or visual
function. "Internal focalization" refers to a narrative that is filtered
through the perspective of a character within the world of the story,
as is the case with most autobiographical comics. "External (or zero)
focalization" is the more subjective or omniscient narration. See also
"ocularization."

Graphic Body Studies An area of scholarship identified by Martha
Stoddard Holmes (2014):

> [A] theory and analysis of graphic representations of embodied
> experiences and social identities, drawing on the work of
> disability studies and other body studies theories but attending
> to the specific attributes of a hybrid genre that draws words and
> writes pictures. (147–8)

Graphic medicine The *Graphic Medicine Manifesto* defines "graphic medicine" as "the intersection of the medium of comics and the discourse of healthcare" (Czerwiec et al. 2015: 1).

Iconic solidarity Thierry Groensteen's (2007) term used to describe the reader's relationship to the comics page as a whole. Images on the comics page exist simultaneously and are taken in by the reader as such. The images are interdependent on the page, and we are aware of their connectedness even as we are focused on a single image. Therefore, the reading experience of the comics page is much more complex than a simple linear reading of images in sequence (18).

Infinite canvas From Scott McCloud's *Reinventing Comics* (2000), this is the idea, with web or digital comics, of using the computer screen as more of a window than a page, meaning the reader could scroll through a comic without the limitations of page size and quantity equated with print. The "infinite" part of the concept means that creators are not bound by any length requirements, page shapes, or reading directions that limit print narratives. Creators could also control information flow and pacing in new ways, and they could incorporate elements like sound and animation to enhance the experience (200–41).

Ironic authentication A term used by Charles Hatfield (2005) to describe "the implicit reinforcement of truth claims through their explicit rejection" (125). Also, "it makes a show of honesty by denying the very possibility of being honest" (126). In a sense, "ironic authentication" is the acknowledgment that the only truth is that no one has access to the "Truth."

Künstlerroman A German term for "artist's novel," it is a subgenre of the *Bildungsroman* that deals with the development and maturity of an artist. For graphic memoirs, then, this would involve the development of the autobiographical subject as a comic book artist, specifically.

Materiality Related to comics, this term refers to the aspects of comics as material or physical objects: the paper, the size, the printing and binding, and so on. The means of distribution for comics may be considered here as well.

Mediality With comics, "mediality" involves the medium through which the comic is communicated: a web comic, an eBook, a pamphlet-sized comic book, a bound graphic novel, and so on.

Minicomic (or mini-comic) As defined by Isaac Cates (2011),

> self-published and usually hand-assembled photocopied comics, made, sold, and traded mainly by amateur cartoonists at small press comics festivals and conventions (or by mail). Although they are often smaller or shorter than standard comics, the

prefix *mini-* is generally understood to refer to the size of the comic's print run, which is frequently only a few hundred. (224 n.9)

Mise en abyme A French term that means literally "placed into abyss," it is used in critical theory to describe a work that contains within it a version of the work itself. In art, this could be represented as a painting of an artist creating the painting. In literature, it could be a novel that features a diegetic novel with the same name, or a play within a play. Comics creators would often use this effect on covers, where, say, Batman and Robin are holding up a copy of the comic we are reading, which shows Batman and Robin holding up the comic, ad infinitum (hence, the term "infinity cover" for such an effect). Many autobiographical creators will use this technique, where the comic appears within the story, often either as a work in progress or as a periodical in a series, the creation and publication of which affects the subject's life in some way.

Monstrator In Thierry Groensteen's (2011) theory of comics narrative, this is the narrator responsible for the image we see on the comic page, as opposed to the text. So, for example, the narrative voice in a caption box can be different from the narrator who provides the visual perspective.

Multimodal With comics, this refers to the function and relationship of the visual and verbal modes (or image and text) inherent in the medium. Comics, therefore, would be considered "multimodal texts."

Narrative theory/ narratology According to Gerald Prince (1987),

> The (structuralist-inspired) theory of narrative. [It] studies the nature, form, and functioning of narrative (regardless of medium of representation) ... More particularly, it examines what all and only narratives have in common ... as well as what enables them to be different from one another, and it attempts to account for the ability to produce and understand them. (65)

Ocularization A term borrowed from film theory, it explains the visual perspective through which we see the story unfold. In other words, we can consider this term related to the "eyes" of the narrator. "Internal ocularization" refers to the visual perspective of a traditional first-person narrator, while "external (or zero) ocularization" refers to a subjective or third-person perspective. See also "focalization."

Paratext Text associated with the book but not part of the actual narrative, like title and publication pages, back cover summaries, author information, acknowledgments and review blurbs.

Pictorial embodiment For Elisabeth El Refaie (2012a), this describes how autobiographical comics creators must draw and redraw themselves throughout the process of creating their works (51). It also addresses the way in which an artist depicts the self.

Picture plane Scott McCloud's (1993) scale for defining artistic style, especially with figure drawing. The picture plane is a triangular spectrum, with realism and abstraction across the bottom, and non-representational style at the top. McCloud places comics artists at different points on the plane dependent on the level of realism or abstraction in their art style. A less realistic, more simplistic or "cartoony" style would be considered "iconic abstraction" and sit on the bottom right side of the spectrum (45–57).

Postmemory Marianne Hirsch's (2011) term for the way in which parents' memories of their own experiences, especially traumatic ones, affect their children. In a sense, postmemory is the child's memory of the parents' memories.

Premeditated commemoration A term used by Elisabeth El Refaie (2012a) for "the self-conscious intervention by an author in his or her life story" (103). Such instances involve the autobiographical creator staging events or otherwise manipulating experiences in order to provide content for his or her story.

Rage comics A highly popular Internet meme that involves comic strips and images depicting crudely drawn figures who often rage at the common indignities of everyday experience. In the final panel, a "rageface" appears to indicate the emotional response. These strips are often anonymous and easily produced by meme generators known as "Rage Makers." The popularity of this meme has also led to various offshoots using repeated faces expressing different emotional responses and reactions.

Small press This type of publisher is usually defined by annual profits or number of titles published in a year. However, the term is also often used to describe a small, independent publisher that is not owned by a large media corporation. These publishers are also often willing to take on risky or alternative projects that larger publishers might shy away from. In terms of autobiographical comics, these presses have been leaders in publishing innovative and important works in the genre.

Visual modality A term used by social semioticians, which refers to "the extent to which an image resembles its objects of representation," with visual or non-linguistic modes serving "the same communicative function as language, but in their own distinctive forms" (El Refaie 2012a: 152).

Web comic A comic that is produced directly for the web medium, to be read primarily on a screen, such as a computer or tablet device.

Zine (or 'zine) Short for "fanzine," which is itself a portmanteau of "fan" and "magazine," a "zine" is an independently self-published work in periodical form, usually produced and assembled with affordable and easily available means of production, like photocopying machines and staplers.

RESOURCES

Primary sources

American Splendor (2003), R. Pulcini and S. S. Berman (dirs.). HBO Films.

Andersen, S. C. (2016), *Adulthood Is a Myth: A Sarah's Scribbles Collection*. Riverside, NJ: Andrews McMeel.

Backderf, D. (2012), *My Friend Dahmer*. New York: Abrams.

Barry, L. (2002), *One Hundred Demons*. Seattle: Sasquatch.

Bashi, P. (2009), *Nylon Road: A Graphic Memoir of Coming of Age in Iran*. New York: St. Martin's.

B., D. [Beauchard, D.] (2006), *Epileptic*. New York: Pantheon.

Bechdel, A. (1989), "The Mitt," *Wimmen's Comix* 15. Auburn, CA: Rip Off Press.

Bechdel, A. (1993), "Coming Out Story," *Gay Comics* 19. Northampton, MA: Kitchen Sink.

Bechdel, A. (2006), *Fun Home: A Family Tragicomic*. Boston: Mariner.

Bechdel, A. (2012), *Are You My Mother?: A Comic Drama*. Boston: Mariner.

Bell, G. (2012), *The Voyeurs*. Minneapolis: Uncivilized Books.

Bell, G. (2014), *Truth Is Fragmentary*. Minneapolis: Uncivilized Books.

Brabner, J. and H. Pekar (2004), *Our Movie Year*. New York: Ballentine.

Brabner, J., H. Pekar, and F. Stack (1994), *Our Cancer Year*. New York: Four Walls Eight Windows.

Brand, M. (1970), "Tirade Funnies," *It Aint Me Babe*. San Francisco: Last Gasp.

Brosh, A. (2013), *Hyperbole and a Half: Unfortunate Situations, Flawed Coping Mechanisms, Mayhem, and Other Things that Happened*. New York: Touchstone.

Brown, C. (1992), *The Playboy: A Comic-Strip Memoir*. Montreal: Drawn & Quarterly.

Brown, C. (1994), *I Never Liked You: A Comic-Strip Narrative*. Montreal: Drawn & Quarterly.

Brown, C. (1998), *The Little Man: Short Strips, 1980–1995*. Montreal: Drawn & Quarterly.

Brown, C. (2011), *Paying for It: A Comic-Strip Memoir about Being a John*. Montreal: Drawn & Quarterly.

Bunjevac, N. (2014), *Fatherland: A Family History*. New York: Liveright.

Campbell, E. (2006), *The Fate of the Artist*. New York: First Second.

Campbell, S. (2015), *These Memories Won't Last*. Available online: http://memories.sutueatsflies.com (accessed May 30, 2016).

Carey, P. and R. Wimberly (2007), *Sentences: The Life of MF Grimm*. New York: Vertigo-DC Comics.

Chast, R. (2014), *Can't We Talk about Something More Pleasant?* New York: Bloomsbury.

Chelsea, D. (2008), "Everybody Gets It Wrong!" *24x2*. Marietta, GA: Top Shelf.

Claytor, R. (2007), *The Collected And Then One Day*. San Diego: Elephant Eater Comics.

Claytor, R. and H. Polkinhorn (2013), *Autobiographical Conversations*. San Diego: Elephant Eater Comics.

Close, D., J. Ostrander and D. Simpson (February 1988), "American Squalor," *Wasteland* 3. New York: DC Comics.

Clowes, D. (1990), "The Stroll," *Eightball* 3. Seattle: Fantagraphics.

Clowes, D. (1991), "Daniel G. Clowes®™ in Just Another Day ...," *Eightball* 5. Seattle: Fantagraphics.

Cole, J. (1944), *Inkie*, *Crack Comics* 34. New York: Quality Comics.

Crumb, R. (1971), "And Now, a Word to You Feminist Women," *Big Ass Comics*. Auburn, CA: Rip Off Press.

Crumb, R. (1972a), "The Confessions of R. Crumb," *The People's Comics*. Northampton, MA: Kitchen Sink.

Crumb, R. (1972b), "The Many Faces of R. Crumb," *XYZ Comics*. Northampton, MA: Kitchen Sink.

Crumb, R. (1981–2), "I Remember the Sixties," *Weirdo* 4. San Francisco: Last Gasp.

Crumb, R. (1988), "Memories Are Made of This," *Weirdo* 22. San Francisco: Last Gasp.

Crumb, R. and A. Kominsky-Crumb (1995), *Self-Loathing Comics*. Seattle: Fantagraphics.

Crumb, R. and A. Kominsky-Crumb (2012), *Drawn Together: The Collected Works of R. and A. Crumb*. New York: Liveright.

Crumb, R., A. Kominsky-Crumb and S. Crumb (1992), *The Complete Dirty Laundry Comics*. San Francisco: Last Gasp.

Cruse, H. (1980a), "Billy Goes Out," *Gay Comix* 1. Northampton, MA: Kitchen Sink.

Cruse, H. (1980b), "Jerry Mack," *Gay Comix* 2. Northampton, MA: Kitchen Sink.

Cruse, H. (1983), "Ready or Not, Here It Comes ... Safe Sex," *Gay Comix* 4. Northampton, MA: Kitchen Sink.

Cruse, H. (1995), *Stuck Rubber Baby*. New York: Paradox Press-DC Comics.

Dahl, K. (2009), *Monsters*. Jackson Heights: Secret Acres.

Davison, A. (1990), *The Spiral Cage*. London: Titan Books.

Doucet, J. (1999), *My New York Diary*. Montreal: Drawn & Quarterly.

Drechsler, D. (1996), *Daddy's Girl*. Seattle: Fantagraphics.

Dunlap-Shohl, P. (2015), *My Degeneration: A Journey through Parkinson's*. University Park: Pennsylvania State University Press.

Eisner, W. (1942), "Self Portrait." *The Spirit*. Newspaper supplement, May 3.

Eisner, W. (1950), "Happy New Year." *The Spirit*. Newspaper supplement, December 31.

Eisner, W. (2007), *Life, in Pictures: Autobiographical Stories*. New York: Norton.

Engelberg, M. (2006), *Cancer Made Me a Shallower Person*. New York: HarperCollins.

Farmer, J. (2014), *Special Exits*. Seattle: Fantagraphics.

Feldstein, A. and W. Wood (1953), "My World," *Weird Science 22*. New York: EC Comics.

Fies, B. (2006), *Mom's Cancer*. New York: Abrams.

Fisher, B. (1919), *Mutt and Jeff*, daily comic strip, February 12.

Fleener, M. (1996), *Life of the Party*. Introduction by Ray Zone. Seattle: Fantagraphics.

Forney, E. (2006), *I Love Led Zeppelin*. Seattle: Fantagraphics.

Forney, E. (2012), *Marbles: Mania, Depression, Michaelangelo, & Me*. New York: Gotham Books.

Frakes, C. (2015), *Prison Island*. San Francisco: Zest Books.

Freedman, M. (2014), *Relatively Indolent but Relentless*. New York: Seven Stories Press.

Giménez, C. (2016), *Paracuellos*. San Diego: IDW.

Glidden, S. (2010), *How to Understand Israel in 60 Days or Less*. New York: Vertigo-DC Comics.

Gloeckner, P. (1998), *A Child's Life and Other Stories*. Berkeley: Frog Books.

Gloeckner, P. (2002), *Diary of a Teenage Girl*. Berkeley: Frog Books.

Green, J. (1969), "Binky Brown Makes Up His Own Puberty Rites," *Yellow Dog 17*. San Francisco: Print Mint.

Green, J. (1972), *Binky Brown Meets the Holy Virgin Mary*. San Francisco: Last Gasp.

Green, J. (1975), "We Fellow Traveleers," *Sacred and Profane*. San Francisco: Last Gasp.

Green, J. (1995), *Justin Green's Binky Brown Sampler*. San Francisco: Last Gasp.

Gregory, D. (2003), *Everyday Matters*. New York: Hyperion.

Harbin, D. (2015), *Diary Comics*. Toronto: Koyama Press.

Hart, T. (2015), *Rosalie Lightning*. New York: St. Martin's.

Hayden, J. (2011), *Underwire*. Marietta, GA: Top Shelf.

Hayden, J. (2015), *The Story of My Tits*. Marietta, GA: Top Shelf.

Hernandez, G. (2013), *Marble Season*. Montreal: Drawn & Quarterly.

Holland, D. (1973), "Fucked Up," *Wimmen's Comix* 3. San Francisco: Last Gasp.

Kane, G. and Friedrich, M. (1969), "His name is ... Kane," *House of Mystery* 180. New York: DC Comics.

Katin, M. (2006), *We Are on Our Own*. Montreal: Drawn & Quarterly.

Katin, M. (2013), *Letting It Go*. Montreal: Drawn & Quarterly.

Kiyama, H. Y. (1998), *Four Immigrants Manga*. Berkeley: Stone Bridge Press.

Kochalka, J. (2007), *American Elf: Book 2: January 1, 2004 to December 31, 2005*. Marietta, GA: Top Shelf.

Kominsky-Crumb, A. (1972), "Goldie: A Neurotic Woman," *Wimmen's Comix* 1. San Francisco: Last Gasp.

Kominsky-Crumb, A. (1975), "Bunch Plays with Herself," *Arcade* 3. San Francisco: Print Mint.

Kominsky-Crumb, A. (1976a), "More of the Bunch," *Twisted Sisters* 1. San Francisco: Last Gasp.

Kominsky-Crumb, A. (1976b), "The Young Bunch: An Unromantic Adventure Story," *Twisted Sisters* 1. San Francisco: Last Gasp.

Kominsky-Crumb, A. (1984), "Mommy Dearest Bunch," *Wimmen's Comix* 9. San Francisco: Last Gasp.

Kominsky-Crumb, A. (1989), "Nose Job," *Wimmen's Comix* 15. Auburn, CA: Rip Off Press.

Kominsky-Crumb, A. (1990), *Love That Bunch*. Seattle: Fantagraphics.

Kominsky-Crumb, A. (2007), *Need More Love: A Graphic Memoir*. London: MQ Publications.

Kottler, D. (1982), "I'm Me," *Gay Comix* 3. Northampton, MA: Kitchen Sink.

Lasko-Gross, M. (2008), *Escape from "Special."* Seattle: Fantagraphics.

Lasko-Gross, M. (2010), *A Mess of Everything*. Seattle: Fantagraphics.

Lay, C. (2008), *The Big Skinny: How I Changed My Fattitude*. New York: Hyperion.

Lee, S. and J. Kirby (1965), *Fantastic Four Annual* 3. California: Marvel Comics Group.

Leguizamo, J., C. Cassano and S. Beyale (2015), *Ghetto Klown*. New York: Abrams.

Lewis, J., A. Aydin and N. Powell (2013), *March: Book 1*. Marietta, GA: Top Shelf.

Lewis, J., A. Aydin and N. Powell (2015), *March: Book 2*. Marietta, GA: Top Shelf.

Lewis, J., A. Aydin and N. Powell (2016), *March: Book 3*. Marietta, GA: Top Shelf.

Libicki, M. (2016), "Jewish Memoir Goes Pow! Zap! Oy!" *Toward a Hot Jew*. Seattle: Fantagraphics.

Linthout, W. (2009), *Years of the Elephant*. Wisbech: Fanfare.

Mack, S. (2004), *Janet and Me: An Illustrated Story of Love and Loss*. New York: Simon and Schuster.

Marchetto, M. A. (2006), *Cancer Vixen*. New York: Pantheon.

Marinaomi. (2011), *Kiss and Tell: A Romantic Resume. Ages 0–22*. New York: Harper.

Marrs, L. (1972), "All in a Day's Work," *Wimmen's Comix* 1. San Francisco: Last Gasp.

Matt, J. (1992), *Peepshow: The Cartoon Diary of Joe Matt*. Montreal: Drawn & Quarterly.

Matt, J. (1996), *The Poor Bastard*. Montreal: Drawn & Quarterly.

Matt, J. (2002), *Fair Weather*. Montreal: Drawn & Quarterly.

Matt, J. (2007), *Spent*. Montreal: Drawn & Quarterly.

Mayer, S. (1937), "Gettin' Up in th' World," *Scribbly*. *The Funnies*. New York: Dell Comics.

Mayer, S. (1942), *Scribbly and the Red Tornado*. *All-American Comics* 45. DC Comics.

Mizuki, S. (2011), *Onward Towards Our Noble Deaths*. Montreal: Drawn & Quarterly.

Nakazawa, K. (1972), *I Saw It!* San Francisco: Last Gasp.

Nakazawa, K. (2004–9), *Barefoot Gen*. San Francisco: Last Gasp.

Okubo, M. (1983), *Citizen 13660*. Seattle: University of Washington Press.

Peeters, F. (2008), *Blue Pills: A Positive Love Story*. London: Jonathan Cape.

Pekar, H. (1978), "Standing Behind Old Jewish Ladies in Supermarket Lines," *American Splendor* 3. Harvey Pekar.

Pekar, H. (1979), "How I Quit Collecting Records and Put Out a Comic Book with the Money I Saved," *American Splendor* 4. Harvey Pekar.

Pekar, H. (1979), "The Young Crumb Story," *American Splendor* 4. Harvey Pekar.

Pekar, H. (1984), "A Marriage Album," *American Splendor* 9. Harvey Pekar.

Pekar, H. (1987), "Another Old Jewish Lady, Another Store," *American Splendor* 12. Harvey Pekar.

Pekar, H. (1988), "My Struggle with Corporate Corruption and Network Philistinism," *American Splendor* 13. Harvey Pekar.

Pekar, H. (1989), "David Letterman Exploitation Issue," *American Splendor* 14. Harvey Pekar.

Penfold, R. B. (2006), *Dragonslippers: This Is What an Abusive Relationship Looks Like*. London: Harper Press.

Porcellino, J. (2000), *Perfect Example*. Montreal: Drawn & Quarterly.

Porcellino, J. (2007), *King-Cat Classix*. Montreal: Drawn & Quarterly.

Porcellino, J. (2014), *The Hospital Suite*. Montreal: Drawn & Quarterly.

Prince, L. (2005), *Will You Still Love Me If I Wet the Bed?* Marietta, GA: Top Shelf.

Prince, L. (2008), *Delayed Replays*. Marietta, GA: Top Shelf.

Prince, L. (2014a), *Alone Forever: The Singles Collection*. Marietta, GA: Top Shelf.

Prince, L. (2014b), *Tomboy*. San Francisco. Zest Books.

Road, C. C. (2012), *Spit and Passion*. New York: Feminist Press.

Robbins, T. (1972), "Sandy Comes Out," *Wimmen's Comix* 1. San Francisco: Last Gasp.

Robbins, T. (1977), "Out of the Closet and into the Frying Pan," *Tits & Clits* 3. Washington, DC: Nanny Goat Productions.

Robbins, T., ed. (1970), *It Aint Me Babe*. San Francisco: Last Gasp.

Rodriguez, S. (1994), *My True Story*. Seattle: Fantagraphics.

Russo, S. and J. Wong (1993), "Rancid Plotte," *The Comics Journal* 162: 79–82.

Ryan, J. (2006), *The Comic Book Holocaust*. Oakland, CA: Buenaventura Press.

Satrapi, M. (2004), *Persepolis: The Story of a Childhood*. New York: Pantheon.

Satrapi, M. (2005), *Persepolis 2: The Story of a Return*. New York: Pantheon.

Satrapi, M. (2007), *The Complete Persepolis*. New York: Pantheon.

Schrag, A. (2008a), *Awkward and Definition: The High School Chronicles of Ariel Schrag*. New York: Touchstone.

Schrag, A. (2008b), *Potential: The High School Chronicles of Ariel Schrag*. New York: Touchstone.

Schrag, A. (2009), *Likewise: The High School Chronicles of Ariel Schrag*. New York: Touchstone.

Seda, D. (1986), *Lonely Night Comics*. San Francisco: Last Gasp.

Seda, D. (2000), *Dori Stories*. Seattle: Fantagraphics.

Seth [Gallant, G.] (1991), "Why?," *Drawn & Quarterly* 4. Montreal: Drawn & Quarterly.

Seth [Gallant, G.] (1996), *It's A Good Life, If You Don't Weaken*. Montreal: Drawn & Quarterly.

Small, D. (2009), *Stitches*. New York: Norton.

Spiegelman, A. (1972), "Maus," *Funny Aminals* 1. San Francisco: Apex Novelties.

Spiegelman, A. (1973a), "Prisoner of the Hell Planet," *Short Order Comix* 1. San Francisco: Head Press.

Spiegelman, A. (1973b), "Skeeter Grant by Skeeter Grant," *Short Order Comix* 1. San Francisco: Head Press.

Spiegelman, A. (1986), *Maus I: My Father Bleeds History*. New York: Pantheon.

Spiegelman, A. (1991), *Maus II: And Here My Troubles Began*. New York: Pantheon.

Spiegelman, A. (2004), *In the Shadow of No Towers*. New York: Pantheon.

Spiegelman, A. (2011), *MetaMaus*. New York: Pantheon.

Spiegelman, A. and F. Mouly, eds (2009), *The Toon Treasury of Classic Children's Comics*. New York: Abrams.

Stein, L. (2015), *Bright-Eyed at Midnight*. Seattle: Fantagraphics.

Sutton, J. (1972), "The Menses Is the Message," *Tits & Clits Comix* 1. Washington, DC: Nanny Goat Productions.

Tatsumi, Y. (2013), *A Drifting Life*. Montreal: Drawn & Quarterly.

Telgemaier, R. (2010), *Smile*. New York: Scholastic.

Telgemaier, R. (2014), *Sisters*. New York: Scholastic.

Thompson, C. (2003), *Blankets: An Illustrated Novel*. Marietta, GA: Top Shelf.

Thrash, M. (2015), *Honor Girl*. Somerville, MA: Candlewick Press.

Tran, G. B. (2010), *Vietnamerica: A Family's Journey*. New York: Villard.

Trondheim, L. (2001), *Nimrod 6*. Seattle: Fantagraphics.

Tyler, C. (2015), *Soldier's Heart: The Campaign to Understand my WWII Father: A Daughter's Memoir*. Seattle: Fantagraphics.

Upton, C. (1990), *Colin Upton's Big Thing*. Canada: Ed Varney.

Walrath, D. (2015), *Aliceheimer's: Alzheimer's Through the Looking Glass*. University Park: Pennsylvania State University Press.

Weaver, L. Q. (2012), *Darkroom: A Memoir in Black and White*. Tuscaloosa: University of Alabama Press.

Weinstein, L. R. (2014), *Carriers*. Available online: http://nautil.us/blog/carriers-a-webcomic-on-health-luck-and-life (accessed May 30, 2016).

Wertz, J. (2015), *Drinking at the Movies*. Toronto: Koyama Press.

Wertz, J. (2007, 2009), *The Fart Party Vols 1 and 2*. New York: Atomic Books.

Williams, I. (2014), *Bad Doctor: The Troubled Life and Times of Dr. Iwan James*. University Park: Pennsylvania State University Press.

Wilson, S. C. (1968), "Head First," *Zap Comics* 2. San Francisco: Apex Novelties.

Wings, M. [Geller, M.] (1973), *Come Out Comix*. Portland, OR: Mary Wings.

Wings, M. [Geller, M.] (1978), *Dyke Shorts*. San Francisco: Print Mint.

Winick, J. (2000), *Pedro and Me*. New York: Henry Holt.

Wojnarowicz, D. and J. Romberger (1996), *7 Miles a Second*. New York: Vertigo-DC Comics.

Wright, A. (2015), *Things to Do in a Retirement Home Trailer Park ... When You're 29 and Unemployed*. University Park: Pennsylvania State University Press.

Critical bibliography

Adams, J. (2008), *Documentary Graphic Novels and Social Realism*. Oxford: Peter Lang.

Allison, M. C. (2014), "(Not) Lost in the Margins: Gender and Identity in Graphic Texts," *Mosaic: A Journal for the Interdisciplinary Study of Literature* 47 (4): 73–97.

Andelman, B. (2005), *Will Eisner: A Spirited Life*. Milwaukie, OR: M Press.

Bakis, M. (2011), *The Graphic Novel Classroom: POWerful Teaching and Learning with Images*. Thousand Oaks, CA: Corwin.

Baur, J. (2012), "Artist alley: Gabrielle Bell semi-autobiographically." Available online: https://www.youtube.com/watch?v=G3oOLsA3HYI (accessed December 14, 2015).

Beaty, B. (2009), "Autobiography as Authenticity," in J. Heer and K. Worcester (eds), *A Comics Studies Reader*. Jackson: University Press of Missouri, 226–35.

Beaty, B. (2011), "Selective Mutual Reinforcement in the Comics of Chester Brown, Joe Matt, and Seth," in M. Chaney (ed.), *Graphic Subjects: Critical Essays on Autobiography and Graphic Novels*. Madison: University of Wisconsin Press, 247–59.

Beaty, B. (2016), "11 million reasons to smile." Available online: http://www.greatestcomicbook.com/blog/2016/3/21/lcsohxnzom3mqdf3n7lwk6zprc65e7 (accessed May 15, 2016).

Bramlett, F. (2015), "The Role of Culture in Comics of the Quotidian," *Journal of Graphic Novels and Comics* 6 (3): 246–59.

Brandt, J. (2014), "Art Spiegelman's *In the Shadow of No Towers* and the Art of Graphic Autofiction," *Journal of Graphic Novels and Comics* 5 (1): 70–78.

Brayshaw, C. (1996), "Joe Matt," *The Comics Journal* 183: 47–75.

Bredehoft, T. (2011), "Style, Voice, and Authorship in Harvey Pekar's (Auto) (Bio)Graphical Comics," *College Literature* 38 (3): 97–110.

Carney, S. (2008), "The Ear of the Eye, or, Do Drawings Make Sounds?," *English Language Notes* 46 (2): 193–209.

Cates, I. (2011), "The Diary Comic," in M. Chaney (ed.), *Graphic Subjects: Critical Essays on Autobiography and Graphic Novels.* Madison: University of Wisconsin Press, 209–26.

Chaney, M. A. (2011a), "Terrors of the Mirrors and the *Mise en Abyme* of Graphic Novel Autobiography," *College Literature* 38 (3): 21–44.

Chaney, M. A., ed. (2011b), *Graphic Subjects: Critical Essays on Autobiography and Graphic Novels.* Madison: University of Wisconsin Press.

Chansky, D. (2011), "From Graphic Narrative to Multi-media Stage: Transmogrifying *The Diary of a Teenage Girl*," *Journal of Adaptation in Film & Performance* 4 (3): 255–74.

Chiu, M. (2008), "Sequencing and Contingent Individualism in the Graphic, Postcolonial Spaces of Satrapi's *Persepolis* and Okubo's *Citizen 13660*," *English Language Notes* 46 (1): 99–114.

Chute, H. L. (2006), "An Interview with Alison Bechdel," *MFS: Modern Fiction Studies* 52 (4): 1004–13.

Chute, H. L. (2007), "Review of *Our Cancer Year, Janet and Me: An Illustrated Story of Love and Loss, Cancer Vixen: A True Story, Mom's Cancer, Blue Pills: A Positive Love Story, Epileptic*, and *Black Hole*," *Literature and Medicine* 26 (2): 413–29.

Chute, H. L. (2008a), "Comics as Literature? Reading Graphic Narrative," *PMLA* 123 (2): 452–65.

Chute, H. L. (2008b), "The Texture of Retracing in Marjane Satrapi's *Persepolis*," *Women's Studies Quarterly* 36 (1/2): 92–110.

Chute, H. L. (2010), *Graphic Women: Life Narrative and Contemporary Comics.* New York: Columbia University Press.

Chute, H. L. (2016), *Disaster Drawn: Visual Witness, Comics, and Documentary Form.* Cambridge, MA: Belknap Press and Harvard University Press.

Clementi, F. K. (2013), "The JAP, the *Yenta* and the *Mame* in Aline Kominksy Crumb's Graphic Imagination," *Journal of Graphic Novels and Comics* 4 (2): 309–31.

Czerwiec, MK, I. Williams, S. M. Squier, M. J. Greene, K. R. Myers, and S. T. Smith (2015), *Graphic Medicine Manifesto.* University Park: Pennsylvania State University Press.

Daly, M. (1993), "Seth, Brown, Matt," *Comics Journal* 162: 51–6.

Darda, J. (2013), "Graphic Ethics: Theorizing the Face in Marjane Satrapi's *Persepolis*," *College Literature* 40 (2): 31–51.

Davis, R. G. (2005), "A Graphic Self: Comics as Autobiography in Marjane Satrapi's *Persepolis*," *Prose Studies: History, Theory, Criticism* 27 (3): 264–79.

Davis, R. G. (2011), "Autographics and the History of the Form: Chronicling Self and Career in Will Eisner's *Life, in Pictures* and Yoshihiro Tatsumi's *A Drifting Life*," *Biography* 34 (2): 253–76.

De Jesús, M. L. (2004a), "Liminality and Mestiza Consciousness in Lynda Barry's *One Hundred Demons*," *MELUS* 29 (1): 219–52.

De Jesús, M. L. (2004b), "Of Monsters and Mothers: Filipina American Identity and Maternal Legacies in Lynda J. Barry's *One Hundred Demons*," *Meridians: Feminism, Race, Transnationalism* 5 (1): 1–26.

Diedrich, L. (2014), "Graphic Analysis: Transitional Phenomena in Alison Bechdel's *Are You My Mother?*" special issue on graphic medicine, *Configurations* 22 (2): 183–203.

Dong, L. (2011), "Thinly Disguised (Autobio)graphical stories: Will Eisner's *Life, in Pictures*," *Shofar: An Interdisciplinary Journal of Jewish Studies* 29 (2): 13–33.

Dong, L., ed. (2012), *Teaching Comics and Graphic Narratives: Essays on Theory, Strategy and Practice*. Jefferson, NC: McFarland.

Donovan, C. (2014), "Representations of Health, Embodiment, and Experience in Graphic Memoir," special issue on graphic medicine, *Configurations* 22 (2): 237–53.

Dueben, A. (2016), "An oral history of *Wimmen's Comix* Part 1 and 2." Available online: http://www.tcj.com/an-oral-history-of-wimmens-comix/ and http://www.tcj.com/an-oral-history-of-wimmens-comix-part-2/ (accessed April 8, 2016).

Earle, H. E. H. (2014), "*My Friend Dahmer*: The Comic as Bildungsroman," *Journal of Graphic Novels and Comics* 5 (4): 429–40.

Elahi, B. (2007), "Frames and Mirrors in Marjane Satrapi's *Persepolis*," *symploke* 15 (1–2): 312–25.

El Refaie, E. (2012a), *Autobiographical Comics: Life Writing in Pictures*. Jackson: University Press of Mississippi.

El Refaie, E. (2012b), "Of Mice, Men, and Monsters: Body Images in David Small's *Stitches: A Memoir*," *Journal of Graphic Novels and Comics* 3 (1): 55–67.

Espiritu, K. (2006), "Putting Grief into Boxes: Trauma and the Crisis of Democracy in Art Spiegelman's *In the Shadow of No Towers*," *Review of Education, Pedagogy, and Cultural Studies* 28 (2): 179–201.

Eveleth, K. W. (2015), "A Vast 'Network of Transversals': Labyrinthine Aesthetics in *Fun Home*," *South Central Review* 32 (3): 88–109.

Fantasia, A. (2011), "The Paterian Bildungsroman Reenvisioned: 'Brain-building' in Alison Bechdel's *Fun Home: A Family Tragicomic*," *Criticism* 53 (1): 83–97.

Fischer, C. and C. Hatfield (2011), "Teeth, Sticks, and Bricks: Calligraphy, Graphic Focalization, and Narrative Braiding in Eddie Campbell's *Alec*," *SubStance* 40 (1): 70–93.

Fox, M. S. (2013), "*Zap Comix* #1." Available online: http://comixjoint. com/zapcomix1-1st.html (accessed January 2, 2016).

Freedman, A. (2009), "Drawing on Modernism in Alison Bechdel's *Fun Home*," *Journal of Modern Literature* 32 (4): 125–40.

Gardner, J. (2008), "Autography's Biography, 1972–2007," *Biography*, 31 (1): 1–26.

Gardner, J. (2012), *Projections: Comics and the History of Twenty-First Century Storytelling*. Stanford, CA: Stanford University Press.

Gardner, J. (2015), "Show me where it hurts: Part 1." Available online: http://www.publicbooks.org/ multigenre/show-me-where-it-hurts-part-1 (accessed May 24, 2016).

Gardner, J. and D. Herman (2011), "Graphic Narratives and Narrative Theory: Introduction," *SubStance* 40 (1): 3–13.

Geis, D. R., ed. (2010), *Considering* Maus: *Approaches to Art Spiegelman's "Survivor's Tale" of the Holocaust*. Tuscaloosa: University of Alabama Press.

Gilmore, L. (1994), *Autobiographics: A Feminist Theory of Women's Autobiography*. Ithaca, NY: Cornell University Press.

Gloeckner, P. (1989), "Comic Books: A Medium Deserving Another Look," *ETC: A Review of General Semantics* 48 (3): 246–7.

Gloeckner, P. (2011), "Autobiography: The Process Negates the Term," in M. Chaney (ed.), *Graphic Subjects: Critical Essays on Autobiography and Graphic Novels*. Madison: University of Wisconsin Press, 178–9.

Gonshak, H. (2009), "Beyond *Maus*: Other Holocaust Graphic Novels," *Shofar: An Interdisciplinary Journal of Jewish Studies* 28 (1): 55–79.

Goodwin, G. M. (2001), "More than a Laughing Matter: Cartoons and Jews," *Modern Judaism* 21 (2): 146–74.

Goulart, R. (1990), "Scribbly," in R. Goulart (ed.), *The Encyclopedia of American Comics, from 1897 to the Present*. New York: Facts on File, 322–3.

Grace, D. and E. Hoffman, eds (2013), *Chester Brown: Conversations*. Jackson: University Press of Mississippi.

Groensteen, T. (2007), *The System of Comics*. Jackson: University Press of Mississippi.

Groensteen, T. (2011), *Comics and Narration*. Jackson: University Press of Mississippi.

Groth, G. (1993) "Harvey Pekar," *Comics Journal* 162: 37–44.

Hall, J., ed. (2012), *No Straight Lines: Four Decades of Queer Comics*. Seattle: Fantagraphics.

Hatfield, C. (2005), *Alternative Comics: An Emerging Literature.* Jackson: University Press of Mississippi.

Hatfield, C. (2014), "Studies in Graphic Selfhood: A Review Essay," *Studies in Comics* 5 (2): 405–24.

Hathaway, R. V. (2011), "Reading Art Spiegelman's *Maus* as Postmodern Ethnography," *Journal of Folklore Research* 48 (3): 249–67.

Herman, D. (2010), "Multimodal Storytelling and Identity Construction in Graphic Narratives," in D. Schiffrin, A. De Fina, and A. Nylund (eds), *Telling Stories: Language, Narrative, and Social Life.* Washington, DC: Georgetown University Press, 195–208.

Herman, D. (2011), "Narrative Worldmaking in Graphic Life Writing," in M. Chaney (ed.), *Graphic Subjects: Critical Essays on Autobiography and Graphic Novels.* Madison: University of Wisconsin Press, 231–43.

Hibbs, B. (2015), "Tilting at windmills: BookScan numbers show big book market growth for comics in 2014." Available online: http://www.comicbookresources.com/article/bookscan-numbers-show-big-book-market-growth-for-comics-in-2014 (accessed December 7, 2015).

Hibbs, B. (2016), "Tilting at windmills: looking at BookScan: 2015." Available online: http://www.comicbookresources.com/article/tilting-at-windmills-bookscan-2015-analysis (accessed March 23, 2016).

Hirsch, M. (2004), "Editor's Column: Collateral Damage," *PMLA* 119 (5): 1209–15.

Hirsch, M. (2011), "Mourning and Postmemory," in M. Chaney (ed.), *Graphic Subjects: Critical Essays on Autobiography and Graphic Novels.* Madison: University of Wisconsin Press, 17–44.

Hoashi, L. (2007), "Fluency in Form: A Survey of the Graphic Memoir," *Missouri Review* 30 (4): 159–74.

Holmes, M. S. (2014), "Cancer Comics: Narrating Cancer through Sequential Art," *Tulsa Studies in Women's Literature* 33 (1): 147–62.

Horstkotte, S. and Pedri, N. (2011), "Focalization in Graphic Narrative," *Narrative* 19 (3): 330–57.

Hutton, R. (2015), "A Mouse in the Bookstore: *Maus* and the Publishing Industry," *South Central Review* 32 (3): 30–44.

Iuliano, F. (2015), "Du côté de *Fun Home*: Alison Bechdel Rewrites Marcel Proust," *Partial Answers: Journal of Literature and the History of Ideas* 13 (2): 287–309.

Jacobs, D. (2008), "Multimodal Constructions of Self: Autobiographical Comics and the Case of Joe Matt's *Peepshow*," *Biography* 31 (1): 59–84.

Jones, M. J. (2007), "Construction of Social Memory through Strategies of Reflexivity: A Case Study in Three Texts by Art Spiegelman," *IJOCA* 9 (2): 373–95.

Kashtan, A. (2013), "My Mother was a Typewriter: *Fun Home* and the Importance of Materiality in Comics Studies," *Journal of Graphic Novels and Comics* 4 (1): 92–116.

Kelley, M. J. (2014), "Mirrored Discourse in Alison Bechdel's *Fun Home*," *Journal of Graphic Novels and Comics* 5 (1): 42–57.

Kirtley, S. (2012), *Lynda Barry: Girlhood through the Looking Glass*. Jackson: University Press of Mississippi.

Køhlert, F. B. (2012), "Female Grotesques: Carnivalesque Subversion in the Comics of Julie Doucet," *Journal of Graphic Novels and Comics* 3 (1): 19–38.

Køhlert, F. B. (2015), "Working it Through: Trauma and Autobiography in Phoebe Gloeckner's *A Child's Life* and *The Diary of a Teenage Girl*," *South Central Review* 32 (3): 124–42.

Larkin, I. (2014), "Absent Eyes, Bodily Trauma and the Perils of Seeing in David Small's *Stitches*," *American Imago*, 71 (2): 183–211.

Lejeune, P. (1989), *On Autobiography*. Minneapolis: University of Minnesota Press.

Levitz, P. (2015), *Will Eisner: Champion of the Graphic Novel*. New York: Abrams.

Lightman, S., ed. (2014), *Graphic Details: Jewish Women's Confessional Comics in Essays and Interviews*. Jefferson, NC: McFarland.

Ludwig, F. A. and G. A. Matte (2012), "Black English in Harvey Pekar's *American Splendor*," *BELT Journal* 3 (1): 146–57.

Marshall, E. and L. Gilmore (2015), "Girlhood in the Gutter: Feminist Graphic Knowledge and the Visualization of Sexual Precarity," *WSQ: Women's Studies Quarterly* 43 (1–2): 95–114.

Mazur, D. and A. Danner (2014), *Comics: A Global History, 1968 to the Present*. London: Thames.

McCloud, S. (1993), *Understanding Comics: The Invisible Art*. Northampton, MA: Kitchen Sink Press.

McCloud, S. (2000), *Reinventing Comics*. New York: Paradox Press-DC Comics.

McGlothlin, E. (2010), "'When Time Stands Still': Traumatic Immediacy and Narrative Organization in Art Spiegelman's *In the Shadow of No Towers*," in S. Baskind and R. Omer-Sherman (eds), *The Jewish Graphic Novel: Critical Approaches*. New Brunswick, NJ: Rutgers University Press, 94–110.

McNicol, S. (2015), "Freedom to Teach: Implications of the Removal of *Persepolis* from Chicago schools," *Journal of Graphic Novels and Comics* 6 (1): 31–41.

Merino, A. (2008), "Feminine Territoriality: Reflections on the Impact of the Underground and Post-underground," trans. E. Polli, *IJOCA* 10 (2): 70–88.

Mickwitz, N. (2016), *Documentary Comics: Graphic Truth-Telling in a Skeptical Age*. New York: Palgrave.

Mihăilescu, D. (2015), "Haunting Spectres of World War II: Memories from a Transgenerational Ethical Perspective in Miriam Katin's *We Are on Our Own* and *Letting It Go*," *Journal of Graphic Novels and Comics* 6 (2): 154–71.

Mikkonen, K. (2012), "Focalization in Comics—from the Specificities of the Medium to Conceptual Reformulation," *Scandinavian Journal of Comic Art* 1 (1): 69–95.

Miller, A. (2011), "Marjane Satrapi's *Persepolis*: Eluding the Frames," *L'Esprit Créateur* 51 (1): 38–52.

Miller, N. K. (2014), "The Trauma of Diagnosis: Picturing Cancer in Graphic Memoir," special issue on graphic medicine, *Configurations* 22 (2): 207–23.

Mitchell, W. J. T. and A. Spiegelman (2014), "Public Conversation: What the %$#! Happened to Comics?," *Critical Inquiry* 40: 20–35.

Morrison, G. (2011), *Supergods: What Masked Vigilantes, Miraculous Mutants, and a Sun God from Smallville Can Teach Us about Being Human*. New York: Spiegel & Grau.

Munson, T. S. (2012), "Transformers and Monkey Kings: Gene Yang's *American Born Chinese* and the Quest for Identity," in Matthew Pustz (ed.), *Comic Books and American Cultural History*. London: Continuum, 171–83.

Novak, R. J. (2013), *Teaching Graphic Novels in the Classroom: Building Literacy and Comprehension*. Waco, TX: Prufrock.

O'Connor, K. (2012), "Penis rays, self-loathing and psychic voodoo: Autobiographical cartoonists on truth and lies." Available online: http://www.theawl.com/2012/08/truth-and-lies-autobiographical-cartoons (accessed December 27, 2015).

Oksman, T. (2007), "Visualizing the Jewish Body in Aline Kominsky Crumb's *Need More Love*," *Studies in Comics* 1 (2): 213–30.

Orbán, K. (2007), "Trauma and Visuality: Art Spiegelman's *Maus* and *In the Shadow of No Towers*," *Representations* 97: 57–89.

Orbán, K. (2015), "Mediating Distant Violence: Reports on Non-photographic Reporting in *The Fixer* and *The Photographer*," *Journal of Graphic Novels and Comics* 6 (2): 122–37.

Pedri, N. (2015), "What's the Matter with Seeing in Graphic Memoir?" *South Central Review* 32 (3): 8–29.

Penaz, M. L. (2009), "Drawing History: Interpretation in the Illustrated Version of the 9/11 Commission Report and Art Spiegelman's *In the Shadow of No Towers* as Historical Biography," *a/b: Auto/Biography Studies* 24 (1): 93–112.

Precup, M. (2015). "'That Medieval Eastern-European Shtetl Family of Yours': Negotiating Jewishness in Aline Kominsky Crumb's *Need More Love* (2007)," *Studies in Comics* 6 (2): 313–27.

Prince, G. (1987), *A Dictionary of Narratology*. Lincoln: University of Nebraska Press.

Reed, L. H. (2010), "(Re)Composing Childhood: Representing the Rhythm of Self in Postmodern Memoir," *JASAT* 41: 17–21.

Reiser, J. (2014), "'Thinking in Cartoons': Reclaiming Spiegelman's *In the Shadow of No Towers*," *Journal of Graphic Novels and Comics* 5 (1): 3–14.

Rerick, M. (2012), "Queering the Museum: Challenging Heteronormative Space in Bechdel's *Fun Home*," *Journal of Graphic Novels and Comics* 3 (2): 223–30.

Rhode, M. G., ed. (2008), *Harvey Pekar: Conversations*. Jackson: University Press of Mississippi.

Rifkind, C. (2008), "Drawn from Memory: Comics Artists and Intergenerational Auto/biography," *Canadian Review of American Studies* 38 (3): 399–427.

Robbins, T. (1999), *From Girls to Grrrlz: A History of Women's Comics from Teens to Zines*. San Francisco: Chronicle.

Robbins, T. (2016), "Introduction," *The Complete Wimmen's Comix*. Seattle: Fantagraphics.

Rohy, V. (2010), "In the Queer Archive: *Fun Home*," *GLQ: A Journal of Lesbian and Gay Studies* 16 (3): 341–61.

Rosenberg, M. (2007), "Multimodality in Phoebe Gloeckner's *Diary of a Teenage Girl*," *IJOCA* 9 (2): 396–412.

Rosencranz, P. (2008), *Rebel Visions: The Underground Comix Revolution—1963–1975*. Seattle: Fantagraphics.

Royal, D. P. (2011), "Jewish Comics: Or, Visualizing Current Jewish Narrative," *Shofar: An Interdisciplinary Journal of Jewish Studies* 29 (2): 1–12.

Sabin, R. (1993), *Adult Comics: An Introduction*. London: Routledge.

Sabin, R. (2001), *Comics, Comix & Graphic Novels: A History of Comic Art*. New York: Phaidon.

Schlam, H. F. (2001), "Contemporary Scribes: Jewish American Cartoonists," *Shofar: An Interdisciplinary Journal of Jewish Studies* 20 (1): 94–112.

Schneider, C. W. (2013), "The Cognitive Grammar of 'I': Viewing Arrangements in Graphic Autobiographies," *Studies in Comics* 4 (2): 307–32.

Schumacher, M. (2010), *Will Eisner: A Dreamer's Life in Comics*. New York: Bloomsbury.

Shannon, E. (2012), "Shameful, Impure Art: Robert Crumb's Autobiographical Comics and the Confessional Poets," *Biography* 35 (4): 627–49.

Sperb, J. (2006), "Removing the Experience: Simulacrum as an Autobiographical Act in *American Splendor*," *Biography* 29 (1): 123–39.

Spiegelman, A. (1995), "Symptoms of Disorder/signs of Genius," in J. Green, *Justin Green's Binky Brown Sampler*. San Francisco: Last Gasp, 4–6.

Squier, S. M. (2008), "Literature and Medicine, Future Tense: Making it Graphic," *Literature and Medicine* 27 (2): 124–52.

Squier, S. M. and J. R. Marks (2014), "Introduction," special issue on graphic medicine, *Configurations* 22 (2): 149–52.

Stamant, N. (2015), "Collections of 'Old Comic Strips' in Art Spiegelman's *In the Shadow of No Towers*," *South Central Review* 32 (3): 70–87.

Stevens, B. (2009), "The Beautiful ambiguity of *Blankets*: Comics representation and religious art." Available online: http://www.english.ufl.edu/imagetext/archives/v5_1/stevens/ (accessed December 4, 2015).

Tabachnick, S. E. (2011), "Autobiography as discovery in *Epileptic*," in M. Chaney (ed.), *Graphic Subjects: Critical Essays on Autobiography and Graphic Novels*. Madison: University of Wisconsin Press, 101–16.

Tabachnick, S. E., ed. (2009), *Teaching the Graphic Novel*. New York: Modern Language Association.

Tabachnick, S. E. (2014), *The Quest for Jewish Belief and Identity in the Graphic Novel*. Tuscaloosa: University of Alabama Press.

Tensuan, T. M. (2006), "Comic Visions and Revisions in the Work of Lynda Barry and Marjane Satrapi," *MFS: Modern Fiction Studies* 52 (4): 947–64.

Tensuan, T. M. (2009), "Crossing the Lines: Graphic (Life) Narratives and Co-laborative Political Transformations," *Biography* 32 (1): 173–89.

Tolmie, J., ed. (2013), *Drawing from Life: Memory and Subjectivity in Comic Art*. Jackson: University Press of Mississippi.

Versaci, R. (2007), *This Book Contains Graphic Language: Comics as Literature*. New York: Continuum.

Versluys, K. (2006), "Art Spiegelman's *In the Shadow of No Towers*: 9/11 and the Representation of Trauma," *MFS: Modern Fiction Studies* 52 (4): 980–1003.

Waples, E. (2014), "Avatars, Illness, and Authority: Embodied Experience in Breast Cancer Autopathographics," special issue on graphic medicine, *Configurations* 22 (2): 153–81.

Warhol, R. (2011), "The Space Between: A Narrative Approach to Alison Bechdel's *Fun Home*," *College Literature* 38 (3): 1–15.

Watson, J. (2008), "Autographic Disclosures and Genealogies of Desire in Alison Bechdel's *Fun Home*," *Biography* 31 (1): 27–58.

Wertham, F. (1954), *Seduction of the Innocent*. New York: Rinehart.

Whitlock, G. (2006), "Autographics: The Seeing 'I' of the Comics," *MFS: Modern Fiction Studies* 52 (4): 965–79.

Whitlock, G. and A. Poletti (2008), "Self-regarding Art," *Biography* 31 (1): v–xxiii.

Williams, I. (2016), "Why 'Graphic Medicine'?" Available online: http://www.graphicmedicine.org/why-graphic-medicine/ (accessed March 27, 2016).

Witek, J. (1989), *Comic Books as History: The Narrative Art of Jack Jackson, Art Spiegelman, and Harvey Pekar*. Jackson: University Press of Mississippi.

Witek, J. (2011), "Justin Green: Autobiography Meets the Comics," in M. Chaney (ed.), *Graphic Subjects: Critical Essays on Autobiography and Graphic Novels*. Madison: University of Wisconsin Press, 227–30.

Witek, J. (2012), "Comics Mode: Caricature and Illustration in the Crumb Family's *Dirty Laundry*," in R. Duncan and M. J. Smith (eds) *Critical Approaches to Comics: Theories and Methods*. New York: Routledge, 27–42.

Wivel, M. (2011), "A house divided: The crisis at L'Association, Part 1 and 2." Available at http://www.tcj.com/a-house-divided-the-crisis-at-l%E2%80%99association-part-1-of-2/& http://www.tcj.com/a-house-divided-the-crisis-at-lassociation-part-2-of-2/ (accessed October 30, 2015).

Wolk, D. (2007), *Reading Comics: How Graphic Novels Work and What They Mean*. Cambridge, MA: Da Capo Press.

Worth, J. (2007), "Unveiling: *Persepolis* as Embodied Performance," *Theatre Research International* 32 (2): 143–60.

Yoe, C., ed. (2013), *Comics about Cartoonists: Stories about the World's Oddest Profession*. San Diego: Yoe-IDW.

Zhou, X. (2007), "Spatial Construction of the 'Enemy Race': Miné Okubo's Visual Strategies in *Citizen 13660*," *MELUS* 32 (3): 51–73.

INDEX

Darda, Joseph 203
Darkroom 114, 118–19
Davis, Rocío 204
Davis, Vanessa 119–20
Davison, Al 122, 124
DC Comics 3, 27, 31, 57 n.4,
    135, 163, 187
Definition 94–5
Deitch, Kim 34, 186
Delayed Replays 101
Delisle, Guy 49, 64
Dell Comics 24
Dharbin 55, 145, 256
Diamond Comic Distributors
    18–19, 135, 138
diary comics 3, 55, 66, 100, 140,
    144–7, 256
Diary Comics 100, 144
Diary of a Teenage Girl 13, 57,
    95, 131–2, 182–7
Dirty Laundry Comics 13, 36, 46,
    157, 162–3, 186
Dirty Plotte 47, 49
distribution 48, 52, 135–8, 140
Do-It-Yourself (DIY) 3, 48,
    52, 134, 256 *see also*
    minicomics
Dong, Lan 79–80, 149 n.12
Doucet, Julie 7–8, 39, 46–7, 49,
    55, 64, 103, 106–7, 110,
    159, 190, 235
Dougan, Michael 49
Dragonslippers 85
Drama 56, 97
Drawing from Life 54
Drawn & Quarterly (publisher)
    48–50, 135, 138, 187–8
Drawn & Quarterly (comic) 49,
    188, 192–3
Dreamer, The 67–8, 149 n.12
Dream of the Rarebit Fiend 22
Drechsler, Debbie 49, 83–4, 86,
    97, 107, 161, 197

Drifting Life, A 49, 96
Drinking at the Movies 102,
    136–7
Dumm, Gary 164, 167
Dunlap-Shohl, Peter 55, 122
Dyke Shorts 37, 40, 111
Dykes to Watch Out For 40, 205

EC Comics 29
Ed the Happy Clown 190
Ego Comme X 51
Eichhorn, Dennis 6, 42, 103, 165,
    168
Eightball 104–5
Eisner, Will 24, 48, 67–8, 119,
    149 n.12, 235
Elahi, Babak 204
Elder, Bill 155
Ellerbisms 145
Ellerby, Mark 145
El Refaie, Elisabeth 1, 3, 9–10,
    18, 32, 35, 48, 54, 62–3,
    70–4, 82 n.8, 123–4, 146,
    155, 158–9, 162, 192,
    198–9, 258–9
  on photography 72–4
  see also pictorial embodiment
Emitown 145, 150 n.21
Engelberg, Miriam 71, 126
Epileptic 51–2, 76, 122, 126–9,
    178
Epstein, Joey 39, 110
Escape from "Special" 81 n.2
"Everybody Gets It Wrong"
    245–7
*Every Girl Is the End of the
    World for Me* 101

Fair Weather 95, 147 n.4, 188–9
fan culture 139
Fantagraphics 48–51, 135
Fantasia, Annette 208
Fantastic Four 30

Mome 49
Momon 82 n.8
Mom's Cancer 55, 127
Monsters 125
monstrator 64, 258
Moore, Alan 65
Moore, Tony 3
Moran, Penny 39, 46
"More of the Bunch" 35, 157, 160
Morrison, Grant 22, 57 n.2
Mouly, Françoise 44, 46, 174
multimodal 6, 9, 79, 258
Mutt and Jeff 22–3
My Degeneration: A Journey through Parkinson's 55, 122
My Friend Dahmer 93, 147 n.3
My True Story 37, 47
"My World" 29–31
Myers, Kimberly R. 54

Nagashimi, Shinji 31
Nakazawa, Keiji 40–1, 71, 83–4, 92, 95, 170–4
narrative medicine *see* graphic medicine
Neaud, Fabrice 51
Need More Love 73, 160, 212 n.3
Néhou, Loïc 51
Nelson, Deborah 217–27
Neufeld, Josh 164
New York Diary 8
Nimrod 51, 64
Noomin, Diane 39, 106–7, 114, 119–20, 148 n.8, 159, 223
Novak, Ryan J. 80

O'Connor, Kim 69
ocularization 63, 258
Okubo, Miné 31
Oliveros, Chris 49
Ollmann, Joe 49

On Autobiography 5
One Hundred Demons 9, 11, 14, 55, 62, 73, 75, 95, 113, 194–9, 214 n.15
Onward Towards Our Noble Deaths 41, 49, 71, 84
Orbán, Katalin 181
Ore wa Mita see *I Saw It!*
Ostrander, John 213 n.6
Our Cancer Year 47, 70, 126, 164, 169, 198
Out of the Inkwell 27

Paley, Nina 246
Palookaville 49, 192–4
Paracuellos 41
paratext 10–11, 65–6, 258
Paying for It 13, 65, 191–2
Pedri, Nancy 63, 81 n. 4
Pedro and Me 112, 122
Peepshow 49, 55, 78–9, 168, 188–90, 194, 214 n.13
Peeters, Frederik 122
Pekar, Harvey 1, 3, 6, 41–4, 47, 49, 64, 70–1, 99–100, 102–3, 126, 134, 163–70, 190, 194, 198, 246
Penhold, Rosalind 85
People's Comics, The 35, 157
Perfect Example 94, 138
Persepolis 1–3, 17, 45, 51–3, 64, 75, 79–80, 84, 93, 95–6, 106, 131–3, 198, 201–5
and adolescence 93, 202
as *Bildungsroman* 95
as canon 1–2
controversy 5, 131–3
and historical trauma 84
style 204
pictorial embodiment 9, 123–4, 158, 162, 258–9
picture plane 2, 64, 71, 203, 259
Picture This 195